THE WORLD OF THE SHOGUN

He threw the young man to the ground, but then he noticed his *mon*: a square with a double line with the number '3' written inside: he was certainly a Kono. Leaning from his saddle, his sword in one hand, Daiko lifted his young adversary and cut off both his legs.

The governor of Tsushima advanced at a gallop with a loud shout of rage. Simultaneously, supporting Kono, three hundred of his vassals moved from the ranks of the Imperial army, in a cloud of red dust. A thousand Minamoto did the same. A clash was imminent. The two armies followed like solid walls.

'Forward!'

Other titles in the Corps d'Elite series:

THE FRENCH FOREIGN LEGION
THE AFRIKA KORPS

THE SAMURAI

Jean Mabire & Yves Breheret

CHARTER
NEW YORK

A DIVISION OF CHARTER COMMUNICATIONS, INC.
A GROSSET & DUNLAP COMPANY

Published in France by Balland, under the title Les Samourai, 1971 © Balland, Paris

Translation copyright © by Allan Wingate (Publishers) Ltd., 1975

Published by arrangement with W. H. Allen Publishers, Inc.

Charter Books
A Division of Charter Communications Inc.
A Grosset & Dunlap Company
360 Park Avenue South
New York, New York 10010

2 4 6 8 0 9 7 5 3 1
Manufactured in the United States of America

Contents

Part I

Seppuku	11
Yoritomo's Iron Fan	20
The Exploits of Yoshitsune	36
When the Divine Winds Blew	53
The Cherry-trees of the Imperial City	71
Black was the Kampaku's Horse	86
A Last Arrow for the Tyrant	99
The Forty-seven Ronin	110

Part II

The Arrival of the 'Pink Noses'	129
Last Civil War	142
Black Dragon against White Bear	153
The Three Minutes of Tsushima	174
The Heroes with the Bamboo Poles	193
The Mikado's Falcons	211
Volunteers for the Jibaku	234
The Kamikaze of the Philippines	247
The Divine Thunder Dies at Okinawa	265
The Twilight of the Samurai	279
Bibliography	286
Periods in Japanese History	288

Part I

Periods in Japanese History

I. Pre-History and Proto-History

Jomon   Ca. 10,000 BC
Yayoi   From 158 BC

II. Ancient History

Tomb Period	270–593	
Asuka Period	593–645	
Nara Period	645–794	
Heian Period	794–1185	
(Fujiwara Regents)	890–1185	
Kamakura Period	1185–1333	(Hojo Regents)
Muromachi Period	1333–1573	(Shogun Ashikaga)
Momoyama Period	1573–1603	(the dictators)
Edo Period	1603–1868	(Shogun Tokugawa)

III. Contemporary History

Meiji Era   1868–1912
Taisho Era   1913–1924
Showa Era   1924–

Seppuku

VERY SLOWLY he drew the sword from its sheath and the blue steel gleamed dully; then he wrapped the blade in a white cloth, leaving five inches of naked steel at the point.

Next he placed the sword, wrapped thus, before him. He raised himself on his knees, then sat back with his legs crossed and undid the fasteners at the neck of his uniform. Slowly, one by one, he undid the small metal buttons, laying bare his brown chest. With a twist of his shoulders, he dropped his jacket on the ground behind him. He unbuckled his belt and opened the top of his trousers. His loin-cloth was dazzlingly white. He used both hands to bare more of his belly. Then he seized the blade of his sword. With his left hand he bunched his belly, his eyes lowered.

The sword had to plunge deep into his entrails a few inches above his navel, a little to the left. In order to make sure that the blade was sharp he rolled up the left leg of his trousers, baring part of his thigh, and then he nicked the skin. Immediately blood filled the wound and trickled down, shining red in the light. His eyes took on the expression of motionless intensity of a bird of prey, but he no longer saw anything. Turning the sword on himself he rose slightly to bend his body towards the point of the blade. The effort that this cost him was revealed by the contraction of his shoulder muscles. He aimed at the left side of his belly. A spasm passed across his face.

Despite the strength which he used against himself he had the impression that it was someone else who had struck him this terrible blow in the side. For a moment or two he felt giddy, and was aware of nothing. The five inches of steel had disappeared completely into his flesh and the white cloth which he was clenching in his fist was held directly against his belly.

He regained consciousness. 'The blade has pierced my abdominal wall,' he said to himself. He was breathing with difficulty. His heart was thumping. From some remote depths of what he could scarcely believe to be himself an abominable pain leapt up. The earth was opening to let the lava of melted rocks escape. Pain advanced at a terrifying speed. He bit his lips to repress an involuntary groan.

'Is this *seppuku*?'* he wondered. Absolute chaos, as if the universe was staggering drunkenly, as if the sky was falling.

His will and his courage which had seemed to him so firm before he had gashed himself were now reduced to the strength of a fine steel thread. He felt an absurd suspicion invade him, like a terrible nausea. His clenched fist was damp. He lowered his eyes without moving his head and saw that his hand and the cloth wrapped round the sword were covered with blood. His loin-cloth also was stained bright red. It seemed incredible that in the midst of such terrible suffering that which could be seen could still be seen and that which existed could still exist.

His pain blazed like the summer sun. It grew continuously. It rose within him.

With his right hand he began to slash with the sword across his belly. Sweat glistened on his forehead. He closed his eyes, then opened them again, as if to realise fully what was happening. His eyes were lustreless, and his gaze was innocent and empty, as that of an animal. The blade met the obstacle of his intestines which trammelled it and the elasticity of which resisted its onslaught. He realised that he needed both hands to keep the blade plunged into his belly.

He pressed down to cut sideways. He gathered all his strength and the gash grew three or four inches larger. Gradually the pain spread from his inmost depths across his whole belly. Bells were ringing wildly. Thousands of them all together. His whole being was shaken with every breath, with every beat of his pulse. He could no longer prevent himself

---

*Seppuku is the honorific term for *hara-kiri*, the self-disembowelling of the ancient samurai.

from groaning. But the blade had reached the level of his navel and when he realised this he regained his courage.

The volume of spilt blood had been increasing steadily and had begun to flow out of the wound to the same rhythm as his pulse-beat. The ground was red.

He had completely disembowelled himself. The blade had no farther to plunge and the point was visible now, shining with grease. A violent wave of nausea swept through him and he gritted his teeth so as not to cry out. Vomiting made the terrible pain yet more terrible and his belly which had remained still until this moment rose suddenly, the wound gaped open and his intestines were spewed out as if the wound were vomiting in its turn. They slipped down without hindrance and lay between his legs like slimy slugs.

His head sank on his chest, his shoulders braced themselves, his eyes half opened and a thin dribble of saliva came from his mouth. There was blood everywhere, he was drenched in it. Helpless and powerless, he sat, one hand on the ground. An acrid stench filled the room. His face was no longer life-like. His eyes were sunken, his lips the colour of chalk. Only his right hand moved, raising itself trembling like a puppet's hand, laboriously gripping the sword which dripped with grease and blood.

Then Morita lifted his sword on his right shoulder and, with a sudden rush of air, slashed off Mishima Yukio's head. 'Madmen! Lunatics!' roared General Mashita, chief of general staff of the Japanese Self-Defence Force. Wounded and tied down in a chair, he had watched helplessly the end of this mad conspiracy. But the pressure on his throat of the sword held by Koga Masayoshi, aged twenty-two, one of Mishima's militiamen, reduced him to silence again.

Morita Masakatsu wrapped Mishima's sword in the white paper he had taken from his pockets and then laid it beside the decapitated body of his master in the midst of the pool of blood. He got his own two swords out of a carefully wrapped parcel.

Koga Hiroyasu, aged twenty-three, took a step forwards and

then stood to attention. He was the *kaishaku** of this second *hari-kiri*. Morita held out to him his large sword which he had drawn lovingly from its sheath.

He knelt, parallel with Mishima's decapitated body, and prepared his own *seppuku*, identical in every gesture with the first. Hiroyasu, behind him, rocked slowly in the median axis of his belly, the Hara, the seat of the equilibrium and the soul; the sword was a blue flash, held in both hands, across his right shoulder.

The horrible ritual was completed more quickly this time. There were two *kiai*, two cries from the belly: that of Morita, disembowelled, and the instantaneous reply of Koga, who two-thirds decapitated him — a refinement according to the most ancient tradition. The horrible, nauseating sound of blood gushing out was heard by all the spectators.

At that instant, at 10.30 in the morning of 25 November 1970, at the headquarters of the Japanese Self-Defence Force in the centre of Tokyo, they broke down the door....

The world-famous writer, Mishima Yukio, aged forty-five, who had frequently been mentioned as a possible winner of the Nobel prize for literature, had attacked the barracks at about nine o'clock at the head of some thirty men of his 'private army', dressed in the former uniforms of the Imperial forces. They brandished samurai swords. The stupefied sentries were immediately rendered powerless. Every order from Mishima — whose expression was infinitely sorrowful — was obeyed instantly.

Followed by four of his 'soldiers' — Morita Masakatsu, the two Kogas and Ogawa Masahira — he rushed into the headquarters offices. They cut down with their swords all the officers they met who looked like intervening.

On the landing of the first floor, outside General Mashita's office, Lieutenant-General Kiyono Fujio was the only one who

*The *kaishaku* is one who cuts off the head of a person in the act of committing *seppuku* by his wish or order.

did not flee before the brandished swords, and who tried to stand up to them. He was stabbed and collapsed, his wounds mortal, while the conspirators stepped over his body which was jerking convulsively. General Mashita, surprised in his office, was wounded, then overcome, and tied up on a chair, his hands bound behind his back.

Mishima sat down opposite him, dramatically sweeping his scattered papers aside with his swords. Slowly he removed his flat peaked cap and tied a white band round his forehead. Then, still silent, he went to open the casement windows which gave on to the barracks square. Obeying his orders, the militiamen again stirred up the bewildered crowd of officer cadets. He was going to harangue them.

Two thousand soldiers were to be assembled at ten o'clock, as well as a number of curious onlookers and the police who did not dare intervene. The militiamen had surged back behind the gates and had barricaded themselves solidly there, taking officers as hostages. 'Pacifism is a threat to our destiny as a nation,' shouted Mishima at the top of his voice.

He was booed.

'Awake, sons of eternal Japan,' he shouted, one fist at his hip, one arm raised towards the sun.

For eight minutes his resounding voice rang out. Then Mishima left the balcony. If the hostile reaction of the soldiers had disappointed him he did not show it. He closed the windows again, clicking his boots on the polished floor, and seized the swords placed on the desk of the commander-in-chief, who was eyeing him, flabbergasted.

'You're completely out of your mind, Mishima. You aren't going to...'

'Kindly be silent,' said Koga Masayoshi, placing the edge of his sword against the General's throat.

'A modern *seppuku*,' murmured the senior officer, 'but why...?'

Before acting out, word for word and gesture for gesture, the death which he had so often described, Mishima Yukio had written at dawn the date – 25 November 1970 – on the last of the three thousand pages of the manuscript of *The Sea of Fertility*, his longest and his greatest novel. Then he had delivered the manuscript to his publisher, four hours before his suicide.

The astonishing neatness of his writing, when he had decided to sacrifice himself, matched the perfection of his *seppuku*. In order to be able to drive a blade very deeply into one's abdomen and open it almost entirely (thirteen centimetres, the autopsy was to say) it was necessary to excel in the literary and martial arts – writing being a martial art.

By his spectacular suicide, Mishima, an impassioned militant nationalist, wished to protest at the refusal to allow Japan to rearm. He had been discovered by Kawabata Yasunari, winner of the 1969 Nobel prize for literature; he had become famous at the age of twenty-four for his first novel, *Confessions of a Mask*, in which his acknowledged homosexuality had created a scandal. Since then he had become a living legend and had set about reinventing the Nô.

Bewildering enough to his compatriots, Mishima proved impenetrable to Western analysis. This is how he appeared at an interview he gave to a French writer.

The man has a pleasing physique, she wrote, with well-developed muscles due to intensive training. But one has the impression that he is sensitive about his small stature since he draws himself up with a sort of aggressiveness.

His features are boldly chiselled, his hair crew-cut, his clothes grey. He wears a polo-necked pullover, and a shirt unbuttoned at the collar.

'Is there a conflict between Japanese tradition and Western influence?' she asked him.

In reply he picked up his cup and put on top of it a sugar bowl which happened to fit exactly.

'You see? That is a house with two storeys. Western man would immediately discover the acceptable way of getting from the ground floor to the first floor: he would build a staircase.'

A brief, chilly smile.

'But for the Oriental,' Mishima continued, 'there is no one way. Each man will find his own: a pole, a rope ladder. An Indian will meditate for twenty years, and then he will go up to the first floor in his imagination. A Zen priest will begin with concentration. He will not concern himself with the technical solution but after his concentration he will perhaps be able to leap directly to the upper floor.'

Mishima laughed.

'With the Western method, I wonder if I am on the first floor.'

The interviewer asked him about his 'army'.

'It's simply twenty-four boys who are training. I am against the security treaty and they are ready to sacrifice their lives if there should be a national crisis. They don't have anything to do with politics, neither of the Right nor the Left. The essential is that they should be able to fight for an idea, even a romantic one. . . .'

Mishima became irritated and bored in a peaceful Japan. In July 1968 he asked for an interview with his former fellow-student, Mr Fukuda, Minister of Finance, and described to him a plan for military and moral rearmament founded on the patriotic tradition and the example of the *kamikaze* (suicide pilots). The most famous Japanese writer, and much admired, he had regularly published excellent novels: *The Temple of the Golden Pavilion, After the Banquet, The Sailor who fell from Grace with the Sea*, for example, in which nightmare swiftly turns into reality. Success did not elude him. He was a public figure and so he put on a publicity show: honorary president of a group of amateur archers, he posed as St Sebastian pierced by arrows. The magazine *Playboy* devoted several pages to him: after months of athletic training he had himself photographed half-naked, brandishing a samurai sword. He devised and acted his own suicide in the film 'Yokoku' of which he wrote the scenario.

His taste for provocation took him further. In 1969 he had a play entitled 'My Friend Hitler' staged in Tokyo. The play had, in fact, nothing to do with the Third Reich, but everything to do with Japan: through the voice of a puppet called Hitler, Mishima sang despair, hatred of the Western world, and love of the warrior ethic. This love cost him dear, since it was out of his own royalties that he raised and trained his private army of twenty-four men, educated in the pure faith of ancestor-worship and the tradition of the samurai. The Imperial Japanese army, however, recognised its military value and invited the 'army' to its major manoeuvres. In June 1969 the magazine of the Ministry of National Defence even began its first issue with a feature on this 'legion'.

Mishima was difficult to pin down. He showed this in his answers to interviewers' questions.

'Are you an exhibitionist?'

'All writers are mental exhibitionists, but I'm a physical one. I can hide behind this mask.'

'Are you faithful to your wife?'

'Yes.' He had married in the traditional fashion followed by seventy per cent of Japanese, by *Miai* (choice by intermediaries).

'What do you think about homosexuality?'

'In our country it is a practice which is older and more natural than love between the two sexes. It was the American missionaries who stopped it.'

'Who are you?'

'A very serious Japanese writer who doesn't care for literature; a bit like a Don Juan who doesn't like women.'

Mishima concluded his self-portrait thus:

'I'm descended from both peasants and samurai. I work like a peasant, but I adhere to the samurai ethic.'

Invited on 13 May 1969 to the Institute of General Culture in Tokyo by the leftist Zenkyoto students, Mishima refused police protection and outraged his hosts.

'In the name of the past, down with the future!' he shouted.

A few months later some sword-waving Zengakuren students diverted a Boeing plane to North Korea. Their opinions had nothing to do with those professed by Mishima, but they were Japanese....

On 25 November 1970, in Tokyo, in Japan, a capitalist country with a highly developed technology and a superpower of tomorrow, the nation was deeply shaken and for good reasons. Even if Mishima Yukio's suicide did not result in a wave of other *seppuku* it would be rash to say that it left people indifferent.

'Mishima must have been insane!' exclaimed Mr Sato, the Prime Minister, when he learned of the conspiracy.

'I condemn this action,' Nakasone Yasuhiro, Minister of State and Director of the Self-Defence Force, was to say later.

These statements reveal a curious ambivalence, because in Japan one does not 'condemn' the insane.

In March 1971, before the 701 chamber of the Tokyo tribunal, the three principal survivors of the conspiracy went on trial. They stood to attention before the judges and claimed in loud, clear voices the right to the ritual death of their leader. Contemporary justice and the samurai tradition met head-on.

On the 'New Tokaido' line, aerodynamic trains run every twenty minutes between Tokyo and Osaka. The nights in Ginza are white with neon lights from one year's end to the next. Nevertheless, at the time of the tea ceremony, just before the curtain rises in the Kabuki theatre, the senseless tragedy of Mishima abolished the notion of time in Japan.

A wandering soul left in search of the eternal samurai.

Yoritomo's Iron Fan

ISLANDS OF fire and wind, the Japanese archipelago is made up of the emerging summits of a huge chain of underwater mountains, the bottom of which lies thousands of feet below the dark waters to one side of the Pacific Ocean. The birth of these islands was part of the volcanic phenomena which geographers call the 'ring of fire of the Pacific'. According to ancient legend, the four jagged-sided islands are set on the back of a large cat-fish which sometimes shakes them in rage.

The forest stretches like a head of hair between the great snow-covered volcanoes and the few plains of the valleys. If it were cut down, Japan would soon disappear, because the forest alone keeps a thin layer of loam in place. In this delightful countryside, a light mist softens the contours and silhouettes the outlines. From the smoking craters to the spring-flowering cherry trees, from the marvellous moonlight to the autumn chrysanthemums, the Japanese cherish their islands, and, living in perfect symbiosis with them, resemble them.

Always struggling with hostile nature, the Japanese people have lived with and tamed its violence. Since the beginning of their history, they have fought with perseverance and ingenuity against earthquakes and tidal waves, fires and tempests. Only the ethic of austerity, perfected in the course of the centuries, and a sharp sense of the need to sacrifice the individual for the group, have enabled them to do so.

From the earliest times, the Japanese have divided their islands into distinct zones: there is the belly and the back, the East and the West. The belly is the historic part, with the town of Kyoto at its centre; that is where most of the events which formed Japanese civilisation occurred. This favoured region of the main island of Honshu is made up of the Kansai plain, stretching from the Inland Sea to the great fissure of Lake Biwa. To the east it extends as far as the foot of Mount Fuji.

With the setting up first at Kamakura, then at Edo,* of the administrative centre of the Empire, the belly of Japan became enlarged. It was in this belly, through which ran the umbilical cord of the Tokaido road, that a city of 100 million inhabitants was built in our time. It was in this world that Mishima Yukio committed *hara-kiri*. It was there that everything began.

Trying to reconcile what seems irreconcilable to Westerners – the past with the present, spirit with matter – the Japanese have evolved in a sort of current which is both alternating and direct: this is the Dô, the way. Mishima's way developed from a long spiritual search whose origins are lost in the mist of Japan and in the night of time. It is difficult for Western man to analyse the concepts of the Japanese soul: there is no need to explain these to the Japanese themselves who feel without knowing. In what veins, at the dawn of the Japanese Middle Ages, did the blood of Mishima Yukio flow? Was he a wandering soul, or inherited chromosomes?

Tombs are not opened in Japan in order to learn the origins of legends and the archaeologists are at a loss: from the first century of our era, they jump to half-legendary centuries, to the days of the grandson of Ninigi, himself grandson of the Sun-Goddess Amaterasu. Jimmu, first human sovereign of Japan, marched from the south to the north of the archipelago and conquered the Ainu barbarians whom he drove back to the east of the island of Hokkaido where they are still: few in numbers, bearded, worshipping the bear, and disappearing quickly – 'Japanised'. That Jimmu once lived is certain: around the year 600 B.C., if one believes Japanese chronology: at about the beginning of our era, according to corrections made in modern times. How is one to know!

It is true that Japan has had only one Imperial dynasty during its history. Its origins, it is said, are divine, since officially

*Former name, until 1868, of Tokyo.

it is descended from celestial beings: the *Kami*. Despite struggles for power, it has never really been usurped.

Japan was first called Wa, from the Chinese word *Wo*, which meant 'harmony', then Ni-hon, in Chinese Ri-Ben, which means 'rising of the sun'. This descriptive term became, in the year 600, an official name. Everything will follow this pattern.

Jimmu's successors went on steadily to conquer the archipelago and dominated progressively the hundred-odd realms of the Ainu aboriginals. They nominated local governors after each conquest.

In these Dark Ages the first rough shape of a society was formed. The family group first, descended from a divine ancestor (*Kami*), companion of Jimmu. The clan, the enlarged family of primitive society, grouped together several families, whose members were set into a hierarchical system from which some of them, real serfs, were soon released. Certain trades were formed into guilds; the dignitaries, at first part of the Imperial family and called *daibu*, were later to become the *daimyo*; the land-holding lords were to become the nobility.

The Emperor was the *Tenno*, supreme head of all these categories. Descended, obscurely, from the Goddess of the Sun, Amaterasu, he was the representative of solar force on the earth. Progressively his power was confined to religious representation, with a corresponding loss of real authority.

The 'Way of the *Kami*', Shinto, appeared at first as a very nebulous religion which had neither permanent sanctuaries, nor sacred images, any more than theology or moral teaching. Its cult was essentially a ritual of purification. The *Kami* were the natural forces, more or less individualised, of legendary gods and of divine ancestors. White creatures were sacrificed to them: for instance, a spotless fowl was skinned alive once a year; or else, during saturnalian orgies, stone phalluses were erected in their honour. Such rituals were calculated to turn away their formidable wrath.

Buddhism reached Japan in the baggage of a Korean ambassador about A.D. 538. The Japanese scoffed at first at these new ideas which divided the court of the *Tenno*, but when the Empress Suiko (554–629), at the age of thirty-nine became a zealous Buddhist on the death of her husband, most of the nobles at the court followed suit. The Japanese, traditionally tolerant in religious matters, never laid down an exclusive form of worship, willingly practising syncretism.

The great families, the clans, gained power, the Fujiwara finally dominating the political and cultural world. It was the Golden Age of Japanese history: a delightful time of refinement with the court at the summit. Poetry had such prestige with the nobility that the most modest writer of impromptu verses could hope for the most flattering success with the ladies and quite unexpected honours: morals were easy and pleasure-seeking in the courts of Old Heian (later known as Kyoto). The life of the nobility was a round of pleasure. Banquets under lights, contemplative walks at night, ritual festivals of nature, popular dances. The year 1000 was a fête; and yet...

The great families were powerful enough to fight each other, most often because polygamy had multiplied the number of descendants of the propertied classes. Under Saga *Tenno*, the direct descendants of the Emperor were reduced to the rank of nobility from the seventh son onwards. Some of these down-graded princes were known by the name of Minamoto, and formed a clan.

Conflicts were sometimes caused by the ambitious: certain titles were coveted, such as those of *Kampaku*; the civil dictator, or *Shogun*, Generalissimo 'against the barbarians'. In 949, a member of the Fujiwara clan was sent to fight against brigands: he became a brigand himself, pillaging and burning.... A Taira, himself also a descendant of an Emperor, seized the province of Kanto (that of the present Tokyo) without having been named as governor. It was a Fujiwara who eliminated this soldier of fortune: the uneasy feudal system of the time was simply a mosaic of similar events.

From the end of the tenth century, the Emperor of Japan

gradually lost his power. The local clan chiefs fought each other maintaining a climate of civil war, while the court, impregnated with Chinese culture, seemed unconcerned with the affairs of the country. The Minamoto clan was eventually to control these squabbles and make itself master. A rough and impassioned era followed a time of soft living and luxury; an era notable for its chivalrous ideals and fidelity to tradition. These were the principles of the first samurai.

The samurai were at first military leaders, direct vassals of the nobles, engaged by them for protection, or having important functions in the administration. They had their own troops and enjoyed the right to ride on horseback when going to war. Little by little, the *bushi*, the ordinary soldiers of peasant origin, became samurai in their turn. It was from the word *bushi* that the *Bushido* code derived. This was written in the seventeenth century and indicated to the samurai his rules of conduct and the right course to follow in daily life as in war. Later, experienced in the martial arts as defined by the 'Way of the bow and the horse', these rough barons denied themselves any association with the effete nobility of the court.

This, then, was the Middle Ages. Comparisons are tempting: for instance, could Yoshitsune not be compared with Roland, the nephew of Charlemagne? No; for, as Mishima said, the thinking of the Japanese was very different.

Yoritomo, chief of the Minamoto clan, tapped his fan on the bulwark of the flagship. His lieutenants were waiting imperturbably till he had finished his silent contemplation of the sunrise to receive their battle orders. But he said nothing.

This morning in April 1185 promised a radiant day. The sun rose into sight, blood-red on the black, deep waters of the Straits of Dan-no-ura, at the far end of the Honshu and Kyushu islands.

The fleet of the Taira, the rival clan, spotted in the night by swift reconnaissance craft, was still hidden by a scatter of fortified, precipitous islets, topped with a cluster of pines which showed in outline against the pearly mist of the east. The Taira could be captured in their nest if Yoritomo wished, but did he so wish? His lack of action suggested otherwise.

'The general fears that the success will again be credited to his brother, Yoshitsune,' whispered one of the crouching officers, bending the wood of his bow with a powerful hand. The iron fan was still tapping on the wood like the chattering of an amorous cormorant.

'I can see Benkei,' whispered an old soldier, stroking his beard. 'He is still watching over Yoshitsune as he sleeps. It is he who tells him which way the wind is blowing. He has slept at his feet for two years, while we have played hide-and-seek on the Inland Sea.'

To the rhythm of his meditation, Yoritomo's fan tapped more loudly: he was imagining the phases of this decisive battle before he was even engaged in it. Already in imagination he was in the heart of the battle. Would he have to sacrifice the young Emperor Antoku and the Empress Mother, whom the Taira would certainly try to take with them in their inescapable rout? Would the Imperial treasure be on the same junk? Would it be opportune if his too-famous half-brother perished in this battle? Such a death would strengthen his legend as a hero, and this made Yoritomo grind his black teeth.

Benkei, yes, that rogue of a monk! He would gladly kill him with his own hands, if they had not been allies temporarily. What a triumph to hang the giant's head from the prow of a ship: the charm which protected Yoshitsune would then be broken and there would remain only the great Minamoto, the only one: Yoritomo!

The red globe, fully emerged, seemed now so close that Yoritomo raised his fan as if to touch it through the fine mist rising from the water. Without looking round, he gave the order: 'Weigh anchor!' The 300 high-sided battle junks lowered their sails of plaited bamboo in one single impressive movement. A favourable wind filled them in a few seconds. The phantom fleet of the early morning, until then motionless, came to life, following in perfect order the plan made the previous evening, while an ant-hill of silent warriors, emerging with their chief from the long paralysis of waiting, prepared for battle.

Yoritomo slowly put on his two-horned helmet, his eyes shining strangely. He was rather small, a little heavy with age, but still the frugal and athletic soldier whom his men had always respected. The head of the clan was wearing black steel armour, like the men around him, and, like them, with three fingers of the right hand together, he stroked the sheath of his sword which he could draw in the twinkling of an eye. This was the only sign that battle was about to begin, for he remained completely calm: he knew that he had already won. It was the third act, the last.

When Yoritomo was born, anyone who was not a Taira was nothing.

Tairo-no-Kiyomori, the most powerful man of his time, cruel, tortuous, ostentatious and corrupt, had profited from the divisions between the clans to obtain the highest honours for his own family and line. Had he not managed to reach the first lower rank at court, one which was only granted, in principle, posthumously? What was more, he had skilfully wormed his way into the graces of the Imperial family and placed his offspring in key posts of power. The Emperor was thus a nephew of the Taira line and the women's apartments in the Imperial palace were filled with their daughters. In order to rule with more freedom and in greater tranquillity, the intriguer had even had the court transferred to Fukuwara, well away from any influence other than his own. Fukuwara was unsuited to the ostentatious life to which the great are inclined, and everyone was discontented, even the common people who lived off their trade with the powerful.

The premonitions of fate were increasing: there were frequent earthquakes and serious epidemics; soon terrible fires ravaged the new capital. Public opinion, in the face of this supernatural wrath, was quickly reversed and the first conspiracies were sparked off....

'The Taira, my lord!' shouted the look-out man.

A finger of sunlight pointing into the straits showed in the distant bluish halo of the mist a dense forest of masts without their rigging. The birds were in their nest. Drawn up in lines, these ships were an easy prey. With a gesture of his fan, Yoritomo ordered the deployment of his fleet. Then he immersed himself once more in his reverie.

After Shirakawa's conspiracy, the ex-Emperor, the son-in-law of the dictator, had been replaced on the Imperial throne by his own son: young Antoku, a child. It was then that Minamoto Yorimasa, father of the *Shogun*, tried to secure the power for his master, Prince Mochihito, son of Shirakawa. He had roused the Minamoto of several provinces along the great routes to Tokaido, Tosando and Hokurikudo. The starting point for the conspirators was to be the monastery of Miidera, where the pretender had taken refuge. But the Taira knew everything: did they not maintain gangs of rascals and urchins as informers to spy on citizens and denounce them?

It was a splendid battle at the break of day, with one against a hundred. Yorimasa had thought up an extraordinary stratagem at the Uji bridge: the Taira cavalry, confused by the mist, had not noticed that he had had the road in the middle of the bridge removed, and they had charged in response to the shouting of the conspirators who were on the other bank. Hundreds of warriors were drowned in the river, hampered by their heavy armour.

For a moment, Minamoto Yorimasa thought he had won, but the law of numbers was to come into play in the succeeding hours. Despite their courage, the Minamoto, of whom not a single one sought to retreat, were all cut down after extraordinary feats of valour. One of the last to fall, Yorimasa, killed himself near to the body of the Imperial prince who had been cut in two by a sword-stroke. Already, on the order of Taira-no-Kiyomori, the monastery of Miidera was blazing like a great bonfire. In the distance, on the mountain tops, all the other great monasteries suspected of having aided the enemies of the Taira were in flames also. This was the beginning of a long-lasting resentment on the part of the monks against the Taira clan. ...

'They are waking up, my lord!'

The Taira look-outs had at last seen the fleet deploying. Yoritomo could hear them calling. No matter, it was too late and the flawless encirclement of the enemy fleet was completed. According to his plan, the tide should prevent them making any coherent manoeuvre to get under way. The fan of battle was tapping again on the gunwale like a cormorant hunting.

Yoritomo had raised the flag of revolt throughout Tokaido in 1181, four years earlier. Kiyomori had promised great wealth to whomever brought him his head. Although pursued by hallucinations in which he saw his victims again, he reproached himself for having shown mercy to the rebel's son. Spared, for some unknown reason, by the despot, young Yoritomo had lived quietly in gilded exile. He feigned to have forgotten all thought of revenge and gave an impression of great frivolousness. 'This Minamoto thinks only of painting his face,' the spies reported.

Whenever he was questioned the son of Yoshitomo replied that he was tired of the political game since he had lit his father's funeral pyre. But it was not so.

After talking all day and drinking *sake* with his many friends – Hojo Tokimasa (a Taira, but one who did not at all like his family), or his foster-brother, Miyoshi-no-Yasunobu – the young man asked his servants to make sure no one was spying on them and then underwent a swift metamorphosis: speedily equipped for war, he leapt on his horse and rode off towards the nearby mountains for martial training which lasted all night. In the morning, weary, he slept late, which made people think him indolent; then he indulged in conversation which made them think him garrulous.

Just once, to the general surprise of the Taira, he came out of his apparent torpor for an unexpected excursion on horseback. This was to kidnap Masako, the Taira daughter of his friend Tokimasa. Her beauty had been so highly praised as to inflame him. Alone, on a dark night, he had slipped stealthily, like a tiger, into the palace of Fukuwara. A guard, not properly awake, had challenged him. The man's head was cut off before he could hear the reply:

'Minamoto!'

Masako, who had been following her seducer without enthusiasm, then hung on his sleeve and no one cared to try to take her from the young man whose broad shoulders and piercing gaze did not encourage the usual pleasantries.

Yoritomo's cousin, Minamoto-no-Yoshinaka, came to visit him frequently: he was planning rebellion in the North. One day in 1180 a messenger arrived: his mount was flecked with foam.

'Yoshinaka has risen in rebellion,' he said simply.

The future *Shogun* equipped himself in the sight of all and went off at a gallop across the dried-up rice-fields where the peasants acclaimed him: Minamoto was going off to attack the Taira once more, twenty years later.

From the beginning of the guerrilla struggle, the young general fixed his base at Kamakura so that he could, from there, incessantly harass the Taira who held Tokaido. He refused at this time any encounter in a set battle with his enemies. The quick ambush and the sudden attack were the essentials of his tactics. Very quickly he had the whole population with him.

The decisive battle for the domination of Tokaido was won almost without any fighting.

Yoritomo had marshalled his troops, who were beginning to fill out and become seasoned, on the banks of a river: they numbered several thousand. The army of the Heike (Taira), a monster war-machine of one hundred thousand men, came to take up their positions towards evening, on the opposite bank. Yoritomo then ordered that thousands of bivouac fires should be lit and he urged all his warriors to talk loudly with great animation. To give an impression of even greater numbers, he had rounded up all the ducks in the countryside and these birds added so great a volume of noise to the night-time chatter that, after a few small skirmishes of no importance, the Taira generals preferred to withdraw with their troops, thinking themselves too greatly outnumbered.

The absurdity of this climb-down was to cause more trouble for the Taira than an actual military defeat. The episode resulted moreover in the death of one man of quality: Kiyomori, the old tyrant, who had been on his deathbed for some weeks, died in a last convulsion of rage.

At the same time, Minamoto-no-Yoshinaka, cousin of the future *Shogun*, was threatening the capital from Shinano. He was the victor of a battle at the foot of Mount Tonami and, enticed by the fine promises of the ex-Emperor, ended by betraying Yoritomo by taking the child *Tenno*, the young Emperor Antoku, to Kyushu. At this time, in 1,182, there were in Japan three seats of government: Fukuwara, the capital of the Taira; the East, with Yoritomo; and Kyushu, with the court.

It was then that Yoshitsune, Yoritomo's half-brother, intervened.

The childhood of this warrior 'without fear or blame' had been in no way comparable to that of Yoritomo. His mother, Tokiwa, was of obscure birth, but of great beauty. She had, according to legend, first place in the heart of Yoshitomo. But when he died she lost everything and took to the roads, fleeing barefoot through the snow, one child at her breast, two others held by their hands.

A soldier of fortune with a pure heart, Yoshitsune possessed only his swords, which a blacksmith uncle had tempered for him when he came of age. It was simply by his skill that he was to recruit his first companion: the giant Benkei, a brigand monk who robbed passers-by in the centre of the town at the turn of a bridge. Yoshitsune, told of this, went alone to challenge the brute.

'Look here, fellow! I've come to deal with you.'

It was a swift duel which remained famous. A passage of arms with two-handed swords meant death when the opponents were good fighters. But this time there was no death and when the terrified onlookers dared to lift their eyes the giant was on his knees prostrating himself before his vanquisher who had disarmed him and spared him – something unknown in such a case in those days. From that day, Benkei followed Yoshitsune and became his faithful servant.

Yoshitsune began a campaign to punish Yoshinaka for his treachery to his brother Yoritomo. He proved to be a great general and at Owaru in December 1182 it was he who ensured the victory of the Minamoto. But now the young hero took political initiatives: immediately after his victory, he and the *Kampaku* Fujiwara-no-Motomichi, the Prime Minister of the period, negotiated a change of sovereign with the ex-Emperor. This latter chose Go-Toba, his grandson, in the place of the absent Emperor, Antoku.

Yoritomo was annoyed. The young knight errant was doing too much for his taste. The year which followed was filled with the exploits of Yoshitsune, who hunted down the Taira on the Inland Sea and dislodged them by wildly audacious exploits from all the positions they still held, destroying their bases.

'My lord, Yoshitsune's men are attacking without us.' In fact, one squadron of the united fleets of the two Minamotos, that of Yoshitsune, to the right, had broken through the line of junks which had been progressing till then like a solid wall, and was now advancing more rapidly. The flagship, carrying on its mainsail the '*mon*', the red circle with Yoshitsune's symbol, had a short lead and sped through the waves directly towards the vessel of the old chief Munmori, whose flag had just been hoisted.

'Lousy dog,' growled Yoritomo, raising his fan of command to direct his fleet and attempt to overtake the thief of glory who had outdistanced him.

The naval battle of Dan-no-ura had begun.

Already, from behind the wooden shields which formed battlements arranged in the length of the junks, a rain of heavily feathered arrows was descending to pierce the flanks of the enemy ships just below the water-line, while other arrows carrying burning oakum lit the first fires of the battle, giving the appearance of fireflies dancing on the blue-green waters.

Yoritomo, in a fury, struck his fan of command on the gunwale: he was almost two kilometres behind. But the tide, as expected, hampered the rudder chains of the Taira, driving their ships on to the reefs of the coast. They were floundering, sails slack, while the sudden assault on the part of the squadron commanded by the impetuous Yoshitsune disorganised their overcrowded ranks.

Ten or twenty vessels, too close to each other, yardarms touching, were in flames already and Yoshitsune's junks hemmed them in, riddling them with arrows. A gigantic howling figurehead, Benkei himself, bent a huge bow at the prow of his master's ship. Far off, Yoritomo on his bridge could distinguish his shouts in the midst of all the uproar. On the waters of the Inland Sea, voices carried as if in an echo chamber. Suddenly, he raised both arms to signal that the course of his fleet be altered by forty-five degrees.

Emerging behind the screen of the line of ships being attacked, a dozen others broke away and slipped off, hugging the reefs of the coast. These had been able to catch the wind and made off quickly. They bore the Imperial *mon*. Yoritomo needed half an hour to reach them with his finest ships. The main part of his fleet, with his half-brother, was intent on the extermination of the Taira. Arrows whistled from the flagship in an attempt not to sink the boats but to capture them.

'Aim for the helmsmen!' ordered Yoritomo.

Pierced by the arrows of the Minamoto marksmen, they abandoned the tillers and slipped into the water. The ships, out of control, began to pile up on the reefs which lay just beneath the surface of the straits.

Yoritomo allowed his junks to tackle the rich ships which

were following, already disabled, and himself headed for the largest of them. He cut across her bows just before the farthest point of Honshu, thus destroying her last chance of escape.

Forced into battle, the Taira were massed in a solid square in the bows to meet their assailants. Their great shields, already bristling with arrows, gave them the air of dragons in a rage. Suddenly, the keel of the great ship scraped on a reef and she grounded.

Yoritomo's brief, savage battle laughter rang out.

From the height of his bridge-deck which overlooked the bow of the first of his adversaries' ships, the avenging Minamoto contemplated his last enemies. Hands on hips, frightening in his controlled ferocity, he saw, behind the screen of the last defenders, the widow of Kiyomori, her veils fluttering in the wind. She was hugging the little Emperor Antoku, who was dressed as a warrior and brandishing a miniature sword as if, pitiful soldier, he thought to defend his throne in the slaughter which was about to take place. The former Empress, daughter of Kiyomori, stood beside them, her hands clasped on her chest. Some scholars of the court, with some monks, their arms folded, surrounded them.

'Women, bring me the child,' said Yoritomo curtly, not yet giving the order to attack to the soldiers who were at his sides, tense as the strings of their bows.

'I wish to salute the Emperor,' he corrected himself, to break the silence which followed his demand, 'and I earnestly request the honour of his being removed from the Taira ship to that of the Minamoto.'

In naming himself, his voice grew suddenly louder and the menace of his tone denied the politeness of the spoken words.

'Come and take him!' roared the captain of the guard.

But a quivering arrow cut off the phrase in his throat and he fell like a log. The fan was lowered. The Minamoto warriors boarded the deck like a glinting wave of steel. They butchered with both hands, cutting off with ferocious cries heads in their crested helmets and hands tensely gripping their weapons, slashing at wood, blood and stray limbs. A long, inhuman cry from a woman interrupted this wild harvesting, as she stood in the middle of the deck, as if in the middle of a field.

'Listen to me, Minamoto!'

The widow, still clutching the Prince Imperial, had climbed on to the gunwale of the poop.

Yoritomo stopped short, his sword on a crushed skull. No sound came from his mouth, open around his black polished teeth.

'I give back the sacred sword to the Emperor.'

She had drawn the emblem from its wrappings and the child in her arms was holding it with difficulty. The wind and the moaning of dying men muffled her next, final words. The woman and the child moved backwards and toppled into the black waters.

When his stupefaction had passed, Yoritomo mowed down the last survivors without mercy. Every man there was heartbroken after the disappearance of the sacred child.

'Dive in, rescue them!' But only the former Empress, who was floating near the reef, could be saved. She was carrying the mirror and the jewel, two of the sacred emblems of the dynasty.

Yoritomo set sail for the scene of the great battle: a fire, which could be seen from afar, now glowed in the straits. His hated half-brother was carrying out the extermination of all who bore the name of Taira. Like a devil, leaping from one ship to the other, sword high, followed by the gigantic Benkei, he looked like an evil *kami*. In the evening, Yoshitsune was still putting to his sword those who had not killed themselves. He boarded the flagship, dripping with blood. He had even slain some enemies by piercing them in the chest with the horns of his helmet.

'Brother,' he said, panting, 'all which is not Minamoto is not born.'

Yoritomo tapped gently with his fan of battle on the side of the ship. He smiled unpleasantly.

'You were not born, Yoshitsune,' he replied. 'You just came into the world.'

Conqueror at the age of thirty-nine, Yoritomo was recognised officially as *Shogun*, and founded the shogunate by establishing his *bakufu* or general headquarters in his old rebel base of Kamakura, which immediately became his capital.

From then on in Japan there were two sovereigns: one, nominal, was the Emperor, or *Tenno*; the other, the effective sovereign, was his premier vassal. The *Shogun* (a title equivalent from then on to that of regent), exercised, in fact, the real authority in the country.

The Exploits of Yoshitsune

LEGEND RECORDS that in the seventh century the Minister Kamatari, the founder of the celebrated family of the Fujiwara, was making a long pilgrimage when he reached a small fishing village named Yui. He then had a dream: a divinity ordered him to bury his *kama*, a large knife in the shape of a matchet, on a nearby hill. The place had then taken the name of Kama-kura: 'the place of the knife'. It was there that Yoritomo had installed his shogunal town, and in the year following the great victory he busied himself in the midst of an ant-hill of workers to build a place worthy of the Minamoto.

The site, in the far east of the country, looked impregnable: around the sanctuary dedicated to Hachiman, *kami* of war, tutelary divinity of his family, the *Shogun* had developed the city in a well-protected valley, watered by the Nameri, surrounded on three sides by high hills and bordered on the south by the sea.

Seven passes gave access to the town across the mountain: the entrances were guarded by *kido*, or wooden doors. Starting at the great sanctuary of Hachiman, a broad avenue, of which the centre was raised some forty inches and formed a path, linked the centre of the town with the sea. On each side of this main artery were to be found the residences of great warriors and the most important personages of the *bakufu*. The residence of the *Shogun* and the government offices were situated to the West of the great sanctuary. They were long, spacious buildings, constructed in the style of Kyoto.

Yoshitsune looked at them for a long time. He handed the reins of his fine horse to Benkei.

'Go,' he said. 'My brother the *Shogun* does not like to be kept waiting.'

Yoritomo, a year after the battle, had put on flesh. Surrounded by his advisers, he drank *sake* slowly and no one spoke. The knight faced him, motionless; having bent almost double in a low bow. His glance detected only feigned indifference and contempt in the crowd. He waited.

The *Shogun* put his goblet on the small table in front of him and remained squatting, legs crossed. He stroked his beard, lifted a mirror to check the whiteness of his face where a thick coating of powder partially concealed the effects of alcohol, then straightened a fold in his sumptuous silk robe, before announcing in a very low, hoarse voice, 'I name you governor of Iyo. Go, your escort is waiting.'

Yoshitsune remained impassive. He would have preferred arrest to this exile, probably under surveillance, and the lack of regard shown by his elder brother spoke volumes of the secret hatred which he was suddenly showing.

But Yoritomo was fanning himself slowly, without raising his eyes: the audience was over. Yoshitsune bowed and turned brusquely on his heels to leave. Thirty armed men, springing from nowhere, surrounded him and marched with him as far as the central avenue. Benkei and the horses found themselves surrounded by an identical troop.

'Master, have you been arrested?' asked the giant.

'No, I'm now governor of Iyo.'

'Much the same thing.'

They rode through the city, which already had more than fifty thousand inhabitants. As they passed they were acclaimed, for these two warriors enjoyed immense popularity.

Shizuka was waiting in a litter. With a simple gesture, the riders signalled to the bearers to join their troop and the dancer's pretty face disappeared behind the curtains.

The small group left the town by the south gate at Cape Inamura. Outside the fortifications, the road passed a narrow beach along which could be seen a line of ships, equipped to shoot arrows. Standing up in his stirrups, Yoshitsune studied the ramparts manned by warriors protected by their shields.

'My brother is a great man,' he said pensively.

Then he rode on in silence, followed by Benkei, like a great shadow, and by Shizuka's litter. Yoritomo's strong-arm men came behind them, lances high, and their horses raised a golden dust as they passed.

Iyo was a monastery for warrior-monks, a frontier fortress set on a deserted hill. Colossal walls safeguarded its foundations and the outer wall was flanked at intervals by wooden buildings, several storeys high, in the form of towers, with loopholes. Great moats filled with greenish water ringed the whole edifice.

'Here we are, then – prisoners!' murmured Benkei, leaning over his horse's withers to pass the postern gate of this lugubrious place. Yoshitsune sniffed the air of the great courtyard. From the neighbouring sanctuary came a smell of incense, full of memories for him. He began to speak of them to his concubine, Shizuka, when her litter came level with his horse.

'I was a *chigo* (a page-boy) once in a monastery like this at Kurama. My mother, before her death, had persuaded a rich relation that I should become a page-boy. I was given rich clothes, had my eyelashes shaved off as they do with girls; I was even given make-up...'

The dancer's very white face showed between the silk curtains: 'You must have been very handsome, my lord!'

'Too much so!'

Yoshitsune gave a brief laugh, shared by Benkei who had been a monk and knew how the lay-brothers felt about their *chigos*.

'But I learned more than such childish things,' the knight went on. 'Each day with my master I recited *sutras*, day and night I studied the Chinese classics, and then, one morning...'

A line of stony-faced monks had replaced the escort of strong-arm men around the little group.

Yoshitsune jumped quickly from his horse, making a clatter with the hobnailed soles of his bear-skin boots.

'Take us to our apartments!' he ordered.

Shizuka's attendant helped her out of the litter, for her limbs had become numb during the long journey. The child she was carrying made her pretty silhouette a little heavy.

Suddenly, the giant Benkei began to shout, 'To the devil with this monk, he's hurting my horse's mouth!'

Then he grabbed the bridles of the two very valuable chestnut stallions, which were his pride, to take them himself to the stables.

These horses had the names of *kami*, so beautiful did their owners consider them. Their tails were bushy and leather saddles decorated with golden stars, covered the entire length of their backs. Fringes and pompoms completed the ornamentation of these noble chargers whose hooves were so delicate that it was necessary, after each outing, to change the shoes which protected them.

'Governor,' said the one-time brigand wryly, on discovering the monastic cells which had been allocated to his master and his followers, 'Governor, where are the coffers containing your armour? Where are your followers? Where are your *saburai* (the guards of this period were named thus). Where are your *bushi*, your foot-soldiers? Where is your power, Yoshitsune?'

'Here,' was the only retort made by his master who, sitting cross-legged on the matting, placed his two swords beside him with infinite respect.

Benkei bowed very low and fell silent. Shizuka, sitting in the shadows, looked at her lord, as one adoring a god.

'Go on with what you were telling me, Yoshitsune,' she whispered softly.

'The other *chigos* in the monastery consented to all sorts of things which I myself refused to do. One day, as I was about to tell you, an old monk wanted me to stand close to him during a ceremony, with a long tube of bamboo so that he could ease his bladder without being inconvenienced. This job was given only to servants of the lower class. I laughed at him. This man would have lost face if suddenly an idea had not struck him: "But I was forgetting," he said, "you are of age." I think he had advanced the date a little to get out of his predicament, but, in any case, I was very happy.'

Yoshitsune went on with his narrative.

'At fifteen,' Yoshitsune continued, 'my life as a man was thus about to begin. The high priest of the Atsuta sanctuary at Nagoya summoned me to remind me of all that this signified. "You will have, from now on, the right to use a *kao* to sign your name because you are now free and have reached your majority. You must wear underpants and a *hakama*, new trousers, and you must coil your hair in a topknot on the top of your head. Finally, for the ceremony of the presentation of your man's hat, you will need a sponsor to give you your name as a man..."'

Shizuka sat listening to this, motionless as an ivory statuette.

'I was called Ushiwaka in my early childhood and, at that time, Shanao,' Yoshitsune went on, 'but I think that I already had a bit of character. I said to Kichiji, the rich merchant who was my companion, "I don't want to go to Oshu as a pageboy! Get me a hat!" He borrowed one which he placed on my head. I was still not satisfied and I showed it immediately. "You want me to be given a name by Hidehira, who is a vassal of the Minamoto," I said. "But I insist that the ceremony takes place here, in the presence of Yoritomo's mother, since all my relations are dead." Kichiji agreed again. The next day I purified myself and I went before the divinities, accompanied by the priest. I had prepared my declaration. I can still remember it.'

Yoshitsune repeated it, word for word, just as he had on that solemn day. 'Being the eighth child of Yoshitomo, I have no objection to being the last. Give me the name of the ninth of the stables on the left, Samakuro, and let my true name be Yoshitsune, since my grandfather was called Tameyoshi...'

Benkei laughed very loudly at the precocious audacity of his lord. Shizuka's servant had a jar of *sake* in her trunk. She put it down on the matting at the feet of the men, and served them. They gulped down the liquid, their morale rising like a well-shot arrow.

'And you, white dove,' asked Benkei, 'what did you do when you came of age?'

'I am of humble origin, my lord, and there was no celebration – on the contrary. My father told me that I should no longer join in games with the boys and my mother put up my hair and painted my teeth black.'

'Your mother knew the customs,' said Shizuka, laughing, 'but she should also have plucked your eyebrows and repainted them on your forehead, as is required for beauty.'

'I am only a peasant, mistress, whereas you became an Imperial concubine immediately.'

The memory of the sacred child, nine years old when he had disappeared in the black waves of Dan-no-ura caused a long silence. Yoshitsune had demanded the most beautiful dancer as part of his booty after the battle.

'Let us drink,' said the knight to Benkei. 'Tomorrow the governor of Iyo will take his writing-brush to address a request to his brother, the *Shogun*, to allow him to leave this place.'

But the messages from the monastery remained unanswered. Shizuka's belly grew rounder. Benkei and his master had only a small courtyard, enclosed by high walls, in which to practise the martial arts each day. The garrison of soldier-monks had been considerably reinforced and the strong-arm men silently crossed their halberds before the 'governor' when he tried to get out of the stronghold.

'For your own safety, you must not go out.'

The knight, after long meditation, which none would have dared to interrupt, had gradually become convinced of the black ingratitude of his brother, Yoritomo. A wild idea came into his head: to lay a complaint with the only authority who was above both of them. He dreamed of going to Kyoto to the court of the *Tenno* himself. But how to escape? A group of cowled pilgrims was crossing the great courtyard of the sanctuary one morning when Benkei, who had been acting piously in order to get out of the stronghold, slapped his forehead.

The giant, bowing his head, moved through the half-darkness in the wake of the monks. A few moments later he came out from the temple, more enormous than usual. Re-entering the stronghold, he threw down in front of his master four sets of old grey hemp clothing.

'There is the road to freedom, my lord.'

The problem of Shizuka and her servant remained. Benkei was not too long in finding a solution.

'Since you are supposed to be travelling with a group of ascetics, it would be better if you appeared to be a page. It would seem natural for you to use make-up and your age would not matter.'

Benkei drew his sword, 'cleaver of rocks', and without remorse, hacked away at Shizuka's beautiful hair till it reached only to her bosom. Then he combed it in the style of a young lad, arranged it on the top of her head, applied a little make-up to her face and painted a delicate pair of eyebrows on her forehead. She dressed herself in five under-kimonos, pulled on a pair of stockings reaching to her thighs, put on a blouse and a silk *hakama*, and straw sandals. At her side she hung a brightly coloured fan and a sword with a red wooden hilt. She also carried a Chinese flute of bamboo, which only men may play, and a midnight-blue brocade bag containing five chapters of the *sutra* of the Lotus, which Benkei hung round her neck. The woman servant, with bigger shoulders, knotted her hair in a topknot like that of a man, and, like a man, bound her forehead with a white linen band before wrapping an ample kimono around herself.

Four furtive shadows approached the door of the stronghold without attracting attention. Gigantic Benkei had changed himself into a very fat man: his false belly was at the same time both baggage and arsenal.

The pseudo-pilgrims had hardly reached the first foothills of the mountain when the alarm bell of the monastery of Iyo rang out. Doubtless, the monks had just discovered the bodies of their brothers whom Benkei had knocked senseless with a speed worthy of a one-time bandit. The fugitives kept up a good pace, turning from time to time to make sure that the dancer, leaning on her servant, was not lagging too far behind. They walked thus all through the night, towards the cold stars shining on the snow-covered summit.

In the morning, Shizuka, exhausted, fell for the first time. Encouraged by her companions, she took the road again, occasionally bathing her sore feet in the icy waters of a mountain stream. Benkei, always alert, was first to hear the riders.

'Yoritomo's men, my lord – probably a group of scouts reconnoitring.'

There were some thirty of them, their horses laboriously climbing the pebbly road, wearing armour and coats of mail with metal protectors for their knees and thighs, and dragon's head helmets on their heads. Swords, five feet long, hung from their belts and in their hands they held octagonal iron bludgeons.

'Charge!'

In twenty wild-cat leaps, Yoshitsune and Benkei dashed forward, swords held high, and charged across the rocks, the two of them against the whole troop. Their mere appearance made some of the horses rear, throwing their riders, while the others, nervous, panicked and circled on the steep slope. One, two, four men fell as steel flashed on steel. A horse, slashed across the neck, dropped like a stone. Benkei had no time to observe the custom of the times, which was to spare horses. He swopped his weapon for a bludgeon which he swung in an awesome manner: a horseman fell with a dull clatter of iron.

The knight Yoshitsune was holding his sword with both hands. He jumped in three strides on an enemy who dared to face him and whose head he struck off. He deflected with the back of his blade the forked arrow which an archer tried to shoot at him and charged at him before he had regained his wits: the man was chopped in two, like a human tree-trunk, while the string of his bow was still vibrating. Benkei killed a horse with a sledge-hammer blow between the eyes, and then its rider, who had fallen towards him. The giant broke a sword which was aimed at his chest and with a back-handed blow made the doomed warrior fly through the air like a blood-stained puppet. The fight was over in a few moments, with a wild rout of the survivors, many of whom staggered and rolled about among the loose rocks on the side of the mountain.

'We're outlaws now,' said Benkei to his master, religiously wiping the blade of his great sword. But the latter was already climbing towards their starting point. His attentive hunter's ear had caught Shizuka's cry.

'It has to be,' said the servant, Kanefusa. 'Her time has come.'

Yoshitsune sat down, as if overwhelmed, beside his mistress.

'Oh! How it hurts!' exclaimed Shizuka, gripping his arm.

She had fainted a few moments earlier when the faithful Benkei had gone down the slope to look for some water. He came back, happy to have found some, and set to massaging the pearly white back of his lord's mistress, who had taken off her clothing and spread it beneath her.

The child was born, without any complications. Benkei wrapped the wailing new-born infant in his monk's cowl and awkwardly cut the baby's umbilical cord with his short sword. Then he washed him with water from the earthenware jar.

'Give him a name immediately,' he said. 'We are in the mountains of Kameware. Since *kame* means tortoise, and they are reputed to live for a very long time, let us join this name with that of *tsuru*, the crane, which they say lives a thousand years, and let us call him Kametsuru.'

'Poor little beggar! Will he even live to grow up?' said Yoshitsune sadly. 'It would be better to abandon him in these mountains while he is still too young to know anything about it!'

At these words, his mistress forgot her recent sufferings.

'How shameful to say such a thing!' she cried. 'Now that he has been lucky enough to enter the world of men, how do you dare to talk of killing him before he has had the chance to see the sun and the moon! He must not die, even if we have to return to Kamakura with him.'

They took once more to the wearisome road under the pines, to the song of many birds. In the evening, they stopped at a hut made of branches, with an interior which was very dark and dirty. But to Shizuka and her son the dried-mud floor of this shelter was a providential protection; soon, overcome by weariness, she slept. Benkei and his master left with the women the small supplies of food which they had and plunged into the darkness to find a village.

The first group of houses they came across in the valley were still locked up, for it was still night. Two movable barriers blocked off the only street, on which a score of wooden houses fronted, roofed with planks and protected from prying eyes by high fences of bamboo trellis work. A dog kept barking somewhere.

'Let us wait,' suggested Benkei.

They went towards the stone walls of a small temple and into the *hondo*, the building in which there was a statue of the god, Amida Butsu, he who welcomes souls in his paradise in the West. Yoshitsune washed himself in the water trough while Benkei rested on the floor reserved for the dances of Nembutsu by Amida's faithful. The neighing of a horse made them start.

'There is a *saburai* in this village,' Yoshitsune decided. 'Let's go and see.'

The barrier had just been opened and immediately they saw the stable from which a horse's head reached out towards the road. Some children had already pointed them out. An armed man greeted them.

'I am the *jito* of this village and I recognise you, Yoshitsune and Benkei. You are welcome in my house.'

To thank him for his courtesy, the knight placed his great sword near his host's on the rack in the entry-hall. His squire followed suit after a moment's hesitation. They ate and drank in silence, before the soldier-administrator of the village gave them the latest news.

'The *Shogun* has put a price on your head, my lord, and also on that of your companion. Yoritomo has sent many warriors after you on the mountain. You must go north, to the Fujiwara of Mutsu.'

The two fugitives were taking a short rest in the home of this old soldier of the Minamoto who respected the outlaws' courage, when the sound of galloping made them start up. Their host called out, 'Don't move! Those are messengers going by.'

'Yoshitsune's concubine has been taken!' shouted one of the riders to the *jito* as he passed. 'She is being taken back to Kamakura to be publicly humiliated. She had a son. He was buried alive on the orders of the *Shogun*. A crazy servant tried to stop them. She clawed at an officer and he chopped her head off.'

Yoshitsune held Benkei back firmly as he tried to get to the door. His eyes were expressionless.

'Let's go to the Fujiwara.'

The two men resumed their long Odyssey. It was to be filled with exploits which would be sung in legends.

On the northern slope of the mountain, in a place named Mitsunokuchi, where the road forked, two local nobles had built a toll-house, protected by stout stakes. Night and day, three hundred guards were constantly on the alert to hold and question all travellers.

One of the guards spoke to the two fugitives. 'Ascetics or not, you must pay the tax. Pay and pass through. By order of the lord of Kamakura, we must support ourselves by collecting payment from all travellers for the right to pass through.'

'That is unheard of!' exclaimed Benkei. 'Since when have the ascetics of Haguro had to pay toll?' As he spoke he braced himself against the heavy timbers which fell on the guards, crushing most of them. Two devils jumped on to the tangled mass of bodies.

'Banzai!'

A rustle of silk: four blades cut through the air and into quivering flesh as the two raging samurai exploded into brief and bloody action. When they pushed their blades back into their scabbards, dead bodies lay in tangled heaps behind them.

But nothing could assuage the knight's sorrow and he separated from his faithful companion when they were close to their objective. Benkei was to return, for good this time, to the monastic life to which he had consecrated his life. Kneeling at the entrance of the temple, the giant blew fiercely on his conch and began to chant in an impressive manner, rolling between his fingers the beads of the rosary hanging from his neck.

'By the *kami* of the three sanctuaries of Kumano, which are the greatest begetters of miracles in Japan, by the hundred thousand guardians of the law of Katsuragi, by the seven great monasteries of Nara, by the Kannon with eleven heads of Hase-dera, may Yoshitsune pass along this road! Hear me, great Bodhisattva: manifest yourself, allow him to reach Oshu safe and sound.'

It was possibly because of the aid of this prayer by his squire that Yoshitsune completed his journey. In 1189, he was staying with the Fujiwara when there came the news that Yoritomo was marching on his host's domain at the head of an enormous army, possibly the strongest ever raised in Japan: 284,000 men.

The sorrowing knight did not hesitate a moment: he could not compromise those who had welcomed him: what was more, he had no appetite for this battle. And so he used his sword. He killed his family – his legal wife, who had rejoined him, and his children. Then he kneeled to commit the traditional *seppuku*.

The hero's last sacrifice was to be in vain: a traitor was already there who was to assassinate Fujiwara-no-Yasuhira, the chief of the clan, and bear his head to the *Shogun*. But Yoritomo also knew the laws of chivalry: beside himself with anger at such baseness, he decapitated the traitor.

For ten years, the *Shogun* was to hear the ever-increasing

verse-chronicle of the exploits of his half-brother, the legendary Yoshitsune, whose preeminence had brought him sorrow in his lifetime. He confided to his wife, Masako, that the shade of the great man pursued him ceaselessly and that he saw him in his dreams, brandishing the sacred sword lost at Dan-no-ura. Was it this vision which made him fall suddenly from his horse in 1199? He was killed thus, instantaneously, at the age of fifty-three.

One corpse among so many others! The tangled labyrinth presented by Japanese history at this period was little more than an uninterrupted series of revolts and murders. But behind the monotonous recitation of these conspiracies lie hidden feats of valour and gallantry. According to the first rule of *Bushido*, one must love life without ever flinching from death.

The careers of Yoritomo's sons were short and wretched. The elder, Yoriie, a slow-witted rake, became a monk. The younger, Sanetomo, a scholar popular at the Imperial court, was to be murdered by his nephew, the Buddhist priest Kugyo. It was then that Hojo Tokimasa, Yoritomo's brother-in-law, and his son Yoshitoki after him, held the position of *Shikken*, that is the *Shogun*'s regent. But who was really governing? A woman: Masako, the *Shogun*'s widow, who had become a Buddhist nun on the death of her husband. The people named her the *ama-shogun*, the nun-general. She it was who faced the rebellion of the Imperial troops in 1221.

It was a time of great confusion. There were four Emperors in Kyoto: the 'first ex-Emperor', Go-Toba; the 'middle ex-Emperor', Juntoku, the younger brother of the former; the 'new ex-Emperor', and the reigning *Tenno*: Kujo, Prince Kamenari, son of the former: he was an infant, three years old.

The *Kampaku*, the civil dictator, belonged to the great family of Fujiwara. It was on his advice that the Emperors ordered the arrest of the civil servants of the shogunate of Kamakura. They declared the *Shikken* Yoshitoki to be a rebel. The war was brief: three corps of troops marched on the capital: 100,000 by way of Tokaido, 50,000 by way of Nakasendo, 40,000 by way of Hokurikudo.

The battle was on!

Izeri Yajiro laid down his brushes with a satisfied air. The men sitting round him looked at him questioningly.

'I am going to read,' he said with a deliberation which was not without affectation, 'the list of family resources which I have drafted for the war which the *bakufu* is embarking on. It corresponds to our sixteen *cho* of land. Here it is: "I, Izeri, vassal of the province of Higo, who entered into religion under the name Saiko, declare respectfully as follows: possessing men, bows, arrows, and horses, Saiko, aged eighty-five years, can no longer walk. Nagahide, his son, possesses bows, arrows, and various weapons: he is sixty-five years old. Tsunehide, his son, who is thirty-eight years old, has a bow, various arrows, armour and a horse. Matsujiro, a relative, aged nineteen, possesses a bow and arrows, various weapons and two servants. Takahide, a grandchild, aged forty years, possesses a bow and arrows, armour, a horse and a servant. All these are under the orders of his lordship, and will serve faithfully. Humbly presented and certified correct as above. The disciple: Saiko."'

'We will leave tomorrow at dawn,' said Nagahide, respectfully rolling up the parchment belonging to the chief of the clan. 'On our way, father, we will leave you at the monastery.'

The old man sighed.

Before going into battle the samurai took a long time checking their equipment and dressing themselves carefully, painting their teeth, arranging their hair, powdering and perfuming themselves. The old man watched them, giving them endless advice.

'It is essential that, even if the enemy takes your head, he should not be able to make fun of your dress. Do not forget to hide in your clothes or your head-dress the holy picture of a protecting divinity and one of the charms I have brought from the sanctuary for you. Do not fear to die in battle: you might follow the endless road of unfulfilled spirits!'

The following day, in the glow of a beautiful morning, he watched them receding into the distance, haloed with crimson light, intoning, 'O, Buddha Amida!'

The *mon*, the family insignia of Izeri's relatives, could not be seen in the long line of battle of the shogunal troops: they wore them on their clothes and all that showed was the distinctive symbols of high-ranking samurai and of *daimyo*, which were held up on banners by servants. It was possible thus to distinguish the wistaria of the Fujiwara, the butterfly of the Taira, the small bamboo of the Minamoto, the two triangles of the Hojo, and the bars within a circle of the Ashikaga. The sixteen-petalled chrysanthemum of the Imperial house did not appear at all: the court did not intervene in this private war; it waited to know who was the victor before taking sides.

The armoured warriors had arrived and already those from Kamakura were speeding their first whistling arrows, to warn and frighten the enemy they were going to attack. Matsujiro waited tensely for his first great battle. 'Hold back your horse,' Nagahide said to him. 'This is the moment for the challenges.'

A single horseman came forward from the ranks of the Imperial army, wearing a lavender cloak over orange-coloured armour. He galloped in front of the enemy ranks, shouting in a powerful voice:

'Since I am a person of small importance, it is possible that no one knows my name: I am a vassal of Lord Ashikaga, Shidara Goro. If there is among you a vassal of the Lords of Rokuhara who wishes to fight with me, let him come forward at a gallop and take the measure of my skill!'

Drawing from his scabbard a three-foot sword, he lifted it in front of his helmet, as if to protect himself from arrows.

The two armies remained motionless, face to face. A minute passed and then an old warrior, who was in the rear ranks of the army of Rokuhara, forced a passage and advanced unsupported. He was wearing armour with black fastenings, and on his head a helmet with a neck protector consisting of five overlapping metal pieces. His chestnut horse was decorated with blue pompoms. He replied at the top of his voice:

'Although I am a stupid man, I have served for many years as a representative of the military government, and though you may despise me, because I am a lay-brother, I belong to the family of General Toshihito, which has provided a long line of warriors. I, Saito Genki...'

As he shouted his name, he was already spurring his horse. He charged, sword held high.

As they met, Shidara seemed the stronger. They clutched each other and both fell. Shidara was on his feet first. He raised his large sword with both hands and swung to chop off his antagonist's head, but Saito, with unbelievable agility, rolled back on himself and parried the blows while on the ground. Then suddenly, with three rapid passes, he struck Shidara who stumbled and staggered, before plunging his sword into the monk's body. The stalwart combatants did not lose their grip on each other as they fell. Their horses came back slowly to sniff the lifeless bodies, joined in death in a brotherly embrace.

But already there came surging from the Kamakura lines a warrior wearing armour enriched with Chinese damask with a helmet on which arrow-heads had been forged. He brandished a five-foot sword, placed it on his shoulder, and set his horse to a gallop just as far as an arrow's distance from the enemy lines. With a loud shout, he announced himself.

'The story of my family is not unknown. Today I see no enemy worth bothering about! I am Daiko Shigenari, personal vassal of the Lord Ashikaga. Is Kono, governor of the island of Tsushima, of whom it is said that he has shown great prowess in past battles, here? If so, let him come forward. We will put on a fine spectacle for the eyes of others!'

While he was speaking, Shigenari gripped his bridle until his horse was blowing foam. A movement began on the right wing of the Imperial army.

'Kono Michiharu is here!'

He was a powerful man and he approached at a gallop.

But suddenly another horseman swept across his path: this was Shichiro Michito, his adopted son, fifteen years old. He rushed towards Daiko who evaded the charge by simply twisting his body and who grabbed him as he passed in a fist of iron. He lifted him in the air by the strap of his armour, saying, 'I do not want to kill a lackey like you!'

He threw the young man to the ground, but then he noticed his *mon*: a square with a double line with the number '3' written inside: he was certainly a Kono. Leaning from his saddle, his sword in one hand, Daiko lifted his young adversary and cut off both his legs.

The governor of Tsushima advanced at a gallop with a loud shout of rage. Simultaneously, supporting Kono, three hundred of his vassals moved from the ranks of the Imperial army, in a cloud of red dust. A thousand Minamoto did the same. A clash was imminent. The two armies followed like solid walls.

'Forward!'

When the Divine Winds Blew

EVEN THE brigands on the roads respected the *shirabyoshi*. If they stopped these female troubadours sometimes, it was so that they could sing for them the exploits of famous warriors. In the exercise of her art, this wandering prostitute was distinguishable by her curious, half-military costume: a tall, stiff bonnet like a man's, and red silk pantaloons twice as long as her legs, so that when she walked they dragged behind her.

Okiku the *shirabyoshi* had decided, after a lot of simpering, to give a performance before some bandits of the Tohoku. She was very young, a little romantic and more affectionate than mercenary. The brigand chief had a long moustache and his eyes became moist when he looked at her.

Hidden behind a low wall, the young girl dressed for the performance while the men waited near the large fire, drinking *sake*, giving great hoots of laughter from time to time, as excited as tom-cats on the tiles. A collective roar marked her entry into the circle.

'Noble lords,' said Okiku, in her small, sharp voice, 'I am going to tell you what happened to the noble hero, Minamoto Yoshitsune, who is not dead, as they say, but still following his glorious career far from here.'

With a tapping of her hand on the tambourine, the entertainer silenced the incredulous murmurs of her audience. Under her make-up, her white face had a tragic fixity. She hid it behind her fan until the silence was complete.

'Yoshitsune still lives.'

So the long narrative began. Okiku mimed, sword and dagger in hand, the quest of the hero whose exploits redoubled in passing through Siberia and from there to Mongolia. Was there a dragon in a river? The fabulous warrior swam to meet it, sword between his teeth, and cut it in two, thus removing its evil spell. He destroyed entire armies single-handed, walked through fire, jumped from precipices, shot his unstoppable arrow between the eyes of legendary giants. Yoshitsune, if things had been thus, would have been ninety years old: but what did that matter? It did not occur to the bandits, who were fascinated by the story. Furthermore, Benkei, brother to all, the miscreant monk with superhuman strength, had rejoined his master to resume his duties in charge of the horses.

'Where are they, Okiku?'

'In China at present. They have already conquered all the North, and soon they will attack towards the South.'

'What name does Yoshitsune use now?'

'The Mongols call him Temujin; but he has become their leader, Genghis Khan.'

'Will he return, Okiku?'

Catastrophe! Catastrophe for Japan if Genghis Khan or his grandson Kublai came seeking vengeance for the wrong done to Yoshitsune....

A falling star zigzagged suddenly through the blue night. The bandits prostrated themselves before the white mask of the *shirabyoshi* which glowed in the last light of the fire.

The number of prophetic visions seen by the monk, Nichiren, increased while he was at Hachiman's sanctuary at Kamakura. 'People of Japan,' he repeated, 'the most powerful monarch of the great Mongol empire is going to send a vast fleet which will decide the destiny of the divine realm.'

This holy man also called for punishment for his country. He considered it corrupt. The sect he had founded, the Hokke-shu, had the stamp of a mystic, nationalistic, fanatical and popular movement.

The Buddhist Church was in fact playing the feudal game, from which it drew substantial profits. Donations (comparable to those of Western nobles) enriched it. Meanwhile, confederations of warrior-monks were formed, such as that on Mount Hiei which consisted of more than three thousand monks. But monastic discipline had become lax: concubinage, the eating of meat, aggressiveness, trickery and violence of every kind were rife.

The monk Nichiren, an isolated visionary, was grieved by this decline. Previously his compatriots had followed the Shinto path, the way of the *kami*, of the spirits: the cult of nature and the Imperial cult, which left an indelible mark on minds, on dress and on architecture.

Since the ninth century, Buddhism had spread over the archipelago as a complementary doctrine. In the first place the wise man, Dengyo Daishi, founder of the monastery of Mount Hiei, to the north of Kyoto, had introduced the *tendai*, the school of liberation by meditation in six stages — reason, discrimination, actual meditation, imitation, partial truth and perfect knowledge. A little later, the *shingon*, also of Chinese origin, preached by Kukai, had refined the philosophy of Buddhism and new sects grew up. Later Jodo and Amidism had come to spread the idea of a gentle redeemer filled with tenderness, who welcomed into his paradise the faithful of goodwill.

'It is a catastrophe!' Nichiren lamented.

In 1260, Kublai became Emperor.

At the head of the Mongol hordes, Kublai made himself the master of Southern China, the last refuge of the national Empire of the *Song*. From Korea, the most recent country to be swallowed up, the conqueror was now thinking of the Japanese archipelago which was reputed to be rich in minerals.

The Khan tried at first to reduce the islands to vassalage by peaceful means. Between 1266 and 1273, six Koreo-Mongol missions tried to negotiate with the Japanese court. The Emperor Yuan, in one of his letters, spoke of Japan as 'a little country' and wished for the setting up of diplomatic relations. But on both sides there was preparation for war: while

Kublai was building a fleet of one thousand ships on the Korean coast, the *Shikken* Hojo Tokimune, hailed at his birth by the oracles as a future saviour of Japan, did not even send the court's reply.

One of the most curious episodes of these preliminaries was the kidnapping, in 1269, of two Japanese from Tsushima. They were taken to Qanbaliq (Peking), and were made much of by the Emperor who entrusted them with a mission to their own government! But this suffered the same failure as the earlier negotiations: the archipelago remained basking in blue light, in a silence no outside voice could pierce.

The samurai of that era, an intrepid and courageous fighter, scorned death. He was not a warrior: he was a peasant, a countryman in the noble and original sense of the word: a man 'of the land' who loved above all else his birthplace, his province, and rejoiced to see peace and order reign there. But in wartime he did his duty with a total selflessness. Certainly he liked to fight sometimes for the simple pleasure of fighting: but he fought above all out of loyalty to his feudal lord in the first place, and, in the second place, for his own folk. He was anxious to bring honour to his family by accomplishing, at the peril of his life, outstanding feats of arms. In adversity, he resigned himself philosophically to suffering the fate of the conquered, or else, weary of running and fighting, he abandoned armour to assume the cowl of a monk, and pray, not for himself, but for the souls of those he had slain in battle.

The samurai fought the better to express his gratitude to him who assured his own and his family's livelihood, and to whom he had sworn fealty in the following terms:

'Now I give my life to the safekeeping of my lord. My life is as light as a feather. I prefer to die facing my enemy than to live turning my back on him.'

This pride, this sense of honour and dignity, was not yet put at the service of the land, of the country as a whole. At this period the idea of Japan as a nation had not yet made its way into men's minds, and the concept of a nation had not yet superseded that of the provinces belonging to the clan. The threat of a Mongol invasion was to mobilise for some time the mental and physical resources of the entire country. Only then did the Japanese recognise that foreigners existed, who might have warlike intentions towards them.

The building of the first great Mongolian fleet was begun in a shipyard in Korea in January 1274. Thirty-five thousand carpenters applied themselves to the speedy building of 300 huge junks, 300 fast boats and 300 small craft. The excellent ships in the style of South China took too much time to complete and the Yuan dynasty had ordered the King of Korea to make haste. Fifteen thousand Mongol and Chinese soldiers were to have sailed in July of the same year, but because of the death of the King of Korea, the embarkation was delayed until 3 October.

Some Koreans had warned the Japanese of the imminence of the attack, for the passing invaders had devastated the Tsushima and Iki islands. The samurai resolutely awaited their landing at Hakata Bay, on the north coast of Kyushu.

The old wall dated from the Nara period in the seventh century A.D. Since dawn, the *Shikken* Tokimune had been perched on the highest part. He kicked the crumbling battlements with his heel and stones rained down on the beach. 'The Taira of Tsushima did not put up any better resistance,' he growled.

Behind him, Nichiren was standing on a promontory, a gaunt shadow among the armed warrior-monks. Gulls by the thousand surged in from the sea, white against the whiteness of the foam on the rough sea, and the mists of the morning. Behind them a tangled forest loomed among the fleecy clouds. 'It's the enemy, my lord!' shouted a young samurai, almost joyously.

Tokimune managed a pale smile and the waiting began.

The perfect proportions of the geography of the gulf were repeated in the ordered grouping of the armies, ranged in a perfect semicircle before and above the old Nara rampart: a coastal fortification forgotten since the times of the former pirates. A cross-wind rattled the *mon* of the great *daimyo*; all were there, side by side for the first time, their horses pawing the ground. On the old wall the human mass was like foliage waving in the breeze, facing the fleet which drew nearer like a large, slow wave from the depths. The ships passed the ends of the bay without any move being made by the defenders: their orders were to wait until the enemy landed.

When the keels of the first ships scraped the pebbles of the beach, the distance of two arrow flights separated the Mongols from the Japanese, but the latter remained impassive. Their archers were waiting, as was customary, until they could see the whites of their enemies' eyes before shooting their whistling arrows. They watched, moreover, with more curiosity than fear, these foreign invaders who formed up into squares as soon as they landed.

On the gunwales of the nearest enemy ships, lines of archers were stringing their short bows and preparing great ballistae, such as the Japanese had never seen before. The shape of their helmets, their clothing and their great shields were objects of astonishment for the samurai. On the bridge of a rated ship, the Chinese commander of the expedition, Wang, began to laugh and his generals followed suit out of politeness, without knowing the reason.

'They're going to let us land,' chuckled Wang. 'They're done for!'

The *Shikken*'s army certainly seemed more contemptible from minute to minute, compared with the Mongols forming up in line on the beach. The critical moment when the invaders could have been thrown back into the sea seemed to have passed. The invaders presented a solid mass whose ships were linked together by chains to make a wall higher than the Nara rampart, and supported the first groups of infantry which had already disembarked. Then a single samurai, caracoling on a horse decorated with pompoms, advanced to face them for the traditional combat challenge.

He was a famous and wealthy warrior: his armour and his weapons looked very splendid. He carried a sword with a golden hilt in a gilded scabbard, attached to a belt of silver chain and protected by a tiger-skin cover. On his back was a quiver of thirty-six arrows, decorated with swans' feathers with stalks of bamboo lightly lacquered between the knots. His bow was ringed in two places and a silver hook fixed above the leather handhold kept the arrow from slipping. Shouting his name aloud, this splendid horseman advanced and challenged a Mongol to come forward to fight with him. All the samurai held their breath. Suddenly, like a swarm of wasps, twenty arrows pierced the horseman and his mount, who both collapsed absurdly at the edge of the tide-line. A second samurai who galloped forward was torn from his saddle by a huge dart from a catapult which pierced him as if he were no more than a butterfly.

A murmur of anger ran through the Japanese ranks: these barbarians had no respect for the laws of 'The Bow and the Horse'! *Shikken* Tokimune could not hold back his troops who were already advancing in a disorderly fashion towards the amphibian fortress. He could only spur his horse to remain in the front line, shouting together with thirty thousand other throats: 'Forward!'

But the furious Japanese charge was stopped dead: the small Mongol bows sent short arrows over a distance of almost 200 metres, whereas the best Japanese bows, much larger and more curved, carried scarcely 100 metres. All the front line of the shogunal troops fell and those following tumbled over the men and horses stretched out on the sand of the beach.

The *Shikken*, with one glance at the convulsed body of one of his officers, realised that the enemy's arrows were tipped with poison. He was signalling to his troops when a heavy rumbling frightened his mount which reared: the Mongols had brought their huge bronze drums, and their loud din terrified the Japanese horses. The ballistae and the catapults made bloody gaps in the ranks of the samurai. Those who, either alone or in small groups, reached the solid line of Mongol infantry were struck from a distance by long spears and failed to penetrate the defence of the wall of great shields.

Nichiren, his arms raised, implored all the *kami* of the skies and at once, went into a kind of trance. His disciples followed suit, their eyes staring.

'Tell Tokimune . . . to retreat . . . quickly. He must assemble another army. He will overcome !'

When the old man's messengers reached the *Shikken* he was just going to order forward the last wave of combatants. Wang's Mongols had landed on the beach strange tubes towards which they held torches : a sudden thunderous sound completely unhorsed an entire line of cavalry; a flash swept behind it, and men rolled on the ground in flames screaming harshly as they died. Tokimune gestured fiercely and the bemused Japanese rapidly withdrew from the beach which was dotted with lifeless bodies : the corpses in their lacquered armour looked like a flight of insects which had been beaten down.

'Go,' said Tokimune to his messenger. 'Call all the samurai of Kyushu and those of Honshu to arms : all quarrels must be forgotten. The enemy is here and has set foot on the sacred soil of Japan. We must vanquish him or perish, all of us. Go !'

Terrible news came in from all round : the Mongol battle corps which had landed at Hakata was not the only one. They were also at Tsushima, which they had taken without striking a blow, and the governor, So-no-Sukekuni, had been killed in battle. Ikishima had been attacked as well. Another force was forming in the bay of Hakozaki in the Chikuzen and was threatening Dazaifu.

Tokimune stayed close to Nichiren, the holy man, in the centre of his camp. The monk restrained him firmly.

'They have taken Imatsu.'

'Don't make a move yet,' said Nichiren, staring at the sky.

'They have occupied six villages on the coast.'

'Wait, Tokimune, wait a little longer!'

Reinforcements were coming in. All the proscribed conspirators, all the *ronin,* and columns of peasants armed with pitchforks, came to replace the dead men who were still lying headless on the beach. Nichiren, motionless, lifted his emaciated arms regularly towards the sky which was imperceptibly darkening. In the evening, the horizon took on a leaden appearance. It was then that a dust-caked messenger, on a horse which collapsed, foaming at the mouth, brought the first good news.

'The *daimyo* of Kyushu have entrenched themselves at Hakozaki. They are resisting the thunder claps. If you cover yourself with animal skins and earth, the flames can be quickly extinguished.'

But Tokimune, fascinated, scarcely listened: he was watching, as were most of the soldiers in his camp, the prodigious results of Nichiren's prayers.

'Look how the sky is darkening . . . look at the sea in the distance, the way it is heaving . . . look at the storm which is blowing up.'

Wang fell dead in a skirmish with the advance guard. A long, feathered Japanese arrow had pierced right through his breastplate and his body. They were building his funeral pyre, facing the angry sea, when one of the Korean helmsmen committed sacrilege by yelling: 'A storm is coming. Weigh anchor! Quick! Quick!'

The first drops of rain extinguished the Chinese general's funeral pyre, while the fleet moved off towards the open sea. A Japanese servant chopped off the head of the leader of the invaders to take it to the *Shikken.*

The typhoon came, like a black, swirling veil, but this frightening phenomenon was welcomed as a refreshing bath by the whole army. Perched on the wall of Hakata, they could see in the distance the wallowing hulls of the enemy vessels, and then their sails being ripped. Each huge wave overturned lines of small boats in a wild bubbling of foam. Other waves again, even higher, rolled the Mongol fleet like a heap of wrecked planks in the cascades of a springtime torrent. The unleashed elements seemed to be responding to the curses called down by Nichiren's outstretched arms and grew more and more violent.

Ships were being wrecked on the rocks at Shiga Point.

'Take their heads!' ordered the *Shikken*.

A group of horsemen sped away, their clothing flapping in the wind. In the morning, hundreds of bloody heads, covered in sand, lay in a heap before Tokimune. The storm abated. A bright ray of red sunshine filtered through the heavy clouds. Nichiren collapsed, exhausted. The divine winds had passed by.

'I will pursue them to Korea!' Hojo Tokimune declared in the euphoria of victory. He immediately ordered a system of naval conscription with a view to manning all the junks of the country. They could not, of course, challenge the enemy on the high seas, but they could render much service along the coasts.

From 1274 to 1296 Japan scarcely demobilised at all. Spurred on by their *Shikken*, who in this way maintained the national unity which had been brought about in their forty-eight hours of great peril, the Japanese carried out intensive training and work on fortifications. Tokimune remembered the long wait on the crumbling ruins of the wall at Hakata: he fortified Kyushu and Nagato against a possible attack from the north; in Kyoto he had the port of Tsuraga placed under permanent guard; finally, in the Bay of Hakata a formidable wall was built on to the old one manned by a permanent garrison.

Years passed under siege. The enemy, however, seemed to have cooled down, and on two occasions Kublai tried to send ambassadors.

'He wants to gain time,' thought Tokimune.

The first envoys of the Mongol Emperor, laden with gold and gifts, disembarked by night at Nagato, at the western point of Honshu. A patrol collected them in the morning and took them to Daizafu and then to Kamakura, because the *Shikken* was at that time carrying out an inspection there.

'We wish to see the Emperor in his palace in Kyoto,' the Khan's envoys moaned. They were on foot, surrounded by horsemen.

'You're dreaming, Chinamen,' laughed a samurai, with a sinister expression. 'Your master has sent you to your deaths – didn't you know?'

A few days later, the mandarins were able to verify the truth of this sally as they passed through the boundaries of the central enclosure in the Japanese leader's camp. They were ushered into a huge square surrounded by motionless troops. Only the rustling in the wind of the streamers on the knights' lances and the stamping of the horses' hooves broke an absolute silence. Three servants bowed, offering *sake* to the ambassadors. They drank it, slowly, and the alcohol made them shudder.

Their hosts, moving aside, made way for six samurai whose swords whistled through the air. The heads of the distinguished envoys fell, leaving their pigtails intact.

'Welcome to Japan,' hissed Tokimune, leaning on the withers of his bay horse which he stroked gently with his fan.

The same scene was to be re-enacted in 1279 at Hakata in the Chikuzen. This time, Kublai Khan's envoys numbered one hundred. They had displayed, on embroidered cloths, the most precious objects of the time. The samurai trampled on them, and the Korean ships carried away coffers quite filled with decapitated heads as so many messages to be returned to their master.

Kublai sent no further ambassadors. In June 1281 his fleet was ready.

From the heights of Chuanchou, on the coast of Fukien, opposite the island of Taiwan, Kublai Khan could see the tall masts of his ships stretching out to the horizon. From his seat on a ceremonial dais he hailed a pale-faced young barbarian in

Manchu costume who had most impolitely found himself a place in front of the dignitaries so as to lose nothing of the spectacle, and who was holding himself curiously erect, his hands on his hips, while all the court remained bowed low in a humble posture.

'Polo, what do you think? Did you ever see such a fleet of ships of war among your Venetians at the other end of the world?'

'Certainly not, great lord,' replied the young, bright-eyed merchant enthusiastically. 'No one will believe me!'

'These three thousand great junks are carrying one hundred thousand of my Chinese, and that's not all!'

'Holy Virgin!' exclaimed Marco Polo in his native language, which the mandarins found very comic – something which, like his blue eyes, had many times saved his life.

'At this moment, while I am speaking, a thousand other ships are leaving Masampo on the southern coast of Korea: they're carrying fifty thousand Mongols and twenty thousand Koreans.'

'Christ's blood! Have they got Greek fire?'

'You mean flame-throwers?'

'Yes, that miraculous invention which lights up the skies at your festivals, great King.'

'All my armies have them.'

'By St Mark, Kublai Khan, who could ever resist your power?'

The fleet was getting under way. Polo noted that he had seen in Zaiton the greatest army in the world setting out to make war on the barbarians of the prohibited islands. He was thought in his time to be an arrant liar.

Nichiren was old now and did not leave his meditations in the Hachiman monastery. His visions were recorded on tablets and messengers riding hell for leather in ceaseless relays carried them to Kamakura. There the Great Council interpreted them both as sacred oracles and as battle orders.

'He foretells contrary winds, Tokimune, and the ebb tide.'

'That means that they're getting under way.'

The wave, in fact, was approaching and was about to break. The first fleet disembarked at Oki. This was the Korean fleet which had taken Tsushima on the way, ravaged Ikishima, and landed at various points along the coast of the Chikuzen between Munakata and the Bay of Hakozaki. The junks were advancing into the bay like a great rampart; they were all linked together by chains.

'Great lord,' pleaded a samurai named Michiari, 'let me attack!'

'Remember the wall of Hakata,' replied Tokimune who was saving his strength and feared to face again the invaders' flame-throwers.

The samurai grumbled. So much the worse for the reckless fellow: his loss would serve as an example!

'Go on then, Michiari!'

One single small boat loaded with volunteers moved in the direction of the solid wall of chain-linked junks. It was so comic, so small, that the entire enemy fleet watched its approach from behind their great leather-covered wooden shields, without even shooting at it. The flagship, thinking that this was a truce mission, sent out signals, and the supreme commander, Admiral Fan Wenhou, an obese pot-bellied man had himself carried to the forward part of his ship to see what was going on.

The Japanese war junk looked like a fisherman's boat facing a cliff as it confronted the huge ship. She came up alongside and the Koreans, much amused, threw grappling anchors. These were immediately grabbed by clusters of black samurai who swarmed up like a flight of large and rather heavy hornets, with their swords between their teeth.

'Forward!'

It was an incredible boarding party of one against a hundred. The surprise was total. Fan Wenhou, who had been knocked over, shouted from the deck, kicking his legs in the air like an overturned tortoise. Beset by five Manchus, Michiari himself, one of the first attackers, upset a brazier between the legs of his adversaries with a quick kick. The fire spread in a flash to the inflammable oil of the flame-throwers set around almost everywhere on the bridge, and the battle continued in the midst of the fire, punctuated by the explosion of earthenware jars.

The crews of the adjacent ships took fright and severed the chains holding them to the flagship which had been transformed into a fireship. The line was broken; the wind, which had quickly set fire to the sails, scattered the fleet in confusion. Some ships collided with each other. Tokimune thought he must be dreaming.

'That impudent fellow! How did he ever do it!'

Michiari came back in the morning, black as a devil, like the other survivors of his crazy escapade. He was pushing in front of him what looked like some large leather bottle wearing a jewelled cap: a high-ranking officer named Wang Kuan, whom he threw down at the feet of the *Shikken*.

'Here's the terror of the Japanese!'

There were a few hiccups at first, then a guttural cackling which grew louder. Tokimune was choking. He coughed and wept . . . then there burst out, loudly, the avenging laughter of the Japanese samurai.

It was only a short interlude: the larger part of the fleet, that from China, arrived in its turn and disembarked at Kyushu. The first contingent, Nichiren had said while he was having a vision, had been undermined by illness. This one, overwhelming in numbers, was brimming with health. Almost immediately, it had successes. Its flame-throwers terrified both men and horses, while the terrible little Mongol bows and ballistae made gaps in the Japanese ranks.

Tokimune decided to dig in. He established himself behind the stone fortifications built in the Bay of Hakozaki and called up from the rest of the archipelago all able-bodied soldiers. Gradually they all arrived. They had to endure: the

Mongols' mortars rained stone cannonballs and burning oil. But the Japanese stood firm. A contingent sought to outflank their fortifications by way of the Hizen: they continued to stand firm.

'The divine winds are coming back,' Nichiren told them. But the battle lasted for several weeks, and each assault became more murderous. Under a sky hopelessly bright, the Mongol hordes forced their way inexorably through the samurai's first lines of defence. The samurai were hacked at furiously and had, it was said, to be killed several times.

It was a soldier-monk of the Hachiman monastery, it seems, who roused the rage of the forgetful gods, by throwing drops of his blood towards the skies, before dying.

The first rumblings of thunder were heard above the explosions of the Mongolian artillery and the invaders all lifted their eyes towards the clear blue sky. The air became heavy and full of menace. The assault stopped suddenly and the attackers began to fall back towards the beach, slowly at first, sponging the sweat and blood from their wounds. Then, as an immense flash of lightning striped the sky where sudden storm clouds were forming rapidly, they began to hurry. Standing on the ramparts, Tokimune raised his sword, like an offering, in his two open hands. Heavy drops of warm rain began to fall, like a giant's tears, on the spiked armour of Kublai Khan's men; they ran back towards their ships, paddling through the curiously still waters of the bay.

'Cut the chains!' shouted the sailors, not caring about the fate of the disembarked troops.

The wave came straight in from the end of the bay, swelling like a rolling-pin picking up a thick dough. The sky and the sea seemed to merge in a sudden diabolic turmoil. Excited by the rain and drenched to the skin, the samurai danced on the ramparts where white flashes of lightning made them look like actors in a shadow show. A Chinese general broke his sword against the rocks muttering inaudible curses upon himself.

The second typhoon of 14 August 1281 was unbelievably

violent and none doubted that it was of supernatural origin. In barely an hour, the greater part of the Sino-Korean fleet went to the bottom of the Bay of Imari. The heavy junks soon began to strike each other like missiles borne on the crests of gigantic waves from the depths which literally exploded and then collapsed like overripe fruits on the rocks in apocalyptic whirlpools. The raging waves dashed themselves against the Japanese fortifications, throwing over the top of the walls a shower of sodden rags and dead bodies, naked and still quivering, their clothes ripped off them in this devil's cauldron.

When the divine winds finally died down, there were dozens of rainbows in the clouds which added to the sacred nature of the sacrifice. The samurai, who had been prostrate before the phenomenon, raised themselves upon their elbows and saw the surface of the bay studded with debris of every sort as far as the eye could see, as if all the sticks of wood in the mountains had suddenly come down, carried by the torrents.

Tokimune was the first to see on the beach of the Island of Takashima, at the entrance to the Gulf of Imari, whole contingents of Chinese seeking in wild disarray to save or pillage among the heaps of wreckage. He thanked the gods for this latest favour.

'You have left us enemies to be sacrificed. We thank you.'

Shoni Kagesuke, a samurai as brave as any, led the final assault. The Chinese, with neither vessels nor guns, had not even the superiority conferred by their archers because the catgut used for their bows had been drenched during the typhoon. The battle, which lasted for two days, was waged with swords and on equal terms.

Isolated on their island, the last of the invaders saw first that all the shores which surrounded them were covered again with a new form of vegetation: the Japanese, all the Japanese, united for the first time in their history, were there: a compact, unmoving, motley wall of humanity – more than 200,000 men, possibly. They formed up in squares and waited. The many tens of thousands of Chinese survivors still constituted a redoubtable army.

At low tide, when the sea had retreated, a broad bank of earth appeared out of the water: a deposit newly formed during the typhoon. Kagesuke took up his position on it, in front of his cavalry, and stood up suddenly in his stirrups, raising a shining sword. 'Forward!'

The whole Japanese nation felt the trembling of the earth when the thousands of horses began a charge which was to become a legend. Tokimune, quivering with pride, presided over this bloody celebration.

'Three prisoners only,' he had said to Kagesuke. 'I want only three, who will be able to tell the Khan what they have seen.'

Coming from a long way away, the cavalry rode at a fast gallop into the bay, raising a wall of spume. This foaming wave rolled towards the squares of Chinese soldiers which disintegrated before they had even been hit. From all round the coastline great shouts re-echoed.

The wave reached the shore, where the Chinese were already trampling each other. The cavalry flung themselves, swords flashing furiously, into the chaos. For hours the samurai hacked and sliced at the jumble of panting bodies, among which organised resistance quickly ceased.

A great surge of heat began to make itself felt towards the middle of the day while heads were still falling. To save damaging the armour and the silken clothing which were part of their booty, the samurai soon began to ask their prisoners to strip naked before they were put to death and the massacre was organised in lines. The Chinese, horror-struck by the waves of blood which ran in wide ditches and spread out to stain the sea with trails of bluish black, obeyed passively. The least dazed of them continued to beseech their unbending conquerors with piercing cries, and some of the young men, trembling with terror, stroked their fine skins provocatively to invite the Japanese to lustful acts which might delay the fatal issue. Their gestures were obscene and explicit.

'Look,' simpered one of them, approaching Kagesuke who had been butchering for so long that his muscles had been numb for hours, 'see what precious booty my body could be.' Taking a deep, ferocious breath, the samurai disembowelled him from throat to sexual organs.

When the slaughter ended there remained a thousand naked men. The samurai were exhausted, spattered all over with blood like butchers. Thirst tormented them all and some no longer had the strength to lift their swords.

'Keep those,' decided their leader. 'Our *Shikken* will choose his messengers from among them.'

Escorted by a huge crowd, the last of the Chinese marched along on their way to the Bay of Hakata where Tokimune had gone to worship the divine winds, the name of which – *Kamikaze* – was to enter into legend and history. It remained for the *Shikken* to choose his messengers. 'You, you and you.'

The young warriors decapitated the others one by one, carefully, as if they had been doing an exercise on the parade ground, discussing their technique at length, taking the measure of each neck before chopping it through with a single blow, to the silken rustle of sharp steel. The animal fear of their victims, their staring eyes, stimulated their skill and flattered their pride.

Kublai Khan, learning of the disaster, decided to prepare a third invasion. His Mongols, however, began to complain: these horsemen did not like overseas expeditions. The Koreans and the Chinese, unwilling servants of the Mongols, began to create serious internal difficulties. When Kublai died in 1294 his successor, Timur, abandoned the preparations.

The Cherry-trees of the Imperial City

THE VICTORY over the Mongols left some men discontented. Rewards had been promised to those who fought well, but they had not been given. The civil wars had brought profits to the conquerors at the expense of the defeated: in this fight the reward was the preservation of the land and its independence, but nothing of advantage to the individual; only ruin and sacrifice for some. On the other hand, the demands of the Buddhist priests, whose prayers had been so anxiously solicited, were in the main, met: their property and their confiscated temples were restored to them, mortgages were reduced, and gifts of land conceded.

Tokimune died in 1284, at the age of thirty-four. His fourteen-year-old son, Sadatoki, succeeded him. A merry-go-round of regents, unworthy puppets, followed. The *bakufu* slid into decadence: homosexuality was officially recognised. The court of Kamakura delighted in staged battles between dogs and those that won, clothed in precious materials, were applauded in the streets. In the countryside, the peasants, weighed down by taxes, starved to death.

The Emperor himself then came on the scene: Go-Daigo, a dissembling and obstinate man who triggered off a conflict with the *Shikken*. A war of monks ensued with varying fortune. Finally, the troops of the *bakufu* rallied to the Emperor: victory went to the court party. On 6 July 1333 Kamakura was taken, the *Shikken* chose suicide, and the restoration followed.

Nakata hid his excitement beneath an impassive manner. He was riding on horseback with great dignity behind his father and another samurai named Sato, but to a fourteen-year-old the road to Kyoto on this spring day in 1380 was fascinating, and his lively eyes missed nothing of the bustle of the Tokaido road.

Nobles, astrologers, and doctors went by in litters, or in carts drawn by oxen. The *grands seigneurs* owned closed carriages, decorated with lacquer and silken curtains, and mounted on great spoked wheels. When crossing a ford, Nakata saw a fat *daimyo* straddled on the shoulders of a very small servant. He chortled with laughter without turning round. Peasants carrying baskets on poles over their shoulders, and chattering monks, kept pace with the horses in unfrequented stretches of the countryside: bandits would not dare to attack samurai. Nakata swelled with self-importance at this mute homage.

By short stages, the travellers moved nearer to the capital, halting sometimes at a shrine, or sometimes at an inn. Young Nakata preferred the inns, for there one could see brazen women: to his great shame, he was still a virgin and every woman he glimpsed gave him a pretext for erotic dreams. Nakata came from the country district of Kanto, where his father, ji-samurai, a peasant-warrior, owned a *yashiki* or small castle surrounded by earth walls and a moat, to which all the local population came whenever there was an alarm, that is to say, often, since civil wars followed the attacks of brigands. The young knight could easily have cornered one of the village girls whom the peasant boys of his own age tumbled in the rice-straw, but he was frightened of not succeeding and that was why he had never accomplished an act as simple as eating and drinking and to which no one at that time paid much attention.

As they rode along, Sato and Nakata's father gossiped about the position of the new *bakufu*.

'The house of Ashikaga is very ancient and noble. It is descended from the Minamoto.'

'Yes, but not through Yoritomo!'

'Was Ashikaga Yoshimitsu wise to establish his shogunate so close to the Imperial Palace?'

'Muromachi will never equal Kamakura,' said Sato sententiously. 'Everything is falling apart. The North is fighting against the South; the *daimyo* against the monks; the monks against the *Shogun*; the *Shogun* against the Emperor! Each year brings some fresh conflict. The samurai are falling...'

'They are made for battle,' replied Nakata's father in a voice loud enough for his son to hear what he was saying.

But Nakata was smelling the perfume of the flowers and the warm scent of the pines. The sun was making little drops of sweat form under the white make-up on his face. He let himself be lulled by the soft tinkle of the little bells on the horses. His hand caressed the smooth metal guard of his sword. A half-naked peasant woman had been planting out her rice. He had seen her from the road unfastening her dress with a graceful movement, and stretching herself, her breasts jutting upwards, towards the blazing sun. He remembered the sight of her body, pure and innocent, bent over the glittering water and haloed with light. It seemed to Nakata that his horse's flanks suddenly felt hotter between his legs.

'Samurai!'

'Yes, Father.' Nakata jumped.

The two warriors eyed each other strangely as they turned in their saddles. They wore the moustaches and the fashionable short, pointed beards which looked like cat whiskers. Their tunics, padded on the shoulders and stamped in the middle of the chest with the same *mon*, made them look so exactly alike that Nakata rubbed his eyes, fearing he was seeing double.

They laughed in chorus. Such were the effects of *sake* on a young man who had not done his exercises for the four days they had been travelling!

'What are you dreaming about, Nakata? About the battles you will be fighting one day?'

'Do you see yourself as a great lord at the court of the *daimyo* in whose house you are going to serve?'

'If you sleep at your age, at ours you'll need a litter to move your fat belly!'

For these pleasantries not to be offensive, they had to come from people he held dear. Just one of these gibes from anyone else would have resulted in bloodshed. Nakata remained impassive and the white make-up hid his flushed face. If they knew – how they would laugh. Nevertheless, the previous year, shortly before he had been dubbed a samurai at the *gempuku*, all the family had lengthily examined the young lad's private parts. He remembered women weighing them gravely in their hands before declaring he was strong and vigorous. Then, a year earlier than the usual age, he had been given his name as a man and had had his hair tied in a topknot under the black hat, the *eboshi*, which he had worn jauntily ever since.

'I have worn my swords since I was three years old,' thought the young man. 'At first they were toys, which my father replaced suitably as I grew older. They were my family's dear and precious weapons. I wear the *hakama*, men's trousers, I drink *sake* like a man, and yet I am still a child, since I have never killed an enemy or enjoyed a woman.'

At these thoughts, the samurai Nakata felt truly desperate. Would he ever become a real warrior like his father whom he had seen decapitate a menacing *ronin* and before his eyes in the firelight embrace his mother as a conscientious man should every evening.

'My son, there is the capital . . .'

The Imperial city of Kyoto, visible from far off, had everything to rouse enthusiasm in a youth from the provinces. Dominated by the sanctuary of Mount Hiei and sectioned by canals fed from the River Kamo, the city covered a square with sides of more than five thousand metres. From east to west ran the great bisecting avenue of Suzaku-oji, ninety metres wide : it had the protective function of limiting damage when fires broke out, a frequent occurrence where houses were built of wood. The town was divided into districts whose boundaries were defined by broad avenues at right angles to each other, and crossed by narrower streets surrounding blocks one hundred metres square.

The Imperial palace was to the north, linked to the town by

a very wide avenue. The Imperial university and the Imperial granaries which backed on to its walls made a separate town of it. The Emperor's other palaces and the most important shrines were scattered all round the town. The shrines of To-ji and Sai-ji, which protected the city, stood on either side of the south gate.

'Do you see the great palace, Nakata?' asked his father. 'There are fourteen gates inside those high walls. Near to the main one, Suzaku-mon, is the guard-post where I had the honour to serve for three months. From here, one can see the buildings which make up the Emperor's home: they are inside a second precinct, enclosed by a double wall in which there are four doors. The *Tenno* lives there with his family, his concubines, his doctors, his astrologers, his archives, his treasures and his weapons. He never goes out except during the periods of ritual impurity to get to another of his palaces.'

'Look!' said Sato. 'Those splendid willows along the great avenues praised by the poets ... and that building under construction down there at the end: that is Muromachi, the new house of the *Shogun* Ashikaga which is now being built. It was a courtier of the Imperial house, Konoe Fusatsugu, who designed it.'

The three horsemen spurred their mounts to go and look more closely at these marvels. The suburbs seemed to them to be intensely alive: a host of pedlars and costermongers were busy there. Nakata wrinkled his nose: a foul smell was coming from the canals. He saw passers-by relieving themselves in the streets without the least embarrassment.

The three samurai went through one of the great fortified gates of the town and mixed with the colourful crowds. Nakata got his father to point out, as they went along, the nobles and the Imperial officials, distinguishable by their traditional garments: each form of dress was the sign of a precise rank and function.

'You'll see that the costumes of the courtiers are even more splendid.'

The young knight recognised by their black head-dresses

those who were of the lesser nobility, like himself. 'That's a good thing,' he thought to himself. 'The chances of an embarrassing mistake are slight when you know precisely with whom you are dealing.' And to reinforce his conviction, he gave a yokel in unbleached smock and linen trousers, who was impeding his horse's passage, a great blow between the shoulderblades with his stirrups.

The houses of the great nobles occupied the districts of an entire *cho*; there were whole blocks of these houses not far from the palace. It was at the house of one of these nobles that young Nakata was to take up his service as a samurai.

The aristocrats of Kyoto distinguished themselves from the ordinary people – the peasants and, particularly the warriors – by observing scrupulously at meals the Buddhist customs concerning meat. As he took his first turn on guard duty with his *daimyo*, however, Nakata noticed that the latter did eat a little fish. From the manner in which his master took his repast Nakata imagined he was on another planet, but he maintained the formal mien and the expressionless features that are *de rigueur* for a samurai in service.

All the same, Nakata was astonished by the abundance of the dishes put before him. In the paternal *yashiki*, during this period of dearth, rice mixed with corn and red millet was the usual food, polished rice being reserved for special holidays. At the end of the meal, Nakata noticed that the *daimyo*'s son, a young man of his own age richly dressed in brocade, with his face made up like that of a courtesan, had himself served a whipped and flavoured ice sherbet.

'These are people of quality,' thought Nakata. 'They have their ice brought down from the mountains, which is the absolute height of refinement.' He exulted in each sign of his master's greatness.

By the time the first really hot days foretold the coming of summer, Nakata was perfectly competent in carrying out his functions in the *daimyo*'s residence. He spent most of his time with the other samurai with whom he practised the martial arts at length each morning from daybreak in a courtyard set aside for this purpose. His skill with the sword had quickly earned him the respect of his peers, and if he still hesitated when they went off to drink *sake* and to gamble in brothels, it was only through fear of losing face, for he had had no opportunity to approach a woman since his arrival in the capital.

The *daimyo* was preparing for his departure to take the thermal waters and to benefit from the fresh mountain air during the summer. Nakata was glad not to be part of the escort and so to be able to stay in the almost deserted palace in the centre of the great town. The *daimyo*'s son, who had been friendly towards him, also remained at Kyoto. This languid young man, who passed his days lolling on cushions, had pleaded fatigue to avoid the journey.

'I'm so bored, Nakata,' he kept saying, yawning, to the young soldier who was stolidly on guard outside his apartments.

Among the nobles of Kyoto, most of whom were idle, and whose lives and movements were circumscribed by the many prohibitions on action or travelling – the *kati-imi* – great importance was attached to amorous relations. These games were the only distractions available to Jiso, the *daimyo*'s son, in his permanent boredom. Before long he confided in Nakata: 'We are going to see a wonderfully beautiful woman this evening. You shall escort me as far as her garden.'

In the sepia dusk the samurai followed his young master over a hedge to see the girls gossiping in their doorway. The silhouette of the lady, with her dress thrown carelessly over her shoulder, was delicate and very child-like. The sound of her voice was just as charming, though full of dignity.

Jiso squeezed his companion's arm so that Nakata felt the long pointed nails scratch him. 'What luck I've had to see her! Yesterday I waited in vain until dawn. She is like a fairy. I have seen the calligraphy of one of her poems: it was wonderfully delicate. Tomorrow I shall hang a message from a branch of the cherry-tree in the front of her house.'

From other samurai, Nakata knew that the beautiful creature's husband was a great noble who rarely left his duties at the palace.

'What will happen if her lord is told? He would surely repudiate her.'

Jiso looked his samurai up and down. 'Between the well-born, that sort of thing is unknown.'

The young samurai could no longer get to sleep on his wooden bed.

'Here is my poem:

> The moon and the flowering of the cherry-trees
> On this wonderful night,
> How I would love to show them to her,
> Who might perhaps understand.'

'But isn't that...'

'Yes,' smiled Jiso, putting down his brush. 'I have copied it from one of the twenty-one Imperial anthologies. That's what one must do.'

On the third night's expedition by the two friends, another poem, written in the same vein, was pushed furtively into Jiso's hand by a serving-woman who fled. The young *daimyo* exclaimed on his lady-love's subtlety.

'Do women always reply like that?' asked Nakata.

'Of course, if they are people of quality! It means that tomorrow night I may go to her bedchamber.'

'Could you not carry her off?' suggested Nakata, fascinated by this romantic game.

'Oh, no! I don't want to have the ridiculous experience of the noble who carried his lady-love off in the dark: when he got home and lifted her veils, he saw that it was her old aunt who had taken her place.'

The young men collapsed with laughter at this thought.

'But I think, Nakata, that for a samurai you pay a lot of attention to these trivialities. They are already beginning to bore me, and I need to catch up on some sleep. Why don't you go in my place tonight? All lovers look the same in the dark and anyway these things are so vulgar. I have had the best of her in her promise: so if her body tempts you . . . . Go on, that's an order!'

Jiso yawned lengthily, haughty and bantering. Then he added, sitting up on his cushions, 'Oh, by the way, I will write out for you tomorrow the poem that it is fitting to send after the night. . . .'

The summer sky shone with a thousand stars and the young man lying in the damp grass turned on his back to name some of them. All the perfume of the cherry-trees and plum-trees was sinking again towards the earth.

Jiso had advised Nakata to put on some form of disguise, but he was loth to do so and had only draped a dark cloak round his shoulders. When the last lights were extinguished in the house, he went forward very softly, the blood throbbing in his temples. The lady's garden said much for her excellent taste, and it looked superb in the moonlight. The minute pond dug in its centre, the 'lake of sentiments', had not a ripple in it and the sky was reflected among the open water-lilies. Nakata went past the little wooden bridge and approached the verandah, trying not to make any noise on the round white pebbles. The entry was closed by a heavy curtain which Nakata lifted gently. In the complete darkness he felt his way with considerable embarrassment. 'The adventure with the old aunt is going to be repeated if I miss my way,' he said to himself. 'I know that women tend to be towards the right, behind the cloth screens of their *kicho*, but where is the lady's *kicho*?'

He was about to retrace his steps when a long sigh, followed by others, guided him on his way. After a moment of walking blindly, the sigh materialised into a warm breath and Nakata sensed two light butterflies on his shoulders: the hands of his chosen one. He stepped back a pace in order to tear off his clothes. Then, naked, in a paroxysm of virility, he clasped her slight body in his arms and pressed her to him. He knew instinctively that the long inactivity of a poetic correspondence must be made up for by brutal action which would restore the male's dignity. He cut short the sweet, warm preliminaries and took her like a veteran, not bothering about her cat-like squeals which made all the other women in the house giggle, attentive and mocking.

Nakata left the garden furtively at the first cock's crow. In the samurai's quarters he undressed completely and washed himself thoroughly in icy water, under the approving eye of an old soldier with whom he afterwards indulged in a bout of fencing of quite remarkable quality.

About midday, the young *daimyo* surly and not fully awake, sent for Nakata to give him the promised note:

> How green are the leaves of the willow!
> This morning more than ever,
> My thoughts are troubled.

'That's what I always say,' commented the *blasé* young man. Then, turning on to his belly, he added, 'I saw the carriage of a lady pass by yesterday. Her brocade sleeves fill my dreams.'

Nakata's days of idleness ended with the autumn. The war against the Yamana was about to break out. *Shogun* Ashikaga mobilised all his forces in order to invade the ten provinces held by the rebels, and the *daimyo* sent his finest samurai, one of whom, the young knight Nakata, was to cover himself with glory.

The Ashikagas' end was wretched. From 1467 to 1477 a series of troubles, known under the name of the war of the Onin era, marked their decline. This war resembled the Thirty Years War in Europe, but lasted only ten years. The brilliant period of Muromachi knew no peace, and its decline was marked by a ferocious civil war which spread even to the streets of Kyoto, where the clans were involved in long-drawn-out trench warfare. The candidates for the shogunate were many, and up to five bogus *Shoguns* set themselves up simultaneously, each one supported by devoted clans striving to gain recognition.

The barbarians arrived during this troubled period.

On a morning in February 1582, in the port of Nagasaki, a rated ship, sails spread, was dragging at its anchors, and the Portuguese captain was becoming impatient.

'Father Mendes, tell them to speed up their farewells, you can talk their language: we're going to miss the tide.'

'Just a moment! They are going to sing a hymn, the *Veni Creator*.'

The cacophony which arose, punctuated by cymbals, made the entire crew laugh until they cried. The four young men in white robes moved unhurriedly through the huge crowd of the subjects of Otomo Sorin, of Arima and of Omura, protectors of the new faith. Everyone wanted to touch the *daimyo*'s envoys who were going to the end of the world, to Rome, to see the living God of these noble strangers.

'Francis would have wished to see this moment,' said an old Jesuit with a face like parchment, to Father Mendes.

'Yes, Father Provincial.'

'What a long way we have come!'

It was scarcely fifty years since the first Portuguese navigators had been cast up on the coast of Tanegashima by a shipwreck. Some traders followed them: they did excellent business. 'Absolutely excellent business: remember how interested they were in our arquebuses: the civil wars were at their height.'

'True, but not many were sold. It was a man named Christian Motta who gave them the first one. When he returned a year later in 1543 to the same place on the Bay of Kumano, a blacksmith named Teppomata, the gun-maker, had begun mass-producing arquebuses, all exactly the same, and in 1546 the administration had already registered more than three thousand!'

On shore, the hymn was ending and the *daimyo* of Arima, Omura and Bungo accompanied to the bridge the four young men, whom the Jesuits were taking with them to Europe. The *daimyo* rested their hands on the young men's shoulders.

'We have chosen young men so that they will not be too old on their return,' said the *daimyo* of Omura to Father Torres, 'and they are samurai so they will be brave in every circumstance.'

'Christian samurai!' said the old Jesuit in surprise. He knew the dislike of the *bushi* for new ideas. 'God's name be praised!'

The faithful on the quays crossed themselves. The caravel got under way swiftly and some small, fast boats escorted it to the open sea. In the evening, the blue archipelago grew blurred, and only the white patch of the snow-topped mountains remained visible, made more splendid by a last ray from the setting sun. The four young travellers, leaning over the rails, bowed low to them, which made Father Torres splutter.

The Jesuit envied the burning faith of St Francis Xavier of the Society of Jesus, the first great evangelist of this part of the world. As for the conversion of the Japanese, he was plagued by doubts and uncertainties. 'Francis was fired with the true zeal of a Spaniard,' he thought. 'I am a Portuguese of little faith.' Nothing stopped Francis: after preaching the Gospel at Goa, in Malabar, in Ceylon and Malacca, he was taken to Japan by a Japanese converted in India. He landed at Kagoshima on 15 August 1549, and began to speak of *Yaso,* of Jesus. The saint was also expert in languages and, with the help of one of the first converts, Yajiro, he quickly established the first catechism in Japanese: the *Kirishitan,* or 'Exposition of the Christian faith'. The Buddhist priests were quick to take offence at this.

Francis journeyed to Hirado, then to Kyoto, in December 1550. He was, however, disappointed: people certainly listened to him, yet he converted only a few. On 20 December 1551 he set off again this time to Goa accompanied by an envoy of the *daimyo* of Dungo, Otomo Sorin, who wanted to initiate commercial relations with the Viceroy. Francis wished ardently to return to Japan, but he died during the journey on 2 December 1552, on the island of San-Chan, near Macao.

'And after him there was the harvest,' interrupted the old Jesuit to whom Father Andres was speaking.

'Certainly, the missionaries arrived in large numbers: Franciscans and Dominicans, according to the mood of the ruler of the moment. They preached in Honshu and in Kyushu, but it was by helping the *daimyo* to profit from the advantages to be conferred by European commerce that they managed to ensure that Christians would be protected!'

'God will know his own, my son!'

The Jesuit agreed, repressing a bitter smile: St Bernard had said these very words as Béziers burned, when genocide had been rife!

'Look at the great personages who have been converted: Otomo Sorin, a rich *daimyo*; Omura Sumitada, who established commercial relations with the Portuguese at Nagasaki.'

'Are you telling me that the 125,000 converts of Kyushu are only concerned with business and worship Christ for profit? And these children we are taking away with us, Father Torres, these pure souls we are to present to His Holiness Pope Gregory XIII, do you doubt their faith? My heart was stirred just now when I learned that they were Christian samurai because I recalled Francis's words and those of Ignatius Loyola: we are the soldiers of Christ. They are ours, Father Torres, body and soul!'

The old Jesuit held out his clenched fist, a reminder of the phrase: 'You must lie in my hands like a dead body.' Torres kissed his hand and went down to the 'tween-deck.

There he had a shock: in the half-light his four protégés were kneeling at their evening prayers. Later, he asked Bernard, the eldest, 'For whom were you praying, my dear son?'

'For my lord, the *Shogun*, to whom my life belongs,' recited the young samurai without hesitation and without lowering his eyes.

'That is good, my son. Sleep now.'

'Like a dead body . . .' murmured Torres, staring at his clenched fist. The creaking of the ship's timbers lulled his sleeplessness for a long time.

The *daimyo* of Omura had been right when he chose the very young as his emissaries: the voyage was long and eventful. The caravel called at Goa in September 1583, but did not reach Lisbon until August 1584. The Jesuit's fiery words had their effect, as the ship continued on its course through the deep sea.

Three years after their departure, in 1585, the four catechumens prostrated themselves at the citadel of St Angelo in Rome before a dying man: Pope Gregory was no longer conscious when the Japanese handed him their credentials and the parchment fell to the ground, slipping from his hand. Torres felt a shiver run down his spine.

With his disciples, the Jesuit attended the coronation of Sixtus V, watching their reactions at seeing the Vatican's pomp. He allowed them to travel the peninsula, showing them Christianity's holy places. It was during their visit to the ruins of the Colosseum, when he evoked memories of the first Christian martyrs, that Bernard asked the question he had so greatly longed to hear. But it was cast in a strange form:

'Father, when shall we be soldiers?'

'You mean to say Jesuits? Soldiers of Christ? Is that your wish?'

'Yes, because you are like the samurai.'

In 1595 the young men went back again to Japan. They had left at the age of fifteen, their heads shaven: they returned in black Western clothes, with white ruffs. They were now twenty-eight and there had been great changes. Nobunaga had overthrown the last Ashikaga *Shogun* before they left, dismissing him as if he had been a mere valet. The 'Lord-Fool', as he was called, was the Jesuits' friend and had often helped them, but later suffering from megalomania, he had started a religion of his own, claiming to be the one god. In his shrine he had himself represented by a sacred stone. This extraordinary phenomenon in a Japan traditionally shared between Shinto and Buddhism had given the monks an excuse to attack the Christian minority: the foreigners, they said, had driven him out of his mind.

The victim of a palace plot, the dictator died bravely by committing *seppuku*, while his son fell at his side, the weapon in his hand. It was for this reason that his shrines continued to exist for a long time, but the Christian community was to suffer persecution.

The four samurai easily obtained permission from their *daimyo* to enter the Society of Jesus. The nobles, sensing that the wind was changing, were only too happy to be rid of them. But the *kami* were to take their revenge against those who had betrayed the faith of their ancestors. The priests of the foreign faith were pursued and arrested. 'Their crime should be punished by death,' was the opinion of their compatriots.

But by what death? That of a warrior allowed to commit *seppuku* and to have his head chopped off by a faithful friend? No. For them one death only was possible, that of their Lord: the Cross. The people said: 'The wrongdoer's torture and not the samurai's sacrifice should be theirs. They no longer belong to Japan!'

They belonged to the catholic, apostolic and Roman Church, which canonised the four martyrs of Nagasaki.

Black was the Kampaku's Horse

THE MONSTROUS little gnome, born in 1536 into the peasant family of Kinoshita, had made his way very successfully. Hiyoshi – that was his first name – was at first a despised convent servant. He was much too ugly for any monk to make him his *chigo*. His passion for learning and his extraordinary skill with weapons dated perhaps from the period of that affront.

'To the devil with monks!' he declared when he reached his majority.

When he was fifteen years old he took the name of Tokichiro. The bandy-legged young man was for a time a stable-lad employed by a noble. A groom made a remark about his deformity, and he killed him instantly. Then he became a brigand, a precocious *ronin*. He felt neither fear nor pity. One day when the civil war was at its height he attacked single-handed a convoy of members of the Imperial administration: a samurai turned his horse towards him, without drawing his sword.

'Your name, brigand!'

'Touch swords with me and you'll know my name.'

'Do you know you could be a soldier despite your hump?'

'Who would take me?'

'I would.'

'What about your gutless men?'

'They fought badly. You would replace them. Follow me... samurai!'

'Kinoshita Tokichiro, my lord.'

From the very first campaign, he was chosen as an officer. His ugliness was such that he fought without a mask and terrified opponents all the more. Du Guesclin, under other skies, was also like this. He rose in his career to become a Marshal of the Empire, who fought on every battlefield, and was at the age of twenty, one of Nobunaga's generals. Nobunaga was rich, clever and cruel, but handsome – a fact which, in the depths of a soul as tortuous as his deformed body, the monstrous manikin never forgave him.

'You are my best general,' the 'Lord-Fool' Nobunaga would say. 'When I have an enemy, I send him to you and he is dead.'

In 1562 Tokichiro adopted the name of Hideyoshi.

Sometimes the dwarf's features blazed with unbearable malice. 'I will step into your shoes, Nobunaga,' he thought to himself. 'I will dishonour your daughters and your sons. You will be left with only one tooth and that will ache.'

Scarcely was the news of the dictator's *seppuku* known in Hideyoshi's camp than he lurched grotesquely towards his horse, which was kept always saddled. Once he was in the saddle, no one dared to laugh at him. To the samurai who ran forward he shouted one word: 'Kyoto!'

The journey on horseback lasted all night. From everywhere galloping shadows rallied to this diabolical horseman who was wearing out all his mounts. In the morning they were crowded in their thousands beneath the walls of the Imperial city, from which clouds of smoke were still rising from the fires started during the latest battles.

The hunchback had negotiated for a long time over the succession to the dead madman: the greatest nobles of Japan to whom he had proposed a new formula for government – a ministry – had been involved in his conspiracy. Who had unleashed hostilities to forestall him? Who?

'Akechi was the chief of the conspirators.'

'Let Akechi be brought to the hills.'

The dwarf's protruding eyes lit up with pleasure at the spectacle and he wiped the thread of spittle, which dribbled always from his lips, with his sleeve. The man who had defied his orders was crucified like *Yaso*, whose followers he had apparently admired. He was hung up, naked, on a beam, and choked slowly, bracing his arms in despair.

'Guard him from a distance during the night,' said the new *Shogun*, 'and do not light any fires. I want the beasts to devour him ... slowly.'

Then he galloped off towards the capital. People grovelled on the ground as he passed. 'My horse is also a god!'

His anger was violent when scholars explained to him, in guarded phrases, that because of his humble origins he could not hold the supreme title.

'Nobunaga's grandson lives: let him reign. I will give him as guardians my generals Niwa, Ikeda and Shibata...'

'The fiends,' murmured the courtiers – this was what they called the gnome's creatures.

'... and myself!' he ended.

Silence fell.

Followed by a single torch-bearer, the monstrous little man walked alone in the night through the palace. He passed unseeing by lines of sentries standing like statues and crossed the deserted courtyards. When his servant opened the door of the stables, the animal heat blew into his face like the blast from an arquebus fired at close range.

He caressed his sick horse for a long time, talking to it as peasant mothers do to children at their breasts. Hideyoshi's brutal face became serious and tender while he was comforting his steed. He whispered confidences to it softly. 'Do you know that those ungrateful men rebelled: Nobunaga and a son of the "fool" whom I had forgotten. I fought them without you, and it was a great battle, but I was sad not to have you with me. In the end they all committed suicide, an immense *seppuku*; you would have plunged your hooves in their blood! On the way back I gave fiefs to the others and I reign alone, all alone. I do that, just think! What's more, I am going to become a great noble. The Minamoto did not want to adopt me; so much the worse for them! I have agreed to become a Fujiwara. They are naming me as *Kampaku*: a noble title, greatly sought after. Are you proud of me, my horse? Get well quickly, because soon I am setting off on the conquest of the whole of Japan: I am going to reunite it as in the days of the *kamikaze*.'

The servant who was carrying the torch heard this incredible monologue without realising that he was seeing one of the most important pages in the history of Japan being turned.

In two campaigns Hideyoshi united the archipelago. Taking advantage of a call for help from the Otomos who were fighting the Shimazus, he intervened at Kyushu and gave the most important fiefs of the island to those who were faithful to him. In the Kanto, the pseudo-Hojos said they were governing in the manner of the *Shikken* whom they claimed as ancestors. An upstart himself, but a genius, the hunchback instantly rendered them harmless.

If writings of the time can be believed, 250,000 men besieged Odawara, their capital. On his great black horse, the little dictator himself directed operations.

'Here, you!' This to a groom carrying a bundle of hay. He was going towards the town, which meant he knew the way. The man would have to tell him or die! This was the breakthrough. The town was taken. The leaders, whether Hojo or not, could slit open their bellies: I allow them this favour. Hideyoshi was becoming more humane as he became powerful...

He appointed an efficient assistant to Kanto: Tokugawa Ieyasu. From now on the archipelago was really unified. The hunchback organised government as he had promised: public works, police, religions, justice, finance, agriculture, the army. He made innovations and rationalisations: he was admired, the deformed *chigo*, who had taken refuge in study because the monks had wanted nothing to do with him.

The *Kampaku* tried first to work out an original political system which Oda Nobunaga had been unable, or unwilling, to create. Although he respected the person of the Emperor, he avoided restoring his authority and intended to remain the sole master: the Emperor's ministers remained, certainly, but only in name.

The monstrous little man had fixed rules of conduct, of work and of philosophy for himself, and these were translated at every turn into maxims. A great builder, he had decided to make Osaka his capital and began this undertaking by building a great castle: this was the most formidable military building operation ever undertaken in Japan.

The castle rose on a rock dominating the swampy plain of the Yodogawa delta. It was surrounded by three separate walls. For three years, thousands of men worked on it, digging moats and building walls made of huge blocks of stone brought from the island of Awaji. Their transport and setting into place filled everyone with astonishment.

Since his accession to power, Hideyoshi had discovered instinctively how to make people forgive his lack of physical charm. He organised sumptuous festivals, of which one, at least, remains unforgettable in the annals of old Japan: the fabulous tea ceremony in 1587 to which all the devotees of this drink in the Empire were invited by an official edict. They were to go to the Kitano forest. There were six thousand guests: nobles, dancers, monks, tradesmen and peasants stayed there for ten days and Hideyoshi tasted everyone's tea while distributing gifts.

The *Kampaku* also knew the history of Japan. After reorganising his country, as in the times of the Mongol invasions, he remembered that two centuries earlier, after the great victory, demobilisation had been a disaster. And so he began to cherish a great project: the revenge of the samurai.

Sô Yoshitomo, *daimyo* of Tsushima, seemed to be dying with shame.

'Your excellencies must wait a little longer,' he stammered.

The three ambassadors from the King of Korea shivered imperceptibly, and the three hundred servants, carrying gifts, who were pressing behind them, murmured like a beehive at this new outrage.

'This is too much,' whispered a mandarin behind his open

fan. 'We have already come once before last year: the monster was fighting in Kanto against the Hojos. We waited for days then, and now it's going to begin again.'

'Nevertheless,' whispered his neighbour, a general, his face bloated with rage under his ferocious dragon helmet, it was he who wanted to re-establish relations. Our king had broken them off after the extortions of the *wako*, those Japanese pirates in the time of the Ashikagas. He sent emissaries: we opened the port of Fusan to Japanese ships. No doubt, he wants something more. But now he sees fit to keep us hanging about! The dwarf is as much of a fool as his one-time master.'

Then a long scream, as of a wounded animal, echoed under the arched roof of the palace. It was interminable, atrocious. The samurai themselves shuddered at it. The *daimyo* Yoshitomo sighed: 'The child is dead.'

A frightening uproar followed the *Kampaku*'s cry. He smashed everything he could lay hands on, he shouted and hit out, he bit the terrified Chinese doctors who protected their faces while uttering little womanish cries.

'He was my son and you have killed him! Curse you!'

The frightened practitioners pretended to take one of his gestures as a dismissal and ran off quickly, holding up the skirts of their long robes. They got their breath back at the end of a corridor:

'The child could not have lived,' whispered one of them. 'You all saw its monstrous head, it was...'

'His son, and he knew it!'

'If it had lived, he would have strangled it with his own hands.'

'Yes, to destroy his own image.'

The *daimyo* Yoshitomo raised the curtain gently and hesitated an instant before the unbelievable sight. The *Kampaku*, crouching on the floor, was weeping like a child, and moaning plaintively. Great sobs shook his small deformed body. Finally the *daimyo* coughed several times: 'The Korean ambassadors, mighty Lord.'

Hideyoshi sat up slowly, wiping away the dribble which was

soiling his silken robe. His staring eyes were more frightening than ever. He looked at his minister as if he was transparent. 'Let them enter,' he said slowly, as if the words were a threat.

A moment later, perched on his high cushions and surrounded by his generals, he interrupted the Korean prince in the middle of the complimentary remarks he was making.

'Shut up, and stay on your knees. Listen carefully to what I say.'

The Korean general made a move as if to draw his sword, but the mandarin stopped him with a scratch from his sharp nails. They continued to bow low.

'Dog and son of a dog,' repeated Hideyoshi complacently. He sniffed back his nasal mucus with pleasure and added, 'Say this to your master, to your dog of a master: in the past you have trampled on the sacred soil of Japan. I have decided to invade China.'

The *Kampaku* paused to savour the effect of his words.

All the courtiers eyed each other interrogatively. These words had been said for the first time. The bowing ambassaadors trembled. 'Dogs! Your country will be my front line and I will lead my troops there myself. Your fate depends on your behaviour.'

The Korean emissaries were already backing away, bowing all the time, when he called them back, shouting, 'I am waiting for your gifts, you dogs!'

While they were paying homage, red-faced, the *daimyo* asked themselves, 'When did he come to this decision?'

'It was just a moment ago,' whispered Yoshitomo to them, 'just a moment ago.'

There was great joy throughout the land while the news flew everywhere like a bird. The *daimyo* raised their troops. Hideyoshi inspected the expeditionary force in April 1592, at Nagoya in the Hizen district. Ninety thousand men had been assembled at the headquarters of the invasion army.

At the head of the troops two generals saluted each other

coldly: Konishi Yukinaga and Kato Kiyomasa were to command the two advance guard corps. Both were good samurai but of humble origins and both had come up in the world with weapons in their hands. The first was the son of an apothecary and the second the son of a blacksmith. But the two men hated each other openly. Konishi, whom the Jesuits called Dom Augustin, had been baptised and commanded the Christians; Kato, a Buddhist of the Nichiren sect, an implacable enemy of Christiantity, commanded the Japanese of Kyushu.

They exchanged a few items of news, rather curtly.

'Our *Kampaku* has arrived alone: is his adopted son not to command the main part of the army now?'

'Hidetsugu refused this honour, it seems, and it is said that our *taiko* was angry about it.'

'Don't try to provoke me! I know perfectly well that Hideyoshi has transferred his title to his adopted son, contenting himself with the title of regent. Here he is!'

Throwing out his small chest on his large horse, Hideyoshi reviewed the troops, looking intently at each face. Each samurai knew that he was noting every detail of his equipment, judging one man, one weapon, one horse among the thousands of others: reading words on their lips without hearing them and discovering the most secret feelings in the depths of their souls. Hideyoshi could put a sword through a man before the victim had thought of defending himself: he hypnotised them. The samurai were proud to have such a leader.

He made his mount carry out an elegant turn in front of the generals.

'Konishi, your Jesuits haven't delivered their Portuguese ships to me...'

Kato sneered contemptuously.

'Nichiren foresaw these times. Did you know that, Kato?'

Konishi laughed quietly. Hideyoshi was already moving away. He was worried.

The great weakness of his expeditionary corps was still the lack of maritime transport. He had had several hundred ships built in the Bay of Ise, but his intelligence services had told him that the Korean Admiral Yi Sun-sin had at his disposal great ships whose hulls he had had covered with metal sheets to enable them to put up stronger resistance to the Japanese.

'I am relying on your fleet,' said Hideyoshi to the *daimyo* of the province of Shima, on the morning of 24 May 1591. At the moment of getting under way he even made this astonishing confession : 'I lack two things at the present time : vessels which our country has not yet built, and a son, which the belly of our Emperor's daughter has not yet given me.'

Konishi landed at Fusan, which he took without striking a blow. Then he set off boldly on the central road of the Korean peninsula, harvesting victories : Tong-nai and Chun-ju. Kato, at his heels, soon made a dash for Kai-nei. The vanguard had made a triumphal progress, and the mass of the army had only to follow. The King of Korea had fled from Seoul to take refuge in China.

Seasoned in war by their ancestral battles and provided with fire-arms, the Japanese, as aggressive as they were intrepid, crushed and trampled down an indolent and peaceful people which had no real army. Twenty days was enough to reach Seoul, the capital, where Hideyoshi erected a bloody pyramid of three thousand heads, cut off in a single moment. The exiled king saw the fall of Pyong Yang, his second capital. The Japanese finally stopped on the Yalu River : Korea had been taken. 'Banzai !' shouted Hideyoshi, allowing his horse to drink water from the river. His wife, Yodo-Gimi, daughter of the Mikado, drew an ideograph on a rock without dismounting. He read it and burst into a loud laugh : 'The Koreans are the dogs of the Japanese' : it was his motto.

From the palace of Seoul, 'the fellow who looks like a monkey' as the vanquished dubbed him, was preparing to reorganise the country. He had shut himself up with the scholars and had forbidden anyone to disturb him. An officer, however, forced his way in : he was white with dust.

'My lord, the dogs are biting: there are uprisings all over the country. Our isolated army corps are being ambushed. The Buddhist priests are peaching a holy war: they have even formed sacred battalions.'

'Give them a blood-bath!' spluttered Hideyoshi. 'Kill all of them, if necessary!'

But the insurrection spread right through the peninsula and the detachments of Japanese troops which were too isolated found themselves chasing phantoms. Worse was to come.

In August 1592 Admiral Yi Sun-sin reappeared off the coast of Fusan and in several engagements his battleships sank and burned the Japanese fleet. The Emperor of China massed an immense army on the Yalu. Despite reinforcements sent by Hideyoshi, they launched a sudden assault. Konishi put up a magnificent defence while waiting for Kato, who delayed on the pretext that attacks from the partisans were hampering his northward move. In January 1593 the Christian general had to fall back on Pyong Yang, and then abandon it for a new retreat towards Seoul. It was winter: his troops were being decimated by the cold.

'I am attacking,' Kato arrogantly assured Hideyoshi.

But he was defeated in his turn and soon the Japanese held only a few places along the coast. The *taiko* decided to negotiate. He began talks with the Chinese ambassadors: his conditions, since he still expected to dictate them, were the surrender of four Korean provinces. Kato protested: he was recalled.

The Emperor of China's reply was received in 1596.

'Never!' growled the hunchback. Seizing a hunting-whip he chased the ambassador who fled before him on his knees, out of his mind with terror.

'What are they asking?' ventured Konishi.

'That I declare myself a vassal of the Emperor!'

All the Japanese burst into spontaneous laughter. But Hideyoshi was weeping in the arms of his general.

So fighting broke out again: in the spring of 1597 a new

force of 100,000 troops was sent to Korea. It was under the command of Kobayakawa, only twenty years old, but advised by Kato, who was emerging from disgrace. A Japanese fleet was rebuilt and Konishi, now an admiral, was given command.

'You will be baptised again,' joked Kato.

'I shall no longer have to wait for your troops!'

But, near to Fusan, there was a surprise: it was Konishi who crushed the Korean fleet. He boarded the flagship, brandishing the cross. As for Kato, he took the citadel of Nangen. The road to Seoul was now open. The two rivals sent the same triumphant message to Kyoto: 'You are victorious, Hideyoshi!'

Riders galloped towards the Imperial city, spreading the news on their way. 'Glory for our arms and the *Kampaku*!' the people exulted.

Hideyoshi had himself carried on a stretcher into the great shrine dedicated to Yoritomo; then he asked to be left alone at the foot of the giant statue of the great *Shogun*. Huge drops of sweat stood in beads on his simian face, because for some days he had been suffering from a bad attack of dysentery which had undermined his health.

'Counsel me, powerful lord! My end is near. Let me have a glimpse of the future, so that I can leave our beloved country in the way of the gods!' For a long time in the half-light he stared at the face of the statue.

'Victory, powerful *Kampaku*!' announced a messenger to the sick man.

'Glory to our Emperor, then,' whispered Hideyoshi. 'But I sense that the fighting must stop!'

Soon afterwards, Chinese and Japanese fought an indecisive battle, with each side claiming victory. The Korean fleet, taken in hand by Yi Sun-sin, harried the Japanese fleet. The autumn of 1598 was harsh: the expeditionary corps was both cold and hungry.

'My dear lord,' said Yodo-Gimi, the Emperor's daughter,

archly, turning her head a little to avoid her husband's breath, 'do you want to see our son?'

'Come close, Hideyori,' murmured the dying man, 'and let me see your fine face. When I commanded the unworthy Hidetsugu to open his belly and I took back my title, you were not even born, but I was waiting for you. I had the heads of his wives and children cut off. You will reign. I have named five regents to govern until you come of age. Two trustworthy men will watch over your education and you are not to leave the fortified castle at Osaka, my *shiro*, my finest stronghold. . . . You will see to that, Ieyasu?'

'I will attend to it most carefully,' replied a fat little man, without moving a muscle of his face. 'He will not go out . . .'

'My son!' whispered Hideyoshi.

He was delirious. The miracle child had been born while he was making war in Korea. On his return, he had had a page-boy beheaded, without giving any reason.

'I have a handsome son,' he said again as he died.

Kato had been besieged for many months in the fortified port of Urusan. He now had no hope and watched from the ramparts while the Chinese army grew in strength. It was setting up siege appartus and guns ready for the final assault. Gunfire made him think for a moment that this was now beginning. His exhausted men moved towards the defences like automatons.

The distant battle soon opened on two fronts. The mist which was hiding the horizon lifted to reveal a powerful charge of Japanese cavalry who swept away the Chinese infantry before they were able to form up. The arquebusiers, who handled their weapons in groups of three, had not even fired their tinders before the samurai horsemen were among them, wielding their swords.

'It's Konishi!' cried Kato ecstatically.

Behind the hills which hid the sea a lurid glow showed that

an intense bombardment had begun. The first troops to land were already visible.

'Come on!' roared Kato. 'We are going to make a sortie!'

When their forces had joined up, the Japanese generals embraced uninhibitedly, but Konishi stiffened suddenly. 'The *Kampaku* is dead. Did you know? His last order was for us to re-embark in good order and honourably.'

'He was the finest of us all.'

Two brothers-in-arms had discovered a common religion.

A Last Arrow for the Tyrant

'AND I, Tokugawa Ieyasu, I refuse...'

The council was ended. Ieyasu, once again, had spoken as the master. At fifty-seven years of age, the first of the five *tairo* (the regents) was a fat little man, smooth-chinned and unyielding, the perfect aristocratic warrior of his day. The *daimyo* Ieyasu never raised his voice; on the contrary, he spoke quietly, to oblige his listeners to pay attention. He was prudent, miserly and sarcastic.

'You were saying, Ishida?'

Ishida Kazushige jumped as if he had been bitten by a serpent: another *tairo*, Masuda Nagamori, immediately sprang to his support. 'I was saying,' he exclaimed in a resonant voice as he turned towards the *Kampaku*'s mother, Yodo-Gimi, 'that we have here an ambitious man, and I would call the fact to the attention of the *churo*, the council of arbitration.'

'Blessed be Hideyoshi, who foresaw everything!' sneered Ieyasu.

The *churo* decided nothing: its three members, Ikoma, Nakamura and Horio, were too afraid of Ieyasu. Everyone returned dissatisfied to his domain, and, once again, conspiracies began to foment – the East against the West and the South; the Shinto leaders against the Christian *daimyo*.

'Ishida and his accomplices have sent a message to all the conspirators,' a spy reported to Ieyasu. 'They are indicting you on thirteen counts and calling to arms all those faithful to young Hideyori.'

'How amusing,' said Ieyasu, 'for am I not his most faithful servant? I shall join their little party... in my own way.'

Civil war was beginning anew.

Ieyasu was a remarkable war leader: a superb strategist, he allowed hostilities to continue without him and weaken the clans. He was waiting until the castle of Fushimi, seat of the *tairo* Ukida, was reduced to ashes and Ukida slit his belly. Until October 1600 he waited in Edo till his army numbered 70,000 men. He waited until the army was perfectly trained to take up its position in phalanx in the manner of the Spanish pikemen, in rectangles of fifty, combining spearmen and arquebusiers. He let several weeks pass without attacking his 90,000 opponents at Sekigahara. Then, suddenly, on the foggy morning of 21 October 1600, he attacked.

'Ho!' roared the *tairo*. 'Down with sedition-mongers!'

But within a few hours Ieyasu's relentless strategy had its effect on their numbers and their courage. His corps of troops manoeuvred in perfect order without apparent haste: reversing their plan of battle, countering attacks with a wall of accurate fire, then suddenly outflanking the weakened positions. When the opposing army had withdrawn its troops from their central positions, as he had foreseen, Ieyasu drew his sword and swept the cavalry forward.

'After work,' he said, 'we can relax!' And he set the example for a merciless massacre.

A few days after this decisive victory, he laid siege to the castle of Sawayama, where the Ishida family had taken refuge. After the attack, he himself stood at the postern-gate through which passed, one by one, his illustrious prisoners. For each he had a caustic comment.

'Ishida, what a surprise! Are you going to ask for arbitration from the council?'

'Dear old Konishi! I thought you were a Jesuit!'

A few days later he had them beheaded on the banks of the river Kamo in the centre of Kyoto, opposite the imperial Palace. Their heads had scarcely fallen before he was remounting his horse. 'Now to the castle of Osaka!'

His most faithful supporters did not open their mouths during the gallop: was Ieyasu going to forswear himself by putting to death Hideyoshi's putative son?

The drawbridges of the formidable citadel had been lowered for the new man of power. Yodo-Gimi, hugging her little prince in her arms, watched the one-time faithful servant approaching. The flagstones echoed under his heavy clogs. By comparison, her dead husband seemed reassuring and tender.

'Beautiful lady,' murmured Ieyasu, 'you have no better friend than I!'

Then he added, for the child's benefit: 'I hope Hideyori is studying hard. Remember your father's wishes, Hideyori: stay quietly in your stronghold. I, moreover, will watch over you as I promised your father....'

So Ieyasu respected the *Kampaku*. He did not do away with him, but in 1603 he restored the shogunate for the benefit of his own family and abdicated immediately in favour of his son, Hidetada. The Tokugawa shogunate was to remain in power until the nineteenth century.

If one wishes to indulge in comparisons, Ieyasu was the Richelieu of Japan. All the administrative structures of the country, as they were to remain for three centuries, dated effectively from his time. Respectful towards the Emperor, he withdrew to the castle of Fushimi which he had had rebuilt, and he continued to assume responsibility for efficient government while devoting himself also to literature and poetry. To be omnipresent, he decentralised the Empire establishing three capitals: that of the *Tenno*, Kyoto, where his official representative supervised the Imperial court; that of the *Kampaku*, Osaka, and that of the *Shogun*, Edo.

The Emperor? He was an abstraction. In 1611 it was Go-Yozei, who abdicated in favour of his son, Go-Minoo. During the civil wars the Mikado lived on small incomes in dilapidated palaces: even their state funerals had to be delayed for lack of money.

In 1603 Ieyasu announced the engagement of his granddaughter, Sen-Hime, to the young *Kampaku*, Hideyori. Was this to herald an era of peace?

Arms crossed, Yodo-Gimi looked at her son. 'Do not accept this invitation, Hideyori, do not leave Osaka.'

'Mother, I have already refused three times. It would be an insult to Ieyasu!'

The old princess shook her head angrily.

At the age of sixteen, the *Kampaku* was an accomplished samurai and also a great noble. The young girls hid as he passed and marvelled at his fine appearance: tall and handsome, a fine horseman and a splendid shot, Hideyori also had a lively mind and great shrewdness. 'He was born to reign,' Yodo-Gimi kept saying.

She said this too often. Ieyasu had heard of it and his invitation was only a pretext to find out from his future son-in-law himself if he had ambitions. To overcome the prejudices of Hideyoshi's widow, he was obliged to guarantee the young man's safety by sending emissaries and by taking an oath.

Two processions started for Kyoto at the same time: Ieyasu's small escort (he never spent a yen more than was necessary) set off from Edo, while Hideyori's magnificent procession left Osaka to the plaudits of a huge crowd.

Ieyasu, first to arrive in the Imperial capital, frowned at so much extravagance. His eyes narrowed when the *Kampaku* himself jumped nimbly from his horse in front of him. He was tall, and possessed of a luminous beauty.

'I thought I was seeing your father,' rasped Ieyasu. 'Tell me . . .' Then he whispered confidentially in his ear: 'Where does the money come from?'

During the sumptuous feasts given in honour of his rival, the fat man seemed to be dozing, his hands crossed over his belly. His plan was soon formed.

The Sumo wrestlers saluted them before confronting each other. They were the best of their time; one weighed two hundred pounds and his opponent almost three hundred.

'Let's have a bet,' said Ieyasu, opening one eye.

'Yes, let's bet,' Hideyori said gaily. 'I'll back the bigger one!'

Ieyasu resumed his apparent doze, thinking: 'He's a

gambler and easily influenced: I'll ruin him: the uncut gem does not sparkle.'

The fat wrestler broke his smaller opponent's back.

So that he could not devote his income to the recruitment and eventual upkeep of troops, Ieyasu led Hideyori into great extravagance. Appealing to his chivalrous spirit, he persuaded him, for example, to commit himself to rebuilding the Hojo shrine which had been destroyed by an earthquake. This the *Kampaku* hastened to do. In 1614 he even invited Ieyasu to a great ceremony to celebrate the completion of this charitable work.

'I have had his name engraved on a bell which we are going to give to one of the shrines,' said the young man to his mother.

'That really is too much of an honour,' said the princess indignantly. She called a servant and whispered a few words to him.

The next day when the bell was unveiled, Ieyasu paled: an ideograph added to his patronymic gave it an offensive meaning. His host, in all innocence, gave him a delighted smile.

'Go back quickly to your castle, putative son,' growled Ieyasu, 'and take care!'

The origins of the outrage were soon known. And much else: for example, that the formidable *shiro* of Osaka was a state within a state where Yodo-Gimi, having decided to acquire power for her son, had called together all the malcontents of the country – the Christians, in particular. Was Hideyori not suspected of being one, secretly? It was Yodo-Gimi who had planned the insult. Ieyasu sent an ultimatum to the *Kampaku*.

'Give me your mother as a hostage, or it will be the worse for you!'

But already the two camps were hastily preparing for war. In December 1614 an army of 70,000 men laid siege to Osaka. The gigantic walls of the great *shiro* were defended by thousands of men and innumerable guns. Its great keeps whose superimposed roofs were embellished with porcelain and gold would be lost in the smoke when thousands of arquebuses let off their projectiles at the same moment in a rain of plunging fire. Hidetada, son of Ieyasu and titular *Shogun*, attacked several times and retreated leaving a carpet of dead bodies before the great moats. The 'Osaka winter campaign' marked time.

'Never look for fish on a tree. This business has gone on too long,' decided the old chief finally. 'I have sent an emissary.'

'To Hideyori, who is swaggering on the walls?'

'No, to his mother. She's a man, that woman!'

'What are your conditions, Father?'

'Only one: that he fills in his moats.'

So it was done; but with much equivocation. Five months, later on 24 May 1615, Ieyasu was back in Osaka with a new army facing the filled-in moats of the great forts. The Tokugawa had lined up 200,000 men for this 'summer campaign': as many as had taken part in the greater wars, although the Japanese population had scarcely increased. It still fluctuated around a total of 25 million souls and was not greatly to exceed this number until the nineteenth century.

Hideyori, for his part, mustered 120,000 soldiers, among whom were found contingents of Christians whose banners bore the effigy of St John, protector of Spain. For several years, the prestige of the Spaniards of Manila had been supplanting that of the Portuguese of Macao in the eyes of the Japanese.

The attack on the *shiro* of Osaka was the last great battle of the Japan of the ancient samurai. It lasted a full month, was distinguished by great feats of arms and ended, traditionally, with great carnage.

The third of June 1615. The Tokugawa's ant-hill army tirelessly made good its losses, and successive betrayals had led to the fall of the first surrounding wall, which was no longer protected by its moats, and then of the second in which mines had made enormous breaches where the best of Hideyori's warriors had died. Ieyasu's sappers were now burrowing like moles towards the keeps and for several nights it had been possible to follow their progress by pressing an ear against the earth. At this very moment they were undoubtedly attacking the foundations. Guns and arquebuses lay on the ground, absurd because they lacked ammunition: even the walls, scraped a hundred times for their saltpetre could no longer provide a charge.

The *Kampaku* gave orders for the glazed tiles to be gathered up, and the crenellations loosened so as still to have some projectiles. The last of his faithful subjects, emaciated by their privations, collected rain – which was unusual at this time of year – in their hats. Their shining eyes showed their pride in the honourable death which was coming to them and they composed poems of farewell, masterpieces which they improved on day by day. Some, crouching in the corner towers, rehearsed already the ritual of the *seppuku*, painstakingly miming each phrase of the gestures.

'We are the last samurai,' the *Kampaku* repeated frequently, proud as a lean wolf. 'Ieyasu is fat: his men are obese. They walk ashamedly behind their mobile stockades.'

Hideyori spat proudly from the top of his stronghold, confronting his destiny. The dowager Yodo-Gimi raised her head placidly from her ideographs to show her proud approval. 'Your father would have called them dogs.'

In the morning, amid an acrid smell of powder, the siege-trenches exploded all together and the debris raised clouds of thick white dust. When this dispersed, large fissures were showing in the building and the troops were making their final assault, yelling ferociously. Hot lead from the arquebuses rained down in front of them, but they came on like the tide.

'Forward!'

The shout burst out from both sides.

A rain of arrows felled the front ranks and immediately savage hand-to-hand fighting began: it was to last for hours. They fought as never before, with swords and stones, fists and teeth! The rubble of the walls was stained with blood. Some breaches were blocked by the piled heaps of corpses; the defenders did not yield even in death. Ieyasu, perched on the debris of the second encircling wall, was smoking a short pipe.

'These Christians really do love their neighbours,' he remarked ironically, to hide his admiration. 'But look, *Shogun*! Do you see what is happening up there!'

The *Kampaku* had just appeared on the tower of the second gateway. He had one arm around his mother's shoulders and she, her face raised, looked radiant and suddenly very young behind her veils. Hideyori raised his sword and slashed through the railings of the window to show himself the better. He shouted his name and the battle below him suddenly ceased.

'Beaten by the rebels, I will destroy myself so as to avenge my wrongs in the hereafter. Watch me closely, so as to learn how a warrior opens his belly when luck runs out.'

Stripping off his armour slowly, piece by piece, he threw it to the foot of the tower. Then he took off the jacket of his narrow-sleeved undergarment, and wearing only brocade trousers . . .

'We are losing face,' Hidetada flung at his father. 'Let us continue the attack.'

'Silence,' said Ieyasu.

The young *Kampaku* cut his flesh in a straight line from left to right. He threw his entrails on to the parapet of the tower. He put his sword in his mouth and threw himself face forward to the ground.

'Sublime!' acknowledged the *Shogun*. 'But his mother?'

'You were not paying attention,' replied Ieyasu. 'She ran a sword through her own breast at the same instant. Remember this scene and never forget the greatness of Japan.' Then, without a pause: 'And now, govern! You must have their heads, every one. Have them cut off. Preserve those of men of importance in the lacquer containers filled with *sake* which I had prepared yesterday.'

A fire, kindled by the last survivors, suddenly lit up the stronghold. The massacre inside was ending among human torches. A child of seven, with a wooden sword – Hideyori's illegitimate son – was brought to Ieyasu.

'Cut off his head!'

'Father, even at Sekigahara...'

'I am getting old: this last battle is decisive. I want it to ensure the position and the inheritance of my descendants.'

Seated in the lotus position, the archer began by meditating. Despite the noise of battle and the smoke from fires which stung his eyes cruelly, he tried to maintain in himself a total silence. Then he knelt down, his bow resting on the ground on his left side. His gaping wound was numbing his shoulder gradually, and he knew that in a few seconds the first shooting pains would stop him from moving.

The arquebusiers were still firing at the last defenders who showed any sign of life, but did not see him motionless in the shadowy corner of the ruins from which he was indistinguishable.

Between the moment when he picked up his bow and the one when he was to speed a last arrow, an interminable time passed, and each of his movements conformed to the most perfect ritual.

The wounded archer raised the axis of his weapon to the level of his head. He turned slowly towards the target. A red mist hid the group of victors at whom he was aiming. His intense concentration blurred the figures, and made gaps in the group. Then the blurred silhouettes became clear and precise again. He shot his arrow, uttering a piercing cry. The archer, the bow, and the arrow were all one. The archer was at the same time arrow and target. A man fell, far below, and the archer also fell, dead.

In an immense curve, the last shot from the ramparts of Osaka had struck Ieyasu, who had had no breastplate. He straightened up and pulled out the arrow himself, saying calmly to the *Shogun*, 'You see, history also is pitiless.'

Then, as his wound was dressed, looking at the little decapitated body at his feet, he blinked back something unthinkable: a tear.

'Even the devil can shed a tear,' remarked a samurai, sliding his sword into its sheath.

Ieyasu died as the result of this wound on 1 June 1616, at the age of seventy-four. A great shrine was built at Nikki to commemorate him. His descendants stayed in power without interruption until 1867.

Ieyasu's 'testament' – a meticulous political and administrative organisation – took the form of a series of laws and regulations relating to administrative, civil, penal and commercial matters, which were not drawn up until after his death. His successors were inspired solely by his ideas. He had restricted himself to laying down the code of the *Kuge* (Nobles) and the *Buke* (samurai): the military caste shed its chivalrous ideal and became no more than a clearly defined and immutable class of society. It comprised all the samurai, including the minor *daimyo* who had an income of less than ten thousand *koku* (five bushels of rice = one *koku*). Thus Ieyasu 'froze' the aristocracy for a long time. He knew that in each family of those defeated at Osaka a stone slab on the family altar was inscribed with the name of the dead man, thus keeping his memory alive. Even if his body had not been found, a lock of hair or an object belonging to him was buried, in place of his ashes, in the cemetery in the garden.

The Portuguese Commandant, Pessoa, had blown up his ship, the *Madre de Dios*, outside Nagasaki on 7 January 1610: the Japanese had wanted to seize it following commercial litigation. The Spanish galleon *San Francisco*, which had on board His Most Catholic Excellency, the governor of the Philippines, Vivero, ran aground at the entrance to the Bay of Edo on 30 September 1609. Many thorny problems resulted.

The Dutch, newcomers and Protestants, disparaged the European Catholics. They doubled the price of pepper in 1599. In 1610 the English East India Company sent out the *Clove*, under the command of John Saris, an Anglican Protestant, who was to represent them in Japan. This presumptuous and narrow-minded man aroused animosity. A struggle for power began between the representatives of the four powers and the two faiths.

Iemitsu, son of Hidetada, succeeded him in 1632. His father had outlawed Christians: he persecuted them. His first edict promised a reward to whomever would disclose a Catholic priest. In 1637 he proscribed the 'perverse religion'. It was forbidden to the Japanese. The half-hearted were forced to abjure, the others were exterminated: in a few years, Christianity became a secret society.

In 1634 Iemitsu prohibited the building of Japanese ships of a greater tonnage than 500 *koku*, thus making any long voyages impossible. In 1638 the Portuguese, who were suspected of having supported an internal rebellion, were refused entry to Japan. In 1639 the archipelago became forbidden territory to anyone, even ambassadors, on pain of death. The Dutch alone kept a small anchorage, the islet of Deshima in the roadstead of Nagasaki. This last point of contact with the land of the Rising Sun was to be for two and a half centuries the only authorised link. What is more the number of ships allowed to dock there was limited, and the crews were not permitted to go ashore.

Thus, Iemitsu closed Japan off completely to the West, renouncing the contribution she could have received from that quarter. From then on, the country could develop only by refining its own culture. Economic expansion was stopped dead. The forbidden islands began a motionless voyage in time, suffused with mystery. 'Flowers of Edo' (fires) might ravage the town; there could be earthquakes; a conspiracy could end in carnage; but no news of these events left the archipelago.

Many isolated islanders have been known to deteriorate, but insularity stimulated the Japanese.

The Forty-seven Ronin

THE SOLITARY voyage of the 'forbidden Japan' of the Tokugawa was a dull period without any event of note.

The *daimyo*, curbed and exploited, found themselves in a precarious financial situation: the collection of taxes was chancy. The circulation of paper money unleashed such inflation that this practice had to be forbidden in 1707. However, the *Shogun* lived in luxury. From 1730 onwards all the nobles fell into the power of the merchant-usurers of Osaka who left them barely enough to keep body and soul together. The government was obliged to announce regularly the cancellation of debts.

The great *daiymo* supported a fairly large number of samurai: since the Tokugawas' reign of peace, all of them had represented a non-productive, inactive class. They derived their livelihood almost exclusively from the labours of the peasants, but all of them enjoyed a sumptuous style of life, generally above their means.

The population of the Empire grew little by little and the influx of country dwellers to the towns completely upset the basis of the Japanese economy. The middle class and the merchants rapidly amassed considerable fortunes and annexed the power which the nobility were gradually losing.

The *bakufu* tried to change this state of affairs by sumptuary laws and confiscations, but nothing could stay the rise of the middle class. These people wanted to see the country opened up to foreigners in order to expand their trade. On this question they were in agreement with the great *daimyo* who saw here a possibility of increasing their resources.

The moral standards of the country were also changing:

after the first efforts of the Tokugawa to fight against the laxity caused by the civil wars, these had been at first simple, austere even, and founded on the *Bushido*. But the *Shoguns*, the nobility, and soon all the ruling class, were swiftly adopting luxurious and extravagant habits.

Classes became interchangeable: warriors became agriculturalists; merchants became warriors, peasants became merchants; but it was especially the samurai and the middle classes who merged with one another; in times of peace, aristocrats must always devote themselves to restoring the fortunes of their houses!

The period of 'splendid isolation' was a time when life was very elegant, but the most sordid poverty existed side by side with the most frivolous ostentation. Kyoto, capital of the divine Emperor, was no more than a town nostalgic for its past, devoting itself to the cultivation of the fine arts and to Imperial ritual. The Emperors were of no real consequence in the unfolding of events. They were no more than a list of names.

Edo, which was to become Tokyo, was a huge head on a very small body: this disproportionately large capital had two million inhabitants, at a time when Paris had no more than half a million. The *shogun*'s palace was the Versailles of Japan. Behind this brilliant decor, Yoshiwara was the best organised of the red-lamp districts. There the rich merchants gave sumptuous banquets, enlivened and embellished by the presence of geishas, the professional dancing girls.

Dress had changed a little: the kimono was now in general use. Although the samurai could still be seen in their traditional dress (sheath-winged armour or robe, trousers and tunic with starched shoulder-straps), the *daimyo* were showing a tendency to become more effeminate, either in their way of life, which did not include virile sports, or in their dress which was becoming more and more softly luxurious.

Politically, socially and economically, Japan was falling rapidly into decadence. However, she had in herself the ability to surmount her difficulties. The spirit of the old samurai lived on. A wonderful and bloody adventure was to symbolise for ever the everlasting nature of law and honour.

In the first days of March 1701 the Emperor Higashiyama sent three ambassadors to Edo to the *Shogun* Tokugawa Tsunayoshi, two to represent him personally and another in the name of the retired Emperor, Reigen.

To receive them, the *Shogun* had appointed two great nobles, of whom Asano Naganori, *daimyo* of the castle of Ako, was to direct the ceremonies. Asano had at first declined this honour, pleading his ignorance of court etiquette. But at the insistence of the other nobles he had finally accepted, on the express condition that he would have the benefit of advice from the grand master of ceremonies of the period, an old man named Kira Yoshihisa. It was a very important matter for Asano: it was, undoubtedly, the most serious mission of his life.

It was the custom in the Edo period for the governor of Kyoto to present himself at the Imperial palace each new year bearing to the Emperor and his family the good wishes of the *Shogun* residing in Edo. In return for this, during the first fine days of spring, the Emperor sent emissaries in his turn to the shogunal court with the duty of expressing his trust in the *Shogun*. This annual mark of respect was like a kind of renewal of investiture. It was, each time, the occasion of an impressive ceremony which the *Shogun* insisted on making as magnificent as possible, for it showed the people that the Emperor supported him.

In fact, the *Shogun* had in his hands all power and all authority. His dictatorship was firmly-based and never disputed. The Emperor, confined to Kyoto, safeguarded by his celestial mandate, descendant of the divinity of the Sun, had only the nominal religious authority conferred on him by his rank. While he reigned like this, without governing, he remained a sacred personage in the eyes of the people, who saw in him a guardian of tradition, the half-divine being who held in his hands the destiny of the country. Without his nomination, previously extorted by force, the *Shogun* would have been a usurper. It was therefore necessary for Asano to carry out his honorary role during the receptions of 12 and 13 March to perfection. This was an affair of state and, above all, a matter of honour.

Kira Yoshihisa, an old, corrupt courtier, demanded sumptuous gifts from all who petitioned him. It was the custom of the time to make such presentations to officials from whom one asked a service, the gifts varying according to the fortune of the petitioner. But Asano Naganori would not hear of this. Brought up according to Confucian principles of uprightness and dignity, he disapproved of a practice which corrupted the servants of the State. Accordingly, though he was advised to scatter gold profusely on Kira's knees, he restricted himself to gifts which were allowed by official usage, and refused to depart from this line of conduct at any price. Asano did not appreciate the customs of Edo and the corrupt mentality of the important people of that period. He maintained that it was Kira's simple duty, as chief of protocol, to teach him the rules of the ceremonial etiquette and considered that it would be discreditable to give him gifts out of proportion to his task.

Kira, a cunning old man, knew that Asano was rich. He had learned that his province brought him each year 53,500 koku of rice and that he was also the owner of a secret method used in a prosperous salt processing industry. 'So?' he growled, bitterly, after receiving the few symbolic gifts which the *diamyo* of Ako had offered him. 'This is all he gives me! If that's the way it is, I shall not help him with any advice, even if he loses face!'

The chief of protocol had only the income that his estate brought him: 4200 bushels of rice annually. However, he led the life of a great noble at the shogunal court, which obliged him to demand payment for every little service. From this misunderstanding was to arise a bloody drama.

On the morning of 12 March, the Imperial envoys were received in private audience by the *Shogun,* and on 13 March a banquet was given in their honour, followed by Nô and Kyogen plays. All this while Asano, not having been able to arrange a single meeting with Councillor Kira, had had to manage as best as he could. He had not, however, cut too sorry a figure, as he was not obliged to appear personally. But the following day – 14 March – the *Shogun* was to give a grand reception to the Imperial envoys before their departure and Asano was to be in charge. Yet he did not really know what he should do, nor where he should stand. He was wandering through the corridors, gnawed by anxiety, when he suddenly saw Kira who was trotting along ahead of him, his hands in his sleeves like a Chinese mandarin, an enigmatic smile on his lips. Asano went up to him, nervously.

'What shall I have to do tomorrow? Tell me quickly!'

'You should have thought about that before,' breathed the old man softly. 'Now I've no longer any time.'

He turned on his heels, leaving Asano out of countenance and furious. Perhaps matters might have rested there, if Kira had not muttered as he went off: 'Good medicine always tastes bitter!'

It was the last straw. Asano, furious with rage, drew his sword and slit the courtier's silken robe with a stroke so subtle that the other was instantly left naked, without his flesh being touched. The grand master of ceremonies howled like a whipped dog. Asano laughed silently.

'You'll remember that!' he mocked.

But Kira, draped in the remnants of his silken robe, yelled out, 'He's mad, a lout, a savage! Help!'

This time the blade cut horizontally. Ever precise, Asano, who knew how to cut off a head, struck only at the open mouth from which this hurtful abuse was issuing, and widened it to the extremities of the jaws in a bloody smile. Kira swallowed and spat out streams of blood. He was choking with it. Onlookers had run forward. They overpowered Asano for fear that he might kill the old man. With a word he reassured them – with a proverb also: 'If you hate your enemy, let him live!'

Kira, still bleeding, was carried out of the shogunal palace.

When the *Shogun* Tsunayoshi, who was taking a bath, heard of the affair, he turned red with rage. First he named another official to replace Asano; then he gave orders for the ceremony to take place in another part of the palace, as the place they were in was stained with Kira's blood. In his wrath the *Shogun* wanted to punish Asano immediately and his counsellors had the greatest difficulty in making him postpone the outcome of this unhappy business until after the departure of the Imperial emissaries.

In the afternoon Asano, who had been under house arrest in the home of a noble named Tamura, received a visit from two judges who announced that the *Shogun* had condemned him to suicide by slitting open his belly. Asano Naganori then wrote his poem of farewell. He spoke in it of his thirty-six years scattered like the petals of flowers not yet fully opened; next, with a hand which did not tremble, he opened his belly from left to right, as a true samurai, and the *kaishaku* chopped off his head with a single stroke of his other sword. The *Shogun* ordered the confiscation of Asano's two houses in Edo, together with his estate in Ako.

When a messenger, white with dust, crossed the drawbridge of the feudal castle, the three hundred warriors of the fallen lord were assembled and already knew what had happened. The news of their master's death had flown the six hundred kilometres like a bird.

The *Shogun*'s messenger, a well-born man, did not bat an eyelid, even though he was expecting at any moment to be cut down by those who had suddenly become *ronin*, soldiers of fortune without protection or resources. He unfolded his manuscript and read it straight off, standing in his stirrups as a herald. It was then that, to his great surprise, the samurai slowly left the precincts and withdrew.

All the previous night, in the dancing light of a huge fire lit at the foot of the stronghold, the warriors had argued about the problem. There were two opposing parties. There were those who accepted the inevitable and bowed to the *Shogun*'s will – had not Asano's brother himself counselled submission? And there were the others. Oishi Kuranosuke was their spokesman.

'With Asano dead,' he intoned in his deep voice, 'would the *Shogun* not accept even his brother who is here to succeed him in the castle? Is the fate of the Naganori sealed for ever? And are we, Asano's faithful warriors, his liegemen, to wander away forgetful of the most sacred of duties?'

Oishi spoke for a long time. The light of the flames danced on his tragically white face. He had rediscovered the grandiloquence of the samurai of ancient days, and his words sent shivers down the spines of his impassive companions. As he spoke his inspired words, their blood warmed and raced.

At the end of his exordium, a cock crowed, announcing the dawn. Without putting it to the vote, fifty warriors spontaneously unsheathed their swords and remained for a long moment impassively facing the fire, each holding in his hand a weapon glinting in the red firelight.

It was on 18 April that the shogunal troops came to take possession of the castle of Ako. The samurai dispersed without offering the slightest resistance. The new lord of the province of Iga, Nagai by name, was riding behind his strong-arm men, a falcon on his glove. The peasants, quite indifferent, watched as they passed. What did it matter to them that one noble rather than another reigned in the castle? They would go on working as before and would pay as much in taxes.

Kira Yoshihisa consulted his mirror once again and groaned. Under his make-up the atrocious wound still gave him the appearance of a baleful *kami*. He thrust the cruel image away and hid himself again behind his open fan. One of the samurai, squatting, his eyes averted out of delicacy, waited for his questions.

'So, you said that there were no more than forty-seven?'

'There were still forty-eight yesterday, my lord, but I was present at a quarrel in an inn where their chief, Oishi, was drunk. A man named Murakami Kiken, also one of Asano's former samurai, had entered, beside himself with anger. He took up his stand firmly in front of Oishi, who was drinking with completely naked geisha girls: "Coward!" he said to him. "Have you forgotten our oath!" At first I thought that Oishi was going to draw his sword, for his hands trembled with pent-up anger. But he began to laugh: he was full of *sake*. "Come and join us and let us laugh together, good companion," he said to the man who had insulted him. It was a terrible thing to ignore such an insult. It made me feel sick.... I managed to draw his sword from its sheath, and the blade was covered with rust.'

'And if it was a trick to distract our attention?'

'Then Oishi would be a hero,' replied Kira's samurai without thinking.

'Watch!' snapped his master drily. 'Watch, and leave me.'

Months passed.

One evening in December 1702 one of the *ronin*, Hara, went to his mother's home, where his young wife and their child also lived. The two women were happy to receive this surprise visit.

'Hara,' his mother said to him, 'I am delighted to see you again. Embrace me without delay. Wash your feet and come in without ceremony.'

He took off his straw sandals and put to one side his big travelling hat. Then he entered the house, followed by his wife who was carrying the child.

The grandmother spoke from her heart. 'Your presence has filled my heart with joy. During your absence, your admirable wife has been like a daughter to me. Look at your lovely little Fusabo, hasn't he grown? He can already walk and say a few words.'

In the meantime Hara's younger brother arrived and all the family was reunited round a little banquet to celebrate the happy return of the head of the family.

'Honoured mother,' said he, 'I think I have found a place with a prince of Kanto who wants me to enter his service. This would retrieve our family fortunes. That is why I am going to Edo. I have come to tell you the good news and to say good-bye.'

The venerable lady looked attentively at her eldest son's face. 'My son,' she said, 'I am happy at your news. But I have the pride of a samurai's mother and I would like to know the real reason for your journey.'

Hara bent his head until it touched the mat to hide his blushes.

At an early hour the next day, the samurai went off quickly so that he would not weaken. Towards midday, he stopped by a tree and opened his box of provisions, where he found rice-cakes which his mother had made for him. He took a piece of one of them and lifted it respectfully to his forehead before beginning his meal. When only one cake remained in the bottom of the box he raised his eyes and saw some pigeons on a branch of the tree. He scattered the remains of his lunch on the ground for them and watched. The birds chirruped for a moment to call their young, to whom they left all the crumbs without taking even one.

'Can human beings learn a lesson from birds about family love?' mused Hara. 'If I go to Edo, it is to die, either fighting, or else by slitting open my belly; I have therefore been telling my mother a great lie. When it is all over, what will she think of me? That my affection was very shallow because I deceived her.'

Hara was unable to continue on his journey with such a weight on his conscience. He turned back immediately along the road to his home, which he reached as the sun was sinking. As soon as he was with the old lady again he went down on his knees at her feet.

'You were not mistaken. I am going to Edo with the intention of avenging my honoured lord. It will therefore be impossible for me ever to see you again. My father is dead, and I should remain here to make you happy: but how can I fulfil my duties as a son and also as a faithful vassal?'

'I was not misled for a single moment,' replied the old lady gently. 'My son, do your duty by your lord, that is the first thing a samurai must consider. Your brother will support me. Let us drink a farewell cup.'

The knight rose the next morning at the break of day and went to wait at the door of his mother's bedroom, knowing she was always up before anyone else in the house. The hours passed. The sun rose high in the sky. It was almost ten in the morning, at the hour of the dragon, when Hara, consumed by anxiety, went into the bedroom and found his mother dead.

Near the wooden head-rest on which the old lady rested her head so as not to untidy her coiffure was a letter stained with blood: 'My dear son, your kindness and your affection are great; happy is the mother of such a son. But it is essential that you should be able to go on your mission without being hindered by any anxiety; otherwise, the enemy would have a chance to see the inside of your helmet. I am therefore about to precede you, my son, to the land of the *kami*. From now on, regard Kira not only as the enemy of your honoured lord, but also as your mother's executioner, and set your comrades an example of heroism. I will die smiling at the blade which cuts the thread of my modest life. My last farewell to your brother, your wife, to little Fusabo, and to you, my dear son. Your Mother.'

'Look, everyone!' exclaimed Hara. 'See what she has done for my sake!'

As he rode towards Edo the knight's expression made even the boldest lower their eyes. They read death in it. Kampei came by another route, and his expression too, was frightening. On his way home from visiting his parents-in-law, he had met Ichimonjiya, the owner of a bawdy house to which his fiancée had sold herself in order to obtain for him the means for his revenge.

Each conspirator, during the months of waiting, had been obliged to swallow insults, refuse challenges and lay false scents, in order to keep the secret. But on the quiet they had amassed funds, hidden arms and armour, conspired together and worked out the details of their plan of attack.

The rendezvous was planned for nightfall on 14 December near to the *yashiki* of Honjo, the fine house where Kira lived in Edo. It stood in an unfrequented district near a great wooden bridge.

Snow was falling. Two boats, the rowers of which had been careful to avoid making any splashing noise, came to rest on the bank. Their prows ran aground, crunching on the frozen grass. Six of the *ronin*, equipped for battle, leaped from each boat. Their breath made puffs of steam in the white moonlight. They were like vigilant dragons. Other phantom-like silhouettes advanced across the bridge at regular intervals, stopping every three paces in order to lull the suspicions of any possible look-outs among Kira's samurai. Only an especially alert eye would have been able to see these intermittent advances which lasted no more than the twinkling of an eye. Only a cat could have seen, during the halts, that the tip of a lance or the curve of a bow was showing above the parapet of the bridge.

The *yashiki* was made up of a group of low buildings at the end of a street in which stood other residences of eminent people. There was no way out of these wooden houses other than the doors which were carefully barricaded at this late hour. But above the snow-covered roofs red sparks from the fires inside the houses showed that people were still awake.

Oishi Kuranosuke, climbing out of a boat, raised his arm. Still silent, his companions took hold of two ladders and some long thick sticks. One by one the other *ronin* leaped across the open space separating the bridge from the nearest buildings.

The ladders were leaned gently against the roof of the house. The band of *ronin* gathered close together in the street, their breath mingling in the cold air.

'Banzai!'

Great roars, held in for two years, burst out over Kira

Yoshihisa who was dozing, huddled in his silken robe, in front of a small fire.

Huge blows from battering rams which shook his door echoed the rhythm of his irregular heart-beats. He began to lose consciousness, for he knew: it was they. Those bad dreams which he attributed to his poor digestion were about this happening. Kira trembled. His fan fell from his hands, uncovering the horrible rictus, and his face was whiter than the cosmetics which he used during his day at the court.

The door gave way. The shouts of the attackers redoubled. Already their horned helmets were emerging on the rooftops, and flashes of cold steel were gleaming in the pale night.

The neighbours who heard the sounds of the attack had understood what it was about. They had been expecting it for a long time. Orders were shouted everywhere in the night. It was an alarm: armed men took up their positions, swords at the ready, before every door. But they were defending only the neutrality of the other houses and did not intervene: this was an affair of honour.

Twelve of Kira's samurai were on guard at Honjo. They reached for their swords and rushed into the courtyards. It was already too late: the attackers caught them, half-naked, leaping through the broken door or jumping from the roofs. They were hit, stabbed by lances, riddled by arrows: they died before even seeing an enemy face.

In an instant, twelve large patches of blood, spreading on the snow, marked the places where they had fallen. One of them, their leader, with some twenty wounds, crawled on his forearms as far as Oishi's feet, pulled himself up and recognised him. He stammered some words which were choked by blood.

'Faithful warriors . . .'

It was a tribute. But a spear pinned him to the ground and he stretched out in a last spasm that raised a flurry of snow.

'Kira!'

Oishi charged, Hara charged, Kampei . . . all of them. They spread through the building, swords bloody, faces furious. Fine draperies and precious vases were destroyed: where was he?

Servants fled into the darkness. Slapped by the flat sides of swords, they all turned, shouting stridently, only to stumble against other demons.

'Kira!'

A court scholar, a friend of the master of ceremonies, came out of an alcove raising both arms. His hands were struck off.

'Kira!'

'He has fled, he is hiding, over there,' gasped a servant. 'There' meant a cupboard in an outbuilding, under dirty linen which was lifted by swords. The linen quaked: Kira was there. He was dragged and carried and pushed to the middle of a snow-covered garden which had been spared by the battle. Torches were lit and stuck in the ground. The *ronin* lined up, awesome in their calmness. This was the great moment, the great hour.

'Lord Kira, send for your swords!'

Not a word came past his chattering teeth. A servant hurried forward and put the condemned man's weapons on a small mat. But he shook his head and remained on his knees, trembling with fear, with shame and with cold.

'I will do it,' said Hara.

Hara smiled gently at this moment. The glare of the torches reflected back from the dazzling snow, was dimmed by the flash of an untarnished blade whipping through the air, followed by a soft, dull thud. Kira's dishonoured head soiled the snow with a scarlet halo.

There was a rattle of swords being pushed back into their sheaths.

Kira's head was then wrapped in white linen and all Asano's samurai left the scene. They took their places in the waiting boats and went down the river as far as the temple of Sengaku-ji, where the mortal remains of their master had been laid. There they solemnly set down Kira's head and the sword which had slain him, together with this declaration:

'The fifteenth year of the era of Genroku, the twelfth

month and the fifteenth day. We have assembled here to offer homage to your memory. We are forty-seven samurai, from Oishi Kuranosuke down to the ordinary foot-soldier, Terasaka Kichiemon, who offer our lives joyfully for you. Reverently, we say this to the spirit of our dead master. On the fourteenth day of the fifteenth month of last year, our revered master attacked Kira Yoshihisa for reasons unknown to us. He was later obliged to kill himself, but Kira lived on. Although after the governmental decree we feared lest this conspiracy might displease our master, we who have eaten his bread can speak these words without blushing: "You shall not live under the same sky, nor tread upon the same earth as your father's enemy or the enemy of your lord". Likewise we would not dare to leave hell and show ourselves in paradise without having completed the work of vengeance which you began. Each day which passed seemed to us as long as three autumns. In fact, we marched for two days through the snow, only stopping once to eat. Even the old and the decrepit, and the sick and the weak, came gladly to offer their lives. Here is Kira's head, and the blade which struck him down. May your hatred be ever assuaged. This is the respectful proclamation of forty-seven samurai. . . .'

Then they gave themselves up. The people of Edo acclaimed them as heroes and the *Shogun* himself admired their constancy and their courage. But the law was the law. First Tsunayoshi decreed that any who attempted to avenge themselves on the forty-seven *ronin* should be considered as criminals, and punished as such. He intended by this measure to discourage in advance any attempts on the part of the Uesugi warriors, who were related to Kira, to seek vengeance.

The shogunal council was later called together to decide what course to take. Its deliberations lasted for months. The discussions ended on 1 February 1703, in the invitation to ritual suicide which would avoid dishonour for the *ronin*.

The atrocious ceremony took place on 4 February. It was held in the open air and began at daybreak. The condemned men, who had been held under guard by *daimyo* of high degree observed all the rules of traditional politeness in such a case. They presented themselves in white linen robes in the precinct which was itself draped in white – the colour of mourning – and which had been properly orientated in relation to the sun, according to the very ancient code of *seppuku*. In the four corners were seated the witnesses or representatives, who were mostly relatives of the condemned men.

Cotton sheets had been spread on the mat-covered floor. The ceremony called for mats to be laid end to end along the path to be taken by the condemned men so that they could walk without sandals: it would not have been proper for them to have lost a sandal on the way. Even the exact point on the horizon which they must face was laid down, and even, most precisely, the particular form of words they must use:

'My lords, I have nothing to say. But, since you have been kind enough to think of me, I beg you to present my respects to your suzerain and also to the gentlemen of your clan who have treated me so well. I should be most obliged if you would be kind enough to give this message to ...'

They then handed over their last poem, destined for someone close to them, a relative or friend, and crouched down, facing the north. The spectators, still and silent, stood around in a semicircle some way off.

The *kaishaku* said: 'Since I am to have the honour of cutting off your head, I should like to borrow your sword for the occasion. It will, I am sure, be some consolation for you to be struck down by a weapon so familiar to you....'

With a gesture, the samurai pointed to his weapons, lying on a small stool beside the bucket where his head would be placed a moment later.

A strong smell of incense was spreading from a large perfume-pan. The man who was about to die had only to stretch out his hand to seize his short sword, lying in front of him, in its wooden sheath. Behind him, his *kaishaku*, his expression showing only a moderate degree of sorrow (as it is laid down), made sure he would depart from this world in a fitting manner.

There is no heroism in knowing how to cut off a head properly, but it would be discreditable to do it clumsily. However, a man must not plead a lack of skill to avoid this obligation, because it is unworthy of a samurai not to know how to behead a man: if it were necessary to ask a stranger to perform this service, it would be almost the equivalent of one's admitting ignorance of the arts of war: a bitter mortification. However, scatter-brained youngsters or individuals likely to lose their composure were avoided.

The *ronins' seppuku* was exemplary. Forty-six heads fell exactly as they should.

One man was missing: the one who had been told, after the attack, to go and tell the Asano family that their master had been avenged. He had presented himself before the council as soon as he returned, but he was acquitted, because the case was closed. He lived on and died at the age of eighty-three: but as he had been one of the forty-seven *ronin* his tomb was placed beside those of his comrades.

To be exact, however, forty-eight venerated tombs lay near the temple of Sengaku-ji. A little while after the funeral rites of the heroes, Murakami Kiken killed himself, alone before the mortal remains of Oishi whom he had once, in the past, called a coward.

He also was to carry out the ritual actions of *seppuku*:

Very slowly he drew the sword from its sheath and the blue steel gleamed dully; then he wrapped the blade in a white cloth, leaving five inches of naked steel at the point . . .

Part II

The Arrival of the 'Pink Noses'

'LAND HO!'

The officer of the watch congratulated the look-out man with a wave of his hand and glued his eye to the telescope: he could just see a well-defined line between the dark blue of the sea and the bright blue of the sky.

It was very warm, this seventh day of July 1853, and sweat was making the American sailors' white linen uniforms stick to their bodies. They had been waiting eight months for this moment.

The top men immediately climbed into the rigging to try to discern the first outlines of this Land of the Rising Sun. Since 24 November, after getting under way off Norfolk, they had sailed by way of Madeira and the Cape before putting into port at Hong Kong and Shanghai. The Pacific Ocean was a continuation of the adventure of the Far West with the same whistling of the wind and the same songs sung by the crew.

'Tell the Commodore!'

Matthew Calbraith Perry was commanding the four ships of the West Indies squadron: the steam frigates *Susquehanna* and *Mississippi* and the corvettes *Plymouth* and *Saratoga*. He was not only a sailor, but a diplomat as well. He carried in his uniform pocket the letter from the State Department of the United States which set out his mission under three headings:

1. Conclude an arrangement for the protection of Americans wrecked off the coasts of Japan.
2. Obtain permission for United States ships to be supplied with water and fuel.
3. Prepare a commercial agreement to buy and sell mixed merchandise of many kinds.

President Fillmore had entrusted to Perry a handwritten letter for Japan's sovereign. However, the Westerners were not very sure at this time who ruled this still mysterious country which in the middle of the nineteenth century, still retained its medieval administrative structures. In Washington, as in St Petersburg, and as in all the European capitals, there was confusion between the *Tenno*, that is to say the Emperor, who was considered divine and reduced to playing only a religious role, and the *Shogun,* or *Sei-i-taishogun* (great chief of the army for the battle against the barbarians), an Imperial civil servant who exercised almost all the political and military powers of the Empire.

Who knew in the West that the name *Mikado* (august door) signified the whole nation and that this nation was led by the *bakufu,* government by the *Shogun* being entirely distinct from that of the Imperial court of the *Tenno*? The first had its seat in Edo (now Tokyo), whereas the second reigned in Kyoto, some 500 kilometres away.

In this still feudal land, four great clans divided the country between them and its history consisted entirely of the rivalries between the Satsuma, the Choshu, the Tosa and the Hizen.

The American fleet approached the Japanese archipelago at the entrance of Edo Bay and anchored off Uraga. Immediately a host of junks surrounded the four steamers. Men armed with swords and lances cruised about under the guns to ask the strangers what they wanted and their tubby boats danced on the lapping waves of the roadstead.

At first, Perry refrained from replying or even making an appearance. He made the 'natives' wait in order to demonstrate the importance of his rank and the pride of his nation. Then the negotiations began.

And difficult negotiations they were : none of the Japanese spoke English and none of the Americans spoke Japanese. They managed finally to communicate after a fashion in Chinese – but not too well. Finally, the semblance of an agreement was reached, equivocal and provisional. The Americans could land on the beach of Kurihama, to the south of Uraga, but must not stay for long.

Perry organised a brief ceremony to hand over the letter from the President of the United States. But to whom? He had some difficulty in finding an authorised representative because he wanted someone of high rank. Two *bugyo* represented the authority of the *Shogun* turn and turn about at Uraga. They went together to the beach to meet the American and accept the document.

The ceremony took place on 14 July and was followed by a procession through the town which gave some military solemnity to this 'friendly' visit.

Commodore Perry had arranged things well: while 800 men remained on board, grouped closely round the guns which were filled to the muzzle with grapeshot, he organised a grand parade through the village of Uraga.

There were no fewer than a thousand seamen, strong-muscled, with unsmiling eyes. They moved with a springing step, rolling like sailors do who have just spent weeks and weeks at sea. Every man carried a weapon: halberd, boarding axe, or just a cutlass. They marched like conquerors rather than as invited guests. They thought themselves at home and were a good head taller than the Japanese as they swung their shoulders and stamped their feet.

The crowd watched without a word but cursed silently. A murmur issued from prudent mouths to attentive ears: 'May the volcanoes heat the sea until it boils them all!' To the Japanese, all of them were barbarians, and they vied with each other to find the most unpleasant description for them: 'Fish eyes' or 'Elephant feet'. The name 'Americans' meant nothing to them. No, they were quite simply the 'Pink Noses'. They were worth less than nothing.

The sailors marked time, made a little dizzy by the heat of the sun and by the crowds. Sweat ran down under their straw hats. The boatswains shouted at them to close their ranks. The able-seamen shuffled their feet, wondering when this wearying procession was going to end and what they would be able to find to drink in this country. They did not like this solid wall of yellow faces, looking both astonished and hostile.

In the midst of the crowd, two samurai stared at these foreign devils and needed no words to know they both thought the same thing. These were warriors, poor and proud. They served their *daimyo* master for an annual salary of 100 measures of rice. But they would have served for nothing, for the simple joy of fighting and even, without fighting, for the sole honour of carrying the two traditional swords.

They had come from Fukuoka and dreamed of serving the *Shogun* for the Emperor. For them, as for all their fellows, the sovereign was a god and the nation a family.

Now at the end of a torrid day, they became furious. The spectacle seemed to them to be quite simply disgraceful.

'Look at those foreigners protected by the *Shogun*'s troops.'

'Look at our brothers prostrating themselves before those animals with men's faces.'

They were exaggerating a little. However, the attitude of passers-by was lacking in pride. They bowed, their eyes closed and their hands on their thighs. This servile attitude seemed inadmissible to the older of the samurai, who said to his companion:

'Toyama san, we cannot accept this. I am too old and I haven't enough time to create another soul. But you . . .'

'Me?' asked the younger man, in a tone in which pride argued with respect. 'What could I do?'

'You could give the Emperor a son. Go back to Fukuoka. "The girded sword is the samurai's soul" – those were the words of the great Tokugawa Ieyasu, which you should repeat to your son every day for twenty years.'

Twenty years to make a man. A life to save Japan. And eternity at the service of the *Shogun* and the Mikado.

The young samurai Toyama fully understood the lesson which his companion had taught him. He asked to touch with his forehead the sword hilt of the man who had spoken these splendid words to him, then he left the crowd to find his horse.

Dusk fell with its fire-like glow making golden avalanches on the mountain sides, and purple reflections on the ocean waves. All the Japanese coastline seemed on fire. But the blood flowing in samurai Toyama's veins burned even more hotly. He pressed the flanks of his mount and took the road to the West, as if he wanted to pursue the sun in a wild ride where only the night awaited him.

While he galloped, the American sailors returned to their ships, whose lights were reflected on the calm waters of the Uraga roadstead.

Agitated by this unexpected disembarkment, Governor Toda sent a messenger to Edo, where the *Shogun* Ieyoshi ruled. The *Shogun* was an old man, sick and frightened, who mistrusted all foreign devils. He maintained that he could not take any decision without consulting public opinion. At this unintentionally witty tribute to democracy from a great feudal lord, Perry weighed anchor and steered a course towards the Ryu-Kyu islands. He promised, before leaving: 'I will come back.'

Five weeks later, on 22 August 1853, it was not in English, but in Russian that there came the shout of a look-out man: '*Zemlia* (land)!' Vice-Admiral Poutiatine had arrived at Nagasaki. He, too, was commanding a squadron of four battleships. He had come to discuss not business, but politics. 'We must settle once and for all the question of the Kuril Islands and of Karafuto (Sakhalin) Island, which we hold jointly with the Japanese,' the Tsar's government had decided.

These foreign warships on the shores of the country of the samurai heralded a revolution. From now on, Japan had to choose: enslavement or power.

When he returned to Fukuoka, the samurai, Toyama, begat a son. It seemed suddenly that all nature was in revolt against the presence of the foreigners. The heavens punished the Japanese who had opened their ports and their doors. There were earthquakes. All the country trembled, as if with a fever, while the snow-covered volcanoes smoked and threw out torrents of fire. The capital, Edo, was partly destroyed. The wood-and-paper houses collapsed, flames devoured the mats and the draught-screens, and the survivors fled, screaming. A rain of ashes beat down like a storm. The sky became black.

But in Fukuoka a male child had been born, with the blood of the samurai in his veins. He clenched his fists, as if holding two swords, and he screamed as if he wanted to paralyse the enemy with his cries.

His father gave him the name of Toyama Mitsuru and swore to his ancestors that this angry baby would never come to terms with the plaguey breed of Christianity which was going to be reborn with the arrival of the foreigners. 'He will be faithful,' he promised. 'He will serve his Emperor and his country.'

One day, the entire yellow race would know the name of this child who was to become the first samurai of the modern world and the master of the most secret Order of Asia: the Black Dragon (Kokuryukai).

But for the time being, in this sad year of 1854, Asia was still enslaved and in chaos. The foreigners swept down on the Empire of the Rising Sun like wolves and vultures. With their iron-clad battleships and their many-coloured flags, they were everywhere. Rivals among themselves, they were united against all who were not white. Did they think they owned the entire world because they sent gunpowder with their words and gold with their missions?

The samurai, Toyama, recited for his friends the sad list of concessions to the foreigners:

'There are the British at Kagoshima, the French at Shimonoseki, the Russians at Nagasaki, the Americans at Yokohama, the Dutch at Deshima. I have come to regret the time when we had only the Spanish and the Portuguese here.'

'Should we make war on them, Toyama san?'

'First we must raise our sons, and the sons of our sons. The real fortress of eternal Japan is to be found deep in the heart of each of us.'

All the samurai were indignant: 'We want to fight here and now!'

Toyama replied: 'I and my men want to triumph later. And for ever.'

This wisdom resembled that of the Emperor Komei, who behaved more as a poet than a leader before the coming of the foreigners. He composed religious verses and organised *harai* (purifications) in the great Shinto sanctuary of Yamada. In the solitude of his palace, the *Tenno* took refuge in the last art of the samurai: calligraphy. With a painstaking brush, he wrote, at the approach of the foreign fleets, what he thought was the only maxim of his reign: 'To the limit of your soul's resources, do your best! Then kneel down and entreat the wind of Ise!'

Emperor Komei knew very well, just as the *Shogun* Iesada, who died without an heir in 1858, five years after his father Ieyoshi, also knew: that to make war you need soldiers. After three centuries of peace there were only heterogeneous military forces in Japan. The warlike exploits of the samurai belonged more to literary legend than to real life.

The nobility was restive and split into two irreconcilable parties. The *daimyo* of the national party were for a fight to the death against the white 'barbarians'. The *bakufu*'s supporters thought the struggle too unequal.

'Why should we refuse to establish relations with the foreigners and to borrow from their arts and their technical knowledge?' they said. 'When we have learned everything from them, we shall be as strong as they are.' Finally, they found a solution agreeable to both parties. To defend themselves against the foreigners, they needed only to imitate them.

The court of Kyoto named Tokugawa Nariaki, *daimyo* of

Mito, as Imperial officer in charge of coastal defences. He was to find his instructors ... in prison. Two officers, Takashima Shuhan and Yagawa Terazaemon, had been arrested and incarcerated for daring to learn from the white barbarians – in fact, from some Dutchmen – something of the use of artillery. They were now rehabilitated and sent to the provinces to teach the samurai European tactics.

The bells of the Buddhist monasteries were melted to make cannons. The ports were fortified. Battleships hoisted the national flag for the first time : a red sun on a white background which was called *hi-no-maru*. Japan was arming herself, but was negotiating at the same time. Peace treaties were signed and foreign consulates were opened on the sacred soil of Japan.

The nationalists fought back, drawing up a moving appeal : 'Are we today to suffer the foreigner to dictate his laws to us and shall we cede to him even an inch of our land?' The manifesto had the merit of candour : 'With the help of the power and authority delegated by the Spirit of Heaven we must always keep in mind our aim of establishing the foundations of our country's supremacy over all other nations.'

The samurai preached rebellion. They coined a slogan which was to spread throughout the country : '*Sonno-joi!*' (Honour the sovereign and drive out the barbarians). They organised armed bands. Not being able to fight against the foreigners, they trained themselves by attacking the peasants and the bourgeoisie. Yoshida Shoin opened a school where he taught physical culture and the martial art. Between lessons, his pupils were supposed to discuss different political doctrines. This continued until the day when Shoin was executed for conspiracy, for his loyalty to the *Tenno* was certainly greater than his loyalty to the *bakufu*.

So the first great theorist of Japanese nationalism was decapitated on 25 October 1859.

Count Ii Naosuke, a septuagenarian who had recently been made a *tairo* (counsellor) to the *Shogun*, emerged as the strong man of Japan. Unlike most of the young officers, he seemed to have decided to open up the country to foreigners. Thus he was signing his death-warrant.

On 24 March 1860 he went in his litter to the *Shogun*'s palace. He had just reached the Sakurada gate. Despite his rugs, he was shivering a little. It was very cold, and day was only just breaking. Large flakes of snow were falling as on the day of the death of the forty-seven *ronin*.

There was a shot! Shouts! This time it was eighteen *ronin* resolved to kill the minister. His escort tried to intervene, but what could be done against these madmen who were brandishing swords and shouting abuse? The soldiers of the guard appeared to be hampered by their heavy capes and some were killed before they had time even to draw their swords from their sheaths.

Ii Naosuke was mortally wounded in the back by the single shot which had given the signal for the killing. One of the conspirators dragged him from his litter and chopped off his head. 'The *tairo* has betrayed the Emperor and the nation in opening up the country to the "animals with men's heads". He is dead. *Sonno-joi!*'

Most of the *ronin* (from the Satsuma clan), under the command of Ozeki Washichiro and Sano Takenosuke, also died during the following days, but their action seemed like an heroic deed, even though the conspiracy had no effect.

Throughout the whole country people searched age-old, collective memory to quote passages in which they accused their victim. 'His crimes are such that neither man nor god could forgive them: we have chastised the guilty man by making ourselves ministers of the divine anger and we await without remorse or regret the death which is destined for us.'

The sacrifice of the samurai devotees of justice whipped up the fanaticism of all their brothers. Armed bands roamed the provinces looking for blood to spill and honour to avenge. On 5 July 1861 fourteen *ronin* attacked the British temporary legation. Two British subjects were wounded, but all the conspirators lost their lives after the failure of this 'commando of hatred'.

Ando Nobumasa, successor to the assassinated *tairo*, wanted to avoid at any price a confrontation between the courts of Kyoto and Edo. The *Tenno* could not clash with the *Shogun* while the foreigners were threatening them. He unfolded his plan to members of the *bakufu*.

'Why should the younger sister of the Emperor not marry the young *Shogun*?'

This provoked a great outburst of violence. A band of *ronin* wanted to repeat the action of the murderers of Ii Naosuke. Ando, badly wounded by four sword-thrusts, defended himself. His escort fought back vigorously. Swords whistled through the air and struck. Blood ran. Men fell everywhere. The six *ronin* were killed fighting or despatched at the end of the affray. But this new example of courage and fanaticism inspired their party with fresh ardour.

As always in Japan, an isolated action was to take on a symbolic value. A samurai from Matsudaira, *daimyo* of Tamba was among the guard at the British legation in Edo. He killed one of the British soldiers with whom he was on sentry duty, and committed suicide. Anarchy spread swiftly. Men died. Houses were burned down. Samurai and *ronin* avenged their ancestors and called the increasing number of assassinations '*tenchu*' (divine punishment).

While the rivalry between the *Shogun* and the Emperor died away in interminable vicissitudes, accompanied by laborious negotiations and invitations to commit suicide, the Japanese learned European military techniques. German instructors arrived at Nagato and Edo; the Japanese manoeuvred in the French style. Japanese even went to Holland to study the building of battleships and the handling of squadrons. The first Japanese battleship, the *Kanrin-Maru*, crossed the Pacific.

The samurai obtained the right of assembly (*Gakushu-in*) during the presidency of Hirano Jiro. But what they really wanted was to fight, not simply to discuss. They decapitated the statues of the *Shoguns* in the temple of Tojin-in. And then they were not slow to begin cutting off live heads.

However, in this climate of violence cherry-trees blossomed and children grew up. Once again it was spring. The Feast of Carp took place on 5 May. Paper fishes floated in the fresh summer breeze above every house. The little children's paper fishes were golden. Those of adults – or of anyone over seven years of age – were painted blue and red.

In this year – 1862 – the young son of the samurai Toyama was seven years old. He watched his fish fluttering above the thatched roof of his home and his father contemplated his son with that expression of mingled anxiety and delight which is typical of everyone who is responsible for a child.

'Grow up quickly, my boy!' he said to himself. 'The Emperor and the nation have need of you.'

Throughout the Japanese archipelago where the clash of swords and the shouts of the *ronin* were resounding, feeling was mounting dangerously against the foreigners and their supporters.

On 14 September 1862, two groups of riders passed each other on the road near Kawasaki: *daimyo* Shimazu Saburo (Hisamitsu) was returning to his estate when he met some English tourists riding in the heart of feudal Japan as calmly as if they were in Devonshire.

They looked each other up and down scornfully. An insult was hurled, and immediately there was a free-for-all. A young merchant from Hong Kong, Richardson, was killed by the samurai. Two of his companions, Marshall and Clarke, were wounded, but they and a woman, Lady Borrodaile, managed to flee and to gallop back to Yokohama.

The British *chargé d'affaires* raged: 'We demand that the guilty men be executed!'

Shimazu Saburo replied to the Emperor: 'I was insulted. My men avenged me.'

Was it to be war? The guns of the Japanese coastal

batteries opened fire on the foreign ships. The bells of the Buddhist monasteries sent more bullets into the sea than prayers to the heavens. The Europeans gave as good as they got. But the gods made their choice between the two sides: a cyclone dispersed a British flotilla.

Was the Emperor, the *Tenno*, going to conduct a war against the barbarians? The samurai who assembled under the command of Fujimoto Tesseki, Matsumoto Kensaburo and Azumi Goro believed he was. They formed a legion and named it *ten chu gumi* (the cohort of celestial anger).

The court took no action. The legion took up arms. There were several months of bitter fighting before these rebellious samurai, who had taken to roaming the countryside and pillaging, were exterminated.

Under the threat of foreign intervention Japan experienced the horrors of civil war. A *rapprochement* took place between the *Shogun* and the Emperor, but their authority scarcely extended beyond the walls of their palaces, which armed bands attacked like the surging waves of a hurricane of violence and murder.

While the British, French and Dutch troops succeeded in landing by force, skirmishes between government troops and insurgents turned into battles. The samurai Takeda advanced towards Kyoto. Loyal troops barred his way and crushed him. The rebel leaders were taken prisoner, and were assembled near Lake Biwa. With exquisite politeness, their conquerors gave them the choice between being beheaded or committing suicide.

Defeated in one place, the samurai were victorious in another. From now on they would have in addition to their two ritual swords, firearms and even cannons. They manoeuvred in the Prussian fashion and formed regular battalions called *ki-hei-tai*. One of their leaders, Takasugi Shinsaku, held out against every attack from the regular troops.

The German instructors had obtained such good results that the *bakufu* also changed to this method: in 1867 a French military mission arrived in Edo – the Gallic cock had crossed the world to challenge the Prussian eagle through two Japanese armies.

But death did not cut down soldiers alone. The *Shogun* Iemochi died six months later, on 3 February 1867, and the *Tenno* Komei on 30 January 1868.

The new Emperor, Mutsuhito, was only fifteen years old. But he was to become the leader of modern Japan, for the Land of the Rising Sun was ripe now for revolution. There was no room any longer for a double-headed leadership. The last *Shogun*, Keiki, abdicated, and his followers fought a hopeless battle. The way ahead became clear and the young Emperor was able to take the oath before the court and the feudal nobility.

This delicate young man with the long face on which he was soon to grow a short, dark beard, seemed to have decided to make old Japan into a young Empire. Silken standards fluttered in the wind and naked swords glinted in the sunshine of the spring of 1868, when he promised:

'Old-fashioned customs and the prejudices of former times are abolished for ever. Equal justice for all shall be my golden rule. Intelligence and merit alone, without discrimination on grounds of class or origin, will be honoured during my reign.'

And the Emperor entered Edo. He changed its name and the town was called from that time onwards Tokyo, the 'capital of the East'.

So began the first year of the Meiji era (the era of enlightened government).

Last Civil War

In 1868 young Toyama Mitsuru was fourteen. He was still living in the province of Fukuoka in Kyushu, the most southerly island of Japan. His father had sent him to a curious school run by Takaba Ran.

'But she's a woman!' expostulated the little boy.

'Yes, indeed, she's a woman. And she is also the only woman who is still a samurai in Japan today.'

Takaba Ran would have been worthy to carry the two swords, and her friends, as well as her enemies, said of her: 'She behaves like a samurai. With men and with women.'

Her school was like both a fortress and a monastery, where swordmanship was as highly regarded as poetry. The head-mistress liked to remind her pupils of the great rules of life, or rather of the only rule, which summed up all the others: honour.

'One day the Emperor addressed a wonderful eulogy to one of his henchmen. But he had put it in the past tense. The recipient understood the meaning of this. He committed *seppuku* so that the facts corresponded to the tense of the verbs.'

For Takaba Ran, there was no heroism without shrewdness. She was the absolute mistress of her school. But it should not be thought that her horizons were bounded by her pupils. She liked to describe her favourite pleasures thus: 'I need good conversation with ten fine men, sixty cups of *sake*, or a good fencing bout.'

These manly passions did not prevent her from recognising 200 different scents or from being able to make tea according to all the traditional rules. But her private life mattered little to her when the existence of the Empire of the Rising Sun was in question.

She lived only for conspiracies and rebellions. She was on the side of all the rebels against all the cowards. And on the side of the outlaws of the mountains against the intriguers of the palaces. She brought up her pupils as she saw fit, singling out the best and directing them along the only road she knew: that of meditation and fighting.

Takaba Ran knew that a child needs its heroes as a samurai his swords. She taught her pupils what the modern hero of the Meiji era should be: 'The more he wants to fight the foreign invaders, the more he needs to understand their techniques.'

These were highly revolutionary words in a world still caught up in the conformism of the old days. But the mistress of the Fukuoka school was less interested in the battle than in victory. She dreamed of a brilliant future for young Toyama Mitsuru, as for the rest of her most gifted pupils.

'The men whose example you should follow are Saigo and Katsu,' she said.

Katsu Kaishu! An invalid at the age of twelve, he became by sheer will-power the best swordsman of Honshu. He taught himself Dutch with the aid of a dictionary which he used from dawn to dusk. He was to become the first Japanese to command a steamship and the first Admiral to cross the Pacific from Yokohama to San Francisco.

Saigo Takamori! As big as a bear from the land of the Ainu, he thought of himself as a theoretician as much as a warrior. He was to give his compatriots the stubborn idea of conquering Korea and was to die revolting against a government which had not understood his dream.

Saigo the soldier and Katsu the sailor – Japan's two horizons. The earth and the water, the mountains and the ocean, the onslaught on the continent of Asia, the conquest of the Pacific Ocean. What would mark the extent of their powers?

'Toyama Mitsuru, samurai's son, you were born for the Empire.'

That was the lesson. When she had finished with lessons, the mistress busied herself with conspiracies. There were always mysterious travellers staying briefly in her home. Sometimes one could make out the outline of a sword showing beneath a kimono.

Young Toyama listened to the strangers, his ear pressed to the thin partition. He had even made a hole so that he could glimpse these men whom he saw as messengers, bringing news of a sublime adventure. One evening, Takaba Ran surprised him. She knew very well that he was spying on her not out of curiosity but out of zealotry. She did not scold him, but explained simply to him the meaning of all that he had seen: 'Japan has remained pure and manly.'

And she then felt obliged to teach him the rule which governed only the best of her pupils: 'Every Japanese is endowed with life by the breath of the gods. For that reason, he can, if his conscience so dictates, place himself above the law ... But in that case he must be ready to sacrifice his life as a token of his sincerity.'

Toyama Mitsuru listened to her with the greatest attention. He showed the sort of fervour which seemed sometimes to take him into another world and caused malicious tongues in the village to allege that he was mentally deranged. But this other world in which he lived was the sixteenth century. The man whose invisible hand he continually held, and who led him through life, was the great hero, Hideyoshi.

'Helped by his example I will revive the time of the samurai.'

'Nothing is revived, Mitsuru, but everything continues.'

The new Emperor made the political decisions from that time onwards. His choice was made. He would negotiate with the 'white barbarians'. Those who insisted on attacking them would have in future to suffer the fate of rebels.

On 8 March 1868, at Sakai, eleven sailors of the French ship *Dupleix* were massacred. The Imperial police were quick to detect the guilty men. There were about forty of them, all of whom claimed this savage deed to be an act of patriotism. Their action was disgraceful, but their motives were not without nobility. Some of them were allowed as a favour the right to commit *hara-kiri*.

Calmly the fanatics lined up and knelt down. The ceremony began. The bellies were opened. The heads rolled on the ground. Those most moved by this sight were the French sailors who watched the condemned men help each other to die. When the eleventh victim had died the captain of the *Dupleix* intervened. 'That's enough. My eleven sailors have been avenged.'

The Japanese seemed not to understand this strange accountancy. It was necessary to insist that they picked up their daggers and their swords and disappeared into the crowd.

Eleven pools of blood dried slowly in the pale March sunlight.

On 5 January 1869 the Emperor received the ministers of the foreign powers in Tokyo. From that date, diplomats had no need to fear attempts on their lives as they went to the Imperial palace. Japanese legations were established in most Western countries: in Paris in 1870, in London in 1872, in Washington, in Vienna and in Rome in 1873, in Berlin and in St Petersburg in 1874. On 25 April 1875 Japan recognised Russia's sovereignty over the islands of Sakhalin, but received in exchange the Kuril Islands.

In the space of a few years old Japan was to change visibly. The Emperor set up a Council of State and a Council of Representatives composed of two chambers: an upper chamber in which sat the *kuge* (nobles), the *daimyo* (provincial chiefs), and the samurai of the victorious clans; and a lower chamber consisting of the samurai elected by all the clans.

The feudal system was to disappear. The clan chiefs themselves decided on what one might call the '*hara-kiri* of privilege'.

On 5 March 1869 the great feudal barons had addressed a petition to their Emperor: 'We renounce our possessions, our rights and our titles.'

The sovereign abolished the titles of *kuge* and *daimyo*. Then he decided that henceforth there would be only two classes of nobles: the first would be the *kazoku* and the second the *shizoku*. This second class was the samurai.

To them the birth of modern Japan seemed a catastrophe. Their land was taken from them and they were given pensions in exchange. There were rumblings of anger. How can you give a pecuniary value to that which has no price: nobility and courage? Gold cannot pay for blood that has been spilt for a man's country. Moreover, the new regime did everything possible to avoid paying these pensions. The small ones were bought back by the authorities for half-a-dozen years' income. Besides, the samurai were paid half in silver and half in government bonds. In August 1876 the government compulsorily converted all pensions into government bonds. But that was nothing beside the fact that the carrying of swords was prohibited from that time onwards.

The samurai were soon to be reconstituted. Modern Japan had to decide how it was going to develop in the future, and war was quickly to become the foremost of the national industries. The old troops of the clans – picturesque and ineffective – were soon to disappear to give place to a national army. The reform of the Imperial guard marked the first stage of this military renascence. But the second stage inaugurated a genuine revolution: military service became compulsory in 1872.

The Imperial edict defined this new army in a quite extraordinary way: 'Adult males capable of doing military service will be recruited to reduce to obedience those who will not submit.'

The samurai had lost their inherent privilege: in future all Japanese would bear arms. Rather than revolt, some of them decided to become officers and to inspire the whole army with the spirit of *Bushido* to the point of creating a real State within a State.

The creator of the Japanese army, Marshal Yamagata,

achieved an astonishing synthesis of the warlike spirit of old Japan and the modern techniques of the European armies. He did not hesitate to call in foreign instructors. In May 1872 a French military mission arrived. Defeat in 1870 in the Franco-Prussian war had made these officers wish to raise an invincible army at the other side of the world. For about ten years they would work to build a formidable military machine. While the French were training the army, the British were organising the navy. The spirit of the former samurai was to reawaken from the spirit of St Cyr and of Portsmouth.

The first barracks were only simple huts, built in the parks of the castles, often at the foot of a former feudal fort. The young peasants exchanged their kimonos and their *getas* (wooden clogs) for the royal-blue uniform with red braid and heavy boots hobnailed in the European fashion. The men were brought on to the strength on 1 December each year and the conscripts were accompanied by the mayors of their villages, by their friends and by all their relatives.

The atmosphere was that of a fairground. The future soldiers went into a roped off enclosure and undressed, lined up in front of their packs like old soldiers. For the first time in their lives they put on that strange garment known as a shirt.

Then they rejoined their families and with them visited the barrack buildings, guided by the seniors from an earlier mobilisation who came from the same village. This was operation 'Open Doors' – all the more surprising as most of them had never in fact seen a door.

At three o'clock in the afternoon a bugle sounded its melancholy notes, and the families had to leave their sons or their brothers. The young soldiers went to take the oath of allegiance before the portraits of the Emperor and the Empress.

The next day the colonel would muster the regiment. The old soldiers to the right, the new ones to the left. Sitting very upright on his white horse, his plume quivering in the cold December wind, he read the Imperial edict on the army which prescribes the five cardinal virtues of the Japanese soldier: fidelity, courtesy, courage, honesty and frugality.

But for all those officers in the service of the new Imperial army, how many unemployed samurai were wandering about the countryside?

The military profession was no longer a profession in the Japan of the seventies. Soldiers were unemployed and Toyama Mitsuru, the son of a samurai, had to earn his living because he was unable to lose his life in battle.

He began his career as an assistant to a potato merchant, then became town-crier of Imperial edicts, before starting to sell clogs.

'Like the great Hideyoshi,' he said in the village, 'I intend to have thirty-seven jobs and to be sacked thirty-seven times.'

He was joking, but laughter is a mask. Times were hard for those of his stamp and of his race. In the whole of Japan, four hundred thousand samurai were out of work, doomed to suffer every sort of adversity, and ready for any adventure.

Toyama Mitsuru already knew about weapons; now he discovered books. One day he told the villagers who were continually astonished by this singular young man: 'I have found my hero.'

'It isn't still Hideyoshi?'

'Not only Hideyoshi. I have discovered a great samurai.'

'What's his name?'

'Napoleon.'

No one in the Japanese archipelago seemed to know this name.

'What island was he born in?'

'In Corsica.'

The samurai could not accept the new order without reacting against it. They found a leader in the person of Saigo Takamori, who, approaching his fiftieth birthday, dreamed of playing an important role in a federated Japan.

Saigo saw only one solution which would restore to the samurai their place in the Empire, and that was to give them an opportunity to fight. In Formosa or in Korea there was no shortage of battlefields. But it was still too soon for a foreign war. The Emperor had sent a mission to the West led by Iwakura and on his return the latter recommended caution.

And so it had to be civil war.

The conversion of pensions, the partition of land, the prohibition of swords, all seemed to be real acts of provocation. From the spring of 1876, revolt was stirring among the samurai of the different clans. A blaze of violence swept over the land in the summer and autumn. The Hizen samurai took the castle of Kumamoto by surprise and massacred the garrison. The Akizuki samurai in Chikuzen attacked Fukuoka. Four hundred samurai marched on Hagi in Nagato. But the government reacted swiftly. Heads fell and the troops broke ranks in disorder.

However, there was still one samurai who did not lose courage and who decided to stake everything for the sake of fidelity to the old order of things and his idea of heroic Japan: Saigo Takamori!

For three years, Saigo had been living in retirement at Kagoshima, where he had established a school of agriculture for young samurai. It was a strange school at which his pupils learned more of swordsmanship than of the use of the plough. All day long the young pupils were trained in the martial arts. At first they fought in single combat, then they faced each other in two lines which advanced and withdrew in turn amid a great din of swords striking on shields. Between the exercises they meditated, to the sound of birdsong from the surrounding countryside.

Saigo knew that you cannot fight guns with bows and arrows. And so he, too, stockpiled modern arms and munitions in his school at Kagoshima. Next he took his pupils to the rifle range and the noise of volley firing resounded lengthily in the cold dawn air. His samurai manoeuvred like Prussians.

The Imperial government could not tolerate such a challenge. In January 1877 it sent a ship to Kagoshima. The captain's instructions were simple and precise: 'to seize all the arms held by Saigo Takamori and his pupils'. But the cadets were quicker than the sailors. As soon as the ship had docked they moved their arsenal and prepared for the attack. The captain could only weigh anchor and admit defeat.

This whole affair seemed so serious that the Minister for the Navy, Kawamura, himself visited Kagoshima in his turn.

'I want to see Saigo.'

It was too late. Saigo had left for the North on 17 February. His pupils had been transformed into a veritable army and he was mustering all the discontented samurai. They now numbered fourteen thousand, but one of the bravest was missing – Toyama Mitsuru. He was already in prison when the rebellion broke out.

Saigo Takamori had explained his plan to his lieutenants:

'We have already roused Kyushu to revolt. Now we are going into Choshu and we shall march on Kyoto.'

Long shouts of enthusiasm answered his declaration. Samurai everywhere took fresh heart and joined Saigo's army.

The first battle was a semi-failure. It was impossible to take Kumamoto by storm. The insurgents left some of their number outside the town and resumed their march northwards.

The Imperial forces had also started to march. At their head was a prince of the blood who had chosen as his chief of staff Yamagata, the creator of the new army. He succeeded in raising the blockade of Kumamoto and then dashed off in pursuit of the samurai.

Everything went badly for Saigo. Kagoshima, his rear base, which he had virtually made into the 'holy city' of the samurai rebellion, had been taken. His friend Kido had fallen in battle. The other provinces refused to join in the uprising.

On 14 August 1876 ten thousand rebels were surrounded at Nabeoka on the northern coast of Hyuga. The battle ended in catastrophe. The Imperial troops and the rebels slit each other's throats with merciless fanaticism.

Was Saigo Takamori going to die in battle with his troops? That would have been to admit defeat. He preferred flight.

'Let us make for the mountain!'

Only two hundred samurai succeeded in pulling out and following him. They did not intend to go to ground, but to live to fight another day.

In small groups the guerrillas reached the mountains. Soon they thought themselves strong enough to go down towards the South, to hustle the opposing forces out of their positions and win back part of Kagoshima. So there was Saigo back home again, giving the lie by his presence to the announcement of his ignominious flight. But bad news overtook him at hurricane speed. 'The Imperial fleet!'

He had to flee yet again. The samurai were surrounded at the foot of Mount Shiroyama. This time there was no longer any question of escape. This was the last battle.

Saigo Takamori was wounded in the thigh. He had only one hope left: to set an example by his death. He disembowelled himself according to the ancient ritual and one of his faithful soldiers cut off his head.

The Imperial troops attacked. All the rebels were either killed or taken prisoner. The victorious Imperial troops exhumed Saigo's head and body and then they gave him a solemn burial in the cemetery of Jokoji. The last samurai rebellion had been crushed at a cost of thirty-five thousand dead.

When the 1877 rebellion ended in a deluge of samurai blood, Toyama Mitsuru was twenty-three years of age. After his dedication to swordsmanship and books he decided to dedicate himself to the gods. But he did not abjure any of his characteristics: he remained both an intellectual and a man of action, a warrior and a scholar. And so he set out on the roads of Japan. There were thirty-three holy high places, living symbols of the nation and its faith; he was to visit twenty-seven of them. He did not withdraw from the world. On the contrary. He continually repeated to himself: 'One must understand before taking action. One must toughen oneself up and meditate.' But Toyama was not a monk. Certainly he could fast for weeks, but he could also devour enormous meals. He could spend whole days in the middle of winter motionless in the snow, but he could also spend whole nights in the company of women, in the most exciting parts of a brothel. One thing alone interested him: learning to dominate himself in order to dominate the enemy.

People began to know Toyama Mitsuru far beyond the confines of his village. What did they say about him? 'He's a funny sort of chap.' That could be taken to mean the best or the worst.

But he cared little about gossip and went his own way, dressed in white, wearing a large conical hat, the back of his kimono stamped with the marks of all the temples he had visited in the course of his pilgrimage.

He loved grandiose landscapes, precipitous mountains and headlong streams. But he also loved the infinite calm of a thatched-roof temple, the *torii* which marked the holy entrance of a sanctuary and the basin of a fountain of pure water. Toyama Mitsuru dreamed of a Japan faithful to its gods and its heroes, its volcanoes and its streams. He hated the regime which from being Imperial was becoming constitutional. He wanted a country pure as the snow and vast as the heavens, a country like a mountain dwarfing the rest of the world, a country which would call to mind an ocean submerging the other continents.

He knew that henceforward there would be an impassable frontier between the orators and the warriors. He had become a monk only to become a better soldier. That was Toyama's policy. At about this time the Tokyo police compiled a dossier on Toyama Mitsuru, born at Fukuoka, five foot eight inches tall. They gave him a label which was to stick to him all his long life: 'dangerous agitator.'

Ever since dedicating his life to patriotism, Toyama Mitsuru had put the Buddhist religion in its place: subservient to the Japanese race. But he claimed to be as strong as the priests. One day he challenged a Zen monk. He knelt before the monk for five days without eating, drinking, sleeping, opening his mouth or moving a finger. At the end of 120 hours the disheartened priest gave up. The samurai had won.

Black Dragon against White Bear

IN THE new Japan of the Meiji era the frontier between religion and politics was as blurred as the line between the sky and the sea on a misty morning. The government had understood perfectly that there can be no political renascence without religious reform. Buddhism was driven out and Shintoism became the State religion. The new faith seemed simple, even if it was divided into innumerable sects: Emperor worship, patriotism and ancestor worship.

On 11 February 1868 the feast of Jimmu-tenno was established, to celebrate the founding of the Empire. Were the sovereigns not descended in a direct line from the goddess Amaterasu? The *kami* continued to watch over Japan, and these divinities, which had emerged from the night of time and the forces of nature, were henceforward to supplant all the foreign spirits.

Toyama Mitsuru was to be as much an ascetic as a conspirator. He liked to climb mountains alone, sleeping in the snow, bathing in the icy water, living off herbs or leaves and remaining silent for several weeks. Only the sacred words: 'O Nobori' (honourable ascension) passed his lips, which were chapped by the cold. If he honoured the gods he also revered the heroes – first and foremost the greatest of them all: Saigo Takamori, the last samurai.

Saigo had been avenged soon after his death. One of his admirers assassinated Okubo Toshimichi, Minister of the Interior. Accomplices were sought everywhere. Naturally, young Toyama found himself in prison again. He was happy to meet there the woman who had made a man of him: Takaba Ran.

But with what could they be reproached? Their conspiracy

was above all a conspiracy of like-minded souls. Their aims were not against the law and could be described quite simply: 'The samurai have suffered a military defeat, but they must be reborn politically.'

Toyama Mitsuru was going to work harder for this rebirth than anyone else and he would not cease until his death – during the Second World War, while the battle in the Pacific was raging – to exalt the Yamato-damashii, that is 'the pure Japanese spirit'.

He wanted to be only a prophet and refused to become a journalist or a politician. Smiling, he denied that he had any ambitions. 'A member of the Diet? I don't speak well enough. Polemicist? I have to think for so long before writing anything that the ink dries at the end of my writing-brush between words.' He did not found a party, but a sect: the *Genyosha*, a patriotic society. In 1881 he gathered together the samurai involved in Saigo Takamori's rebellion and he planned assassinations, one of which was to cost the Queen of Korea her life.

From then onwards the future of Japan lay in conquest. Urged on by the military clique, the Emperor declared war on China on 1 August 1894. Forty-one million Japanese rushed to attack 350 million Chinese. It was the contest of David and Goliath, re-enacted in a Far Eastern setting.

The Empire of the Rising Sun had its own party of violent opposition: an army of 250,000 men, all austere fanatics. The officers and even the junior officers, all of whom were of peasant origin had all been to the Shikangakko military academy in Tokyo, where the instructors combined the traditions of the French military academy of St Cyr and of the Prussian Junkers with those of the samurai.

The regiments of infantry (hohei), of cavalry (kihei), of artillery (hôhei), the corps of engineers (kôhei) and even the army service corps (shichôhei) were all educated in the hard school of *Bushido*. They would go to war with their samurai swords hanging from their black leather sword belts, whose copper buckles were decorated with five-pointed stars.

Europe paid scant attention to the conflict between Japan, the young wolf, newly arrived on history's scene, and China, the old dragon which had been sleeping for centuries. The cause of this conflict was Korea, of which scarcely anyone had heard at this time. However, since the beginning of our own period, China and Japan have not ceased to quarrel – with varying success and failure – over the possession of this peninsula which, squat as a Chinese junk, thrusts out into the sea between their two lands. For centuries the land of the Calm Morning seemed to present a permanent invitation to whomever wished to seize her.

On 11 September 1894 Japan – reorganised, powerful, and aggressive – attacked in the Gulf of Po-hai (Petchili) and in less than two hours disabled half the Chinese fleet which had been drawn up in an archaic formation. Then Japanese troops landed in Korea, took Port Arthur, and soon penetrated Manchuria and marched on Peking. These movements were accomplished at lightning speed without a single error or hesitation. Westerners put forward an explanation which was to be used for half a century! 'The Japanese have become the Prussians of Asia.'

The treaty of Shimonoseki soon finished this lightning war: China recognised Korea's independence and ceded to her conqueror the peninsula of Liao-tung with Port Arthur, as well as the islands of Formosa and the Pescadores. The entire world marvelled at the audacity of the 'little Japanese', who had dared to attack such a powerful opponent. In the eyes of indulgent Westerners the 'Japs' had immediately become history's favourite child: the child prodigy whom one admires without taking too seriously.

The Japanese soon took advantage of the affection they had inspired: not only did they quickly inundate European markets with the products of their budding industrialisation, but they also sent thousands of their people to Germany, France and England: small, intelligent, politely smiling and inscrutable men poured into technical colleges, dockyards, and armaments factories, there to study with hungry enthusiasm the most modern techniques.

But although the Japanese knew very well what was going on in the rest of the world, the rest of the world was completely unaware of what was happening in Japan. Nobody suspected that in Tokyo and Yokohama ambitious men, far from being content with the laurels they had won, were laying plans for several decades ahead, were checking and criticising every one of their achievements, mercilessly applying literally the Japanese proverb: 'In victory, tighten the strings of your helmet.'

However, the Mikado's subjects, who thought they had gained the ascendancy in the Far East, had soon to change their tune. The great European powers – Russia, France and Germany – under the pretext of safeguarding Chinese independence, joined forces to oppose them and to demand the restitution of Port Arthur and of Liao-tung. The Japanese yielded with a deep feeling of frustration and bitterness.

The Empire of the Rising Sun was now faced by the formidable Muscovite Empire – a more redoubtable adversary than ancient, crumbling China. Since the conquest of Siberia by Ivan the Terrible, the Russians had wished to make the Pacific their natural frontier. In 1860 they had begun to build, in a well-protected bay, the port of Vladivostok – an ambitious name which means 'Mastery of the East'. The Trans-Siberian railway which ended there had, however, to make an enormous detour of some 500 kilometres, the length of Manchuria, to reach its terminus. In 1896 Russian diplomats persuaded China, 'grateful for their intervention at the time of the negotiations with Japan', to allow them to run the Trans-Siberian railway through Manchuria.

On the heels of the railway came the Cossacks – to protect it. Two years later, the Chinese chancellor Li Hung-chang, ceded to Russia on a twenty-five-year lease the peninsula of Liao-tung and Port Arthur, both evacuated by the Japanese.

The Russians thought this quarter-century was going to last a thousand years, and they feverishly prepared to make the territory a gigantic entrenched camp. Port Arthur appeared as the symbol of the Tsar's power in the East.

For the Japanese it was both an affront and a danger. The Liao-tung peninsula became a huge thorn in their *amour-propre*. 'We don't want the blue and white cross of St Andrew flying over the Yellow Sea,' they raged.

But the Russians laughed at the puny little soldiers who were getting so excited at the gates of their new Empire. 'It will perhaps be centuries before the Japanese army acquires the sort of morale on which the organisation of European armies is based', Wanowski, the Russian military attaché in Toyko, wrote derisively. At Port Arthur the officers celebrated with Crimean champagne and then smashed their glasses against the granite walls of the citadel.

One man was less inclined than any other Japanese to recognise the new frontier. Toyama Mitsuru became the moving spirit behind a huge secret society which spread from Turkestan to Manchuria. Its roots were to be found in the Indian resistance to the British occupation and its first members had been recently gathered together by Nana Sahib at the time of the Indian Mutiny. Toyama Mitsuru founded the Japanese branch of this invisible army, sworn to drive the Whites out of the Yellow world. He called it *Kokuryukai*. The literal translation of this is one to make you either tremble with fear or smile: 'The Black Dragon Society'. The Black Dragon is the Japanese name of the river which marks the western frontier between the White and Yellow peoples: the Amur (Hei-lung-chiang in Chinese). So Toyama intended to show that for him and the men who were faithful to him this was Japan's only western frontier in the heart of Asia.

His enterprise caused surprise and anxiety. 'The River Amur,' stormed the Minister for Foreign Affairs, the Marquis Okuma Shigenobu, 'the River Amur . . . and why not Lake Baikal?' But the Black Dragon laughed at the ironic comments of those who did not believe in the resurrection of the samurai.

Toyama Mitsuru ordered his disciples to meet every 3 February in the temple where forty-seven stone lanterns commemorated the sacrifice of the forty-seven *ronin*.

His secret society was to expand to the dimensions of a country, an empire, a continent. Sometimes some of its chiefs and some of its members were known, but for the most part the Black Dragon remained a formidable iceberg, the extent of whose invisible part no one could guess. Its rites and its crimes were to weave the bloody background of a Japan that had at last been awakened from its ancestral slumbers.

Its vengeance was often as difficult to prove as it was slow to reveal itself. However, Marquis Okuma's barouche was eventually blown up by a booby trap. The man responsible, a student by the name of Kurushima Tsuneki, cut his throat. He, at least, would say nothing. The police, as certain as they were powerless, arrested Toyama Mitsuru again.

Letters arrived by the hundred at the Ministry of the Interior. Some contained an amputated finger and a short explanatory note: 'We will endure anything in order to have Toyama set free.' Uncertain and indecisive, the government gave in: Toyama was set free.

What did this modern samurai do? He went unconcernedly to his 'victim's' home. Marquis Okuma received him extremely politely, hopping on his one leg. 'I must apologise for not being able to kneel to take tea.'

When his guest, whom he considered as being also his would-be assassin, was taking his leave, the marquis said, 'Did it occur to you, Toyama, to bring me back my leg?'

The man from the Black Dragon bowed with feigned respect and answered coldly, 'A good official must be ready to give a leg for the Emperor.'

Toyama Mitsuru had himself drafted the 'blood oath' which every member of the Society had to take by reciting the sacred formula:

'My blood, dedicated from my birth to that which flows in

the veins of all the descendants of the goddess, Amaterasu, this blood which I shed in this cup to mingle with that of my brothers, this blood is a token of my sincerity.'

Then the petitioner continued, when it was no longer possible to distinguish his blood from that of his fellow-conspirators and comrades-in-arms: 'I swear on this blood of the sons of Japan, I swear to shed all my heart's blood for the glory and the life of the august sovereign, for the grandeur of the Empire, and to help its defenders to chastise its enemies. I swear also to shed this blood to free all my Asian brothers and to bring them the supreme enlightenment: Banzai!'

Later on Uchida Ryohei would preside over the Black Dragon, but Toyama Mitsuru would always remain its true chief, its inspiration and an example to all.

The man whom police reports had recently described as a 'dangerous agitator' now wielded power. The government was aware of this and at the Council of Ministers when his name was mentioned there was always someone to say: 'He can lay hands on ten million yens and arm a hundred thousand men.'

One day in 1902 Toyama Mitsuru went to see Aoki, the new Minister for Foreign Affairs, in his office. He considered Aoki's policy towards Russia to be insufficiently bold. He spoke to him in a parable. 'Last night I had a strange dream. Demons were climbing up over a precipice and I was fighting the king of the devils. When I had vanquished him he was no more than a puff of smoke. Odd, don't you think?'

'Very odd!'

Aoki became anti-Russian, but was replaced by another minister whose name was Ito.

In July 1903 a young sub-lieutenant, a disciple of the Black Dragon, came to see Toyama Mitsuru. He seemed to be burdened with a grave secret which the wise man was not slow to uncover.

'You intend to kill a man.'

'That's right, master.'

'You must follow the dictates of your conscience. But spare one man alone: Ito.'

'But it is he whom I must kill! I and my brother-officers have sworn to do so.'

'Perhaps you have. But Toyama has not yet spoken to him.'

The master of the Black Dragon decided to approach the minister. He went to Tokyo with three friends, and succeeded in arranging a meeting immediately, so great were the respect and the fear which he inspired.

'Who is the greatest person in the Empire?' Toyama asked Ito.

The minister did not hesitate: 'Our divine sovereign.'

'And who is the greatest of all his subjects?'

Ito did not reply, so Toyama answered for him. 'It must be you, Ito.'

And he shook his hand with immense vigour. The minister understood the lesson immediately and joined the pro-war party.

Among the military leaders, General Nogi and Admiral Togo could barely conceal their impatience to cross swords with the Russians. But Viscount Hayashi – who, nevertheless, shared their enthusiasm – said: 'The Japanese must remain quiet in order to allay suspicions.'

In his palace on the Golden Mountain, overlooking Port Arthur, Admiral Eugene Alexeieff, illegitimate son of the Tsar Alexander II, lived like an Oriental prince. A 'ukase' of 12 August 1903 had even conferred on him the title of Viceroy. On 6 February 1904 he frowned and adjusted his monocle when Vice-Admiral Stark was unexpectedly announced.

'Your Excellency,' mumbled the old sailor, 'you did not reply to my note: the Japanese consul of Chin Fu appeared this morning with a steamship: he is evacuating all Japanese nationals.'

'The yellow monkeys are going? Good riddance!'

'We have identified the official who was with him: it was one of Togo's officers. He was calmly making sketches of the vessels in the outer roadstead.'

'Those people like to educate themselves.'

'I confirm my request to put the fleet under orders, to send out the destroyers which are anchored in the inner roadstead as forward cover and to put out torpedo nets.'

'And I repeat my orders, Stark: wait!'

The staff officers repressed a smile: the whole fleet knew the fateful three words written in green ink which had appeared at the end of all reports for years: 'No, not yet!'

Alexieff slowly stroked his beard and said unkindly: 'Go back to your drinking, Stark. That's all you're good for.'

Back on his ship, the *Petropavlosk*, the commander of the China Sea fleet opened several bottles of the vodka with which he ordinarily sought to mitigate his boredom, and then, for the first time for a long while, he gave orders – those he could give on his own initiative: the recall on board ship of all officers and ratings on leave, the severance of all communications with land until dawn, and guard duty for the battleship *Retvisan* and the cruiser *Pallada*.

It was an inky black night. Stark was keeping a look-out on the bridge. From time to time the strains of a waltz were borne to him on the cold wind; the Viceroy was holding a reception.

For a moment he imagined the bemedalled uniforms of the ninety officers and the despot's aides-de-camp – all different whirling beneath the chandeliers of the great rooms.

The captain of the *Petropavlosk* reported to him, and his commander asked: 'Where are our reconnaissance vessels?'

'The *Bestraschny* and the *Rastoropny*? They are in open water south of Encounter Rock.'

'That's too far away. Get the gunboat *Gilliak* under way.'

'She has engine trouble.'

They were suffering from poor maintenance by the barrack-ships.

'Order out the *Bobr*....'

It was almost midnight. The Viceroy's violins struck up the 'Emperor Waltz'.

The officers' heels clicked together in the wardroom of the *Mikasa*. Togo, who sometimes remembered the British sense of humour, had said: 'Good bear-hunting!' He added for the benefit of the rest of the men: 'We're going to drive the bear out of his hole.'

The admiral of the Imperial Japanese fleet had put to sea two days previously, at the very moment when the Japanese ambassador at St Petersburg was telling the Russian Minister for Foreign Affairs that diplomatic relations had been broken off. A few hours before, the Tsar's two look-out ships in the China Sea, the *Bestraschny* and the *Rastoropny*, had sighted the Japanese ships. Steaming full ahead in the dark night, the Russian ships attempted to make for Port Arthur to give the alarm, but respected the Viceroy's strict orders not to engage in combat. For the same reason they did not use their radio equipment, which was, in any case in a very bad state of repair.

At midnight precisely the Japanese destroyer flotilla, which had advanced to within 400 metres of the fleet lying at anchor, launched its torpedoes in three successive waves. Sixteen black steel sharks sped towards the seven battleships and the nine cruisers in a matter of seconds. Three of them hit their targets: the *Pallada*, a first-class cruiser built in Russia in 1902, was hit amidships in her boilers, and immediately took a list of ten degrees. Struck in the stern, near her rudder, the *Cesarevitch*, a battleship built in France in 1901, was equipped with internal armour-plating, which prevented an explosion. As for the *Retvisan*, a cruiser built in America in 1900, she had a gash thirty feet long in her fore-part and was shipping water in torrents.

The whole action lasted less than half an hour. When the first unaimed shots were fired in the darkness by the Russian ships their assailants were already far away.

At Port Arthur, General Stoessel, commander of the Kuantung Army was talking angrily on the telephone. The navy's general staff was replying evasively: 'Practice firing, Excellency.'

Exhausted, Stark simply showed his note of that morning to his officers. The paper, crumpled by his rage and his tears, bore the instruction in green ink: 'Not yet, wait!' The three best ships of the fleet were already out of action.

The vice-admiral had some more vodka sent up to him.

In the early hours of the following day Alexeieff saw through his powerful binoculars a sight which made him tremble with rage: on the horizon, just below Port Arthur, the Viceroy could observe the Imperial Japanese fleet of Admiral Togo.

The admiral's flag was fluttering on the mainmast of the most perfect battleship of the time: the *Mikasa*, 15,300 tons, nineteen knots, with artillery and armour-plating superior to that of the most modern British battleships. Then came four ships of the line of equal worth and three of a slightly inferior class. A hedge of destroyers was belching black smoke in front of the large vessels. Alexeieff roared out to Stark the order for which he had so long been hoping: 'Attack!'

The vice-admiral was already striding through the gardens of the Golden Mountain, his sword in his hand, when an aide-de-camp caught up with him:

'His Excellency desires me to state his orders more explicitly: attack, but remain within range of the guns of the fort.'

Stark unhurriedly resumed the descent to the roadstead: he was not to be allowed to engage in a real battle. The long-distance artillery duel would reveal only one thing: the Japanese guns of equal calibre had a range twenty per cent greater than that of his own.

After these two incidents the aides-de-camp were terrified to go into Alexeieff's office. Scowling, he was dictating his first war report. He had scarcely finished when he had to add a postscript: a new encounter had just taken place at Chemulpo!

In the roadstead of this neutral port situated on the west coast of Korea, not far from Seoul, were several ships of different nationalities and two Russian vessels: the cruiser *Varyag* and the *Koreietz*, an old gunboat, poorly armed and without armour-plating. It was at this port, linked by a railway line with Seoul, the capital, that the Japanese Admiral Uryu had decided quietly to land his army while the Russians were still unaware that they were at war.

On 9 March, the landings completed, the Japanese admiral demanded that Captain Rudneff, captain of the *Varyag*, should come out of the port and fight, or be dislodged. A naval battle in a neutral port where there were ships of all nationalities – British, French, Italian, American and Korean – was unthinkable. Rudneff had his crew sing the national anthem and took the *Varyag* through the channel, followed by the *Koreietz*, both ships dressed overall.

In a half-circle in front of the port nine vessels of Uryu's divison were waiting. When the distance between the adversaries was no more than 7000 metres, the leading battleship, the *Asama*, opened fire.

Rudneff fought like a demon, striving with his cruiser to protect the gunboat, only one of whose guns had sufficient range to hit the enemy. The two ships did not disengage until they had exhausted their ammunition: they were floating wrecks when they returned to Chemulpo. The two captains, after a rapid consultation, decided to scuttle their vessels.

Thirteen hours after the beginning of hostilities the Russians had already lost five ships. The following day the minelayer *Ienissei* hit one of her own mines at Dalny and sank in fifteen minutes: the *Boyarin*, sent to her assistance, suffered exactly the same fate.

Alexeieff was almost apoplectic. 'Two days of war, seven ships! And they haven't even declared war!'

Stark was drinking like a fish in his wardroom. 'Yellow monkeys, eh? First-class marksmen – trained by the English! They have range-finders, guns and shells which outclass our own, radio communications! Makaroff was right when he said that you could not accomplish in time of war what you had not learned in time of peace.'

On 17 February 1904 sailors of the Russian fleet at Port Arthur cheered when they learned that they were at last to have a chief: Admiral Makaroff, commanding officer of the naval station of Kronstadt, had been appointed Commander-in-Chief of the naval forces of East Asia.

'We must wake up!' exclaimed 'The Beard' when he arrived in the beleaguered stronghold on 8 March. The sailors were able to confirm that two characteristics attributed to him by his legendary reputation were correct: he was a great talker and he had an immense blond beard which was ruffled by the breeze.

The white admiral was there and the duel could begin.

'Makaroff,' said Togo simply.

He put down his table-napkin and closed his eyes for a moment. His officers held their forks suspended in mid-air so as not to disturb his meditation. The wardroom of the *Asama* was completely Westernised, and nothing, apart from the narrow eyes of its occupants, recalled old Japan, except, perhaps, for civilities of this sort.

'I translated his *Discussion of Questions in Naval Tactics*,' said Togo at last, 'when I was director of the Naval College. That remarkable work has always been more or less my model. I recommend you all to study it....'

He read the telegram again as it lay on the spotless white tablecloth: 'There is much talk in the military and naval circles of Port Arthur of the imminent arrival of Admiral Makaroff and this news is causing hope and excitement.' Japanese intelligence knew everything, always, immediately, while the Russians, who had alienated the sympathy of the Chinese spies, were reduced simply to guessing at their adversaries' intentions. 'We are the same age,' said the admiral, thinking aloud. He allowed a further period of silence to elapse before reeling off the biographical details of his new enemy for the benefit of his staff officers.

'Makaroff is of humble origins: he is the son of a leading seaman and that's why the sailors love him. He is an astute man: when he was a sub-lieutenant he invented a collision mat to be placed over a hole in a ship's side below the waterline, and all navies adopted this idea. He is bold and fearless: during the Russo-Turkish war of 1878 he distinguished himself by forcing an entry at night to the port of Batum, destroying there a number of enemy ships by the use of torpedoes: these were the first self-propelling torpedoes. Makaroff is full of ideas: he is the inventor of a caisson which enables ships to be repaired without their having to go into dock. He also invented an armour-piercing shell.

'He has published works on oceanography, the development of personality, artillery and ice-breakers . . .'

'And his men call him "The Beard",' laughed a young officer.

He stopped short: beneath his gaze, Admiral Togo's beard, pointed, majestic, grey with a silvery sheen, seemed to bristle like the fur of a wild animal.

The Englishman behaved discreetly, dined in his cabin and appeared only rarely on the bridge. 'I'm off now,' he would say to his opposite numbers among the engineers. Moreover, it was understood that he would go ashore as soon as he had finished supervising the seagoing trials of his firm's equipment.

This evening, however, he stayed on a little later than usual, smoking his pipe near a casemate, watching the red sun sink in the yellow sea. 'It's like your flag, Yoshihita . . .'

The young sub-lieutenant with whom he had stayed in Hiroshima was his only friend on board. The young man bowed very low to salute him.

'I bet £100 on Togo in Hong Kong,' went on the Englishman. 'I hope Makaroff doesn't ruin me.'

'The English are the only people to bet on a Japanese victory.'

The British officer puffed at his pipe. 'It's not just because of friendship ordinary between islanders, Yoshihita. Your Togo has a bit of the Nelson touch. He'll win.'

'I'll tell you about his first feat of arms,' said the young sub-lieutenant suddenly. 'Do you know that in 1863, at the age of fifteen, Togo Heihachiro was one of the defenders of Kagoshima?'

And he went on: 'He was a young samurai with a shaved head. He had studied only Japanese ideographs, the writings of Confucius and sabre-fencing. When Kupper's Western fleet arrived on a punitive expedition, Togo in his lacquered armour was on the ramparts with the others. They loaded their old mortars with stone bullets – they were muzzle-loaded. They could hear the sailors laughing behind the armour-plating.'

'It was simply a massacre, wasn't it?'

'Yes, but more than that, it was a terrible humiliation. When Kupper returned their fire everything crumbled: the ramparts, the old guns, the samurai, and, more than anything, a certain sense of the greatness of Japan. Young Togo didn't forget. He remained an officer in the feudal navy of Satsuma, but when he was twenty-three he left with some other young men for your training college in Plymouth.'

'You mean the Royal Naval College at Greenwich on the Thames, the way into the Royal Navy "by the hawse-hole",' the Englishman corrected him.

'Togo rose from the ranks, it's true, but four years later when he got back he had as much technical know-how as any Western officer. The war with China was also a college education.'

'I know the rest of the story, my friend,' said the Englishman. He emptied the ash from his pipe which had gone out and added, thoughtfully, 'But because of the ramparts of Kagoshima I think I'll send a message to Hong Kong.'

'Is it urgent?'

'Very. Now I'm going to bet £200 on Togo.'

The next day the British press agencies began to link the names of Makaroff and Togo in their cables. Headlines in all the great European newspapers read: 'Duel Between White and Yellow Admirals.'

On land the winter campaign continued. Japanese soldiers carrying thirty-kilo packs advanced sixty kilometres a day along the miserable, muddy roads of Korea, despite cold, fatigue and privation. The Russian troops confined themselves to defensive action and proved to be unskilful at manoeuvring; they beat precipitate retreats every time the Japanese carried out a fairly large turning movement. Their incapability stemmed primarily from the Russian general staff's attachment to railway lines. It was not a question of strategy, but simply one of comfort. Thus, at the beginning of the war, Admiral Alexeieff had at his disposal a special train which consisted of passenger coaches, restaurant cars and sleeping cars: the general staff was made up of such a crowd of bemedalled officers! When this special train moved, a pilot train, the 'shield', preceded it for fear of a mine or an ambush. The Viceroy hated travelling at night and rose late, so his train spent most of its time in a siding, or at a station. He did not like his slumbers to be disturbed by train whistles either, so all traffic in the district was halted.

On board their ships his Japanese adversaries lived like monks. Togo mounted guard in front of Port Arthur. Patiently and secretly. Daily intelligence telegrams reported Makaroff's actions and movements. 'Repairs to the damaged ships are speeding up ... Land fortifications are improving.'

Moreover, inspired by the bearded giant, the Tsar's fleet was regaining its strength. On 10 March a lively battle took place between two Russian destroyers and the first flotilla of Japanese destroyers under Admiral Deva. As soon as the signal station on the Golden Mountain signalled that the battle had begun, Makaroff got his swiftest cruisers under way: the *Askold* and the *Novik*. They arrived too late: the *Steregustchy* was sinking with her captain on board; but the leading Japanese destroyer, the *Akebono*, had been hit by twenty-seven projectiles and the Japanese fleet was being led by a floating wreck.

Togo nodded. 'Makaroff is fighting back,' he said.

Some hours later the yellow admiral was himself setting the range-finder of the *Yashima*'s 305 guns. Like a surgeon operating in front of his young house surgeons, he gave a running commentary on his manoeuvres for the benefit of the silent young officers.

'We know,' said Togo, 'that at low tide the entrance to Port Arthur has a depth of only nine metres of water, which makes it impossible for large enemy battleships to come out. They are at present all together in the deep waters of the roadstead and we are going to pound them with shells.'

'We can't see anything, Admiral,' said a sub-lieutenant in astonishment.

The old samurai's dark eyes glowed gently.

'My boy, our battleships have been moored broadside on in the Bay of the Pigeon: is that by chance? I shall bombard the roadstead across the small hills of the Liao-Tichan ... Fire!'

The first wave of enormous shells passed with a dull, throbbing sound over the forward Russian lines. A long time afterwards the first explosions began to set alight the fortress, the dock sheds, the roads and the ships.

Alexeieff roared. 'Makaroff, are you going to allow us to be shelled? Make a sortie.'

'It's too soon,' replied the admiral on the telephone, tugging his beard to prevent himself from laughing. 'I'm waiting for the tide; but I have a solution ...'

The bombardment, which although inaccurate, was very wearing for the nerves of the besieged men, lasted for several hours. Makaroff was preparing his reply: an exercise in the art of the rapid sortie.

The next day, four hours before dawn, he had succeeded in equipping twenty ships in two and a half hours, where Stark would have taken twelve! A counter-battery and a telephone set had been installed on the hilltop of Liao-Tichan. On 22 March, when the battleships *Fuji* and *Yashima* were about to reopen their indirect bombardment, accurate firing barred their way to the Bay of the Pigeon. Suddenly two black trails of smoke appeared between the cliffs. Togo identified his adversaries with his binoculars: 'The *Pobieda* and the *Retvisan*.'

The first cones of fire narrowly missed his ships.

'They're aiming better.'

Two bull's-eyes on the *Fuji* where fires were started.

'Much better.'

A third silhouette hove in sight. Togo had difficulty in identifying it through the smoke of his guns which were firing continually on two fronts: the coastal guns were getting dangerous.

'It's the *Petropavlosk* . . . with Makaroff's flag!'

Four battleships were following the white admiral. For the first time Togo made for the open sea, and, followed by the crippled *Fuji*, the *Yashima* fled, accompanied by spouts of water.

The Japanese leader's face clouded. Suddenly he saw again the ramparts of Kagoshima.

'They have run the blockade,' he cabled to Tokyo. 'I am laying mines.'

On 12 April 1904 the sea was growing rather rough and a snowstorm had set up an impenetrable screen. Togo had had his flag hoisted on board the *Mikasa*. He signalled to the *Koryu Maru*, which was setting out to lay mines at the entrance to the enemy's harbour: 'Good luck!'

The searchlights of the coastal batteries were sweeping the sea in vain: there was only thick white cloud. However, through this cotton-wool curtain an attentive ear could make out the muffled 'tack-tack' of the little black steamers which were steadily laying their deadly mines.

Hardly a mile away, Makaroff himself was mounting guard on the bridge of the cruiser which was guarding the entrance to the port. He had turned up the collar of his watch-coat and was amusing himself by studying the shapes of the snowflakes which were alighting to melt on the glass before him. Every now and then he would give a mechanical order.

'Tomorrow morning we shall have to order out the minesweepers.'

Togo, also, was awake. This sleepless night would decide his fate. He knew that. With the tip of his finger he drew ideographs on the frosted glass of the bridge. He guessed what Makaroff was going to do.

'Send six destroyers to Liao-Tichan.'

At the same time – just before midnight – Makaroff moved his pawn in this strange game of chess:

'A flotilla of destroyers to the Elliot Islands! I want to reconnoitre the whereabouts of the Japanese forces.'

Four hours later, just before dawn, two of the Russian destroyers, the *Strachny* and the *Smalny*, had lost their bearings in the cotton-wool.

Lieutenant Maleiff, in command of the *Strachny*, was anxious: the shapes he had been following for a few minutes were . . .

'It's the Japs! General fire!'

Too late, for at that very moment a deluge crashed down on his little ship, which suddenly reared up. One of the Japanese shells had exploded a torpedo in its tube.

The *Strachny* was scarcely afloat.

The long, black wolves came to within seventy metres, aiming and firing continuously almost at point-blank range. Maleiff, bleeding profusely, pushed away the inert body of a gunner and manned the gun himself. Men jumped into the icy water, their clothing in flames. The *Strachny* sank. Maleiff was the last to jump: the whole affair had lasted no more than five minutes.

The ripples had not disappeared from the green water in which a few survivors were floundering when the five funnels of the cruiser *Bayan*, alerted by the *Smalny*, appeared. Day was dawning. Suddenly, from the south, Admiral Deva's third detachment arrived. A gun battle began immediately. The *Bayan* was firing with all her guns, abandoning her rescue operation. Both Makaroff and Togo gave the same order at the same moment:

'Action!'

'Banzai!'

Makaroff came to the rescue: engines full steam ahead, guns ready, the *Petropavlosk* appeared on the scene, followed by the *Poltava*, the *Askold*, *the Diana* and the *Novik*.

Togo had seven battleships in line and two new vessels which had just come from Europe: the *Nichin* and the *Kasuga*. English instructors were standing beside each officer.

Togo had the advantage this time in guns, in numbers and in power: he was sailing full steam ahead, straight for the Russian fleet, which was following Admiral Deva's flotillas.

Checkmate!

8.40 a.m.: Makaroff saw, understood and ordered a half-turn. 'The bear is looking for his lair,' commented Togo. The *Mikasa*, his flagship, came within four nautical miles of the Russian *Diana*, the rear ship. He did not fire.

9.15 a.m.: Makaroff would soon be protected by the batteries of Port Arthur. Still Togo did not fire.

The *Peverest*, the *Pobieda* and the *Sebastopol* joined the other battleships. Makaroff ordered single line ahead.

'Fire, for God's sake!' he muttered in his beard at his strange adversary.

All the Japanese were staring at the flagship's yardarm, but the *Mikasa* remained uncommunicative. Togo gave an order changing course, but not the order to open fire.

'It's odd,' said the Englishman, sucking his pipe.

9.45 a.m.: the atmosphere was suddenly shattered by four terrific explosions: the *Petropavlosk* had blown up: she had touched a mine. Her boilers exploded at the same time as the explosives and eighteen mines which were on board. Her hull flew through the air in pieces in a great whirlwind of yellow smoke. The foremast hung for a moment in mid-air. The propellers turned wildly, and then everything fell back into the sea amid a great whirlpool. When the undertow from the sinking of the great ship caused the *Mikasa* to shudder slightly, Togo aroused himself from his happy torpor.

'Makaroff was a fine sailor,' he said simply. And he saluted.

On the fortifications of Port Arthur, the Russian garrison, who had seen the whole battle, broke down and wept. On the Golden Mountain, the Grand Duke Boris fainted at the sight. The Tsar's vanquished flotilla returned to its anchorage. Suddenly there was another conflagration: the *Pobieda* had also touched a mine. Again Togo saluted on his bridge.

The *Petropavlosk* had gone down with 600 men and 31 officers on board, among them Admiral Makaroff, commander of the Imperial Russian fleet.

The next day Togo replied to the telegram of congratulations which he had received from the Mikado: 'The victory of Port Arthur was due primarily to the strength and to the virtues of Your Majesty.'

The Three Minutes of Tsushima

WITH MAKAROFF dead, the Russian fleet had lost its spirit. Even the land forces were prostrated. While ever greater numbers of Japanese disembarked in Manchuria with each new day, and while the armies of Nogi, Oku and Kuroki took the offensive, General Kuropatkin (1848-1925), a cautious bureaucrat, beat to windward and abandoned one by one his strongest positions.

The Russian soldiers deserved at that time their nickname of 'grey martyrs', for, wearing tattered boots made of waste pieces of leather, in temperatures of lower than twenty degrees of frost, they had fallen back into the Manchurian mountains, starving and pursued by the Japanese troops, who had been galvanised by their first victories.

On 5 May the Tsar decided that the incompetent Alexeieff should leave Port Arthur, which was likely to be under siege in a matter of hours. He was to take command of the Mukden sector – less dangerous, it was thought. The ground defence of Port Arthur was entrusted to General Stoessel: Nogi was approaching. The fleet was under the command of Admiral Whitheft. Togo was mounting guard.

But in St Petersburg at this time there was great joy. Tsar Nicholas had decided to send a fleet to the Pacific.

All European Russia was working feverishly to put this tremendous plan into effect. Factories and shipyards hummed busily day and night: there were steam hammers and hammer drills; mechanical cranes held enormous armour-plates suspended in mid-air; the long black stocks of guns rose threateningly along the horizon. Gradually, the new national armada was being born, built by Russian workmen, in Russian workshops, to Russian specifications: the fleet which would punish Togo and avenge 13 April.

In the spring of 1904 the whole world was talking about this unheard-of project to arm a fleet and to send it to fight more than 20,000 miles away. Wagers were laid on how they would refuel on such a long journey, how they would effect repairs without any base, and at the end how they would fare when they met the Japanese ships.

'The Russian fleet will consist of forty ships and ten thousand men, a veritable floating town with its shops, its hospitals and its arsenals....'

'Impressive,' concluded Togo, putting down his pince-nez which he never used in front of his officers.

'The English newspapers are very well informed,' said Marquess Ito, Minister of War, who was inspecting the fleet. 'I think this adversary will show up here before the end of the year. By that time, you will have finished with the Port Arthur fleet.'

'I have lost some ships,' Togo explained. 'Not in battle, but through a series of accidents which occurred as if the gods wanted to test our endurance: the *Yoshino* was in a collision; the *Miyako* struck a mine, as did the *Hazure*, and the *Kaymon*, and yesterday, on 26 July, the *Chiyoda*. My sailors are saying that Makaroff is getting his own back.'

'Togo Heihachiro,' replied Ito sternly, 'Japan is a poor country. If a second fleet appears in the Straits of Korea you will have to defeat it, for that will be the decisive time for our land. In order to do this, the first fleet must already have been put out of action. If it has not been put out of action, our expeditionary force will be in the same position as Bonaparte in Egypt. So you must take Port Arthur and beat Kuropatkin. You will make arrangements with Nogi.'

And the Marquess abruptly took his fan from the sleeve of his Western suit – a sign of intense concentration.

Ito always wore a tail-coat, but sometimes the former

samurai reappeared in the statesman: for instance, in February 1904, just after the first attack on Port Arthur, in the royal palace at Seoul.

It took Marquess Ito three nights to make the King of Korea ratify the protectorate treaty which would hand over his country to Japan. The Marquess had convened the Great Council: the King, all the ministers and the dignitaries were present. It was night-time, as Korean etiquette demands: silence and darkness are best for reflection.

The first night, Ito spoke eloquently, but the Council was hostile towards him. His speeches were in vain: failure for the Japanese.

The second night there was the same resistance. The Marquess changed his tactics and his tone: he began to threaten. He intimidated the Koreans, but he did not persuade them. They did not want to die fighting the Russians.

Came the third and final night. Violence was expected, for the Japanese troops who were occupying the country 'amicably' were on alert. An old Korean general had just committed suicide so as not to be present at his country's capitulation. Some members of the Council made as if to withdraw: this was the signal. The Japanese troops who were surrounding the palace broke into the hall where the Council was sitting. Marquess Ito placed before the King the agreement to the protectorate, which had been prepared in advance.

'The royal seal is not on it,' stammered the sovereign.

'You refuse to give your assent? But I shall have it even so,' growled Ito.

Japanese soldiers went on his orders to fetch the seal. Ito took it and handed it to the Chancellor. The latter did not move. Then the Marquess took his hand and forced him to place the seal at the bottom of the agreement, which had been unrolled before him.

'Thank you, Your Majesty,' said Ito politely to the King.

The day after this historic night the Japanese government announced the good news to an astonished world in the following terms: 'As the Korean government was unable to safeguard the interests and well-being of the country, we have amicably relieved them of this responsibility.'

Marquess Ito stared for a moment at his open fan: his hand was Seoul, the right edge was Vladivostok in the Sea of Japan, the left, Port Arthur in the Yellow Sea, and on the half-circle the mother-of-pearl fasteners had names: Mukden in the west, Kharbin in the centre, Ninguta in the north.

'Togo,' he said, 'our armies are making progress everywhere. Take care of your fleet because everything depends on you.'

The Admiral of the Imperial Fleet prostrated himself in the traditional manner on his *tatami*.

'It is impossible to wait,' Togo had told Nogi. 'We must take the High Mountain.'

The General and the Admiral were alike in some ways. Both of them were old samurai and both had chosen the square beard and Western uniform. But the precise bow of the army commander when he agreed to the sacrifice of his troops to avoid the fleet having to go into a mine-field was no mere formality: it signified the acceptance of the sacrifice.

The attack was a massacre. Before the hills and the forts, densely covered with barbed wire, whole battalions lay slashed to pieces. When a redoubt was captured the Russians blew it up and took shelter in order to counter-attack behind a heap of stones, of earth and of corpses. The conquest of the position known as the White Wolf cost the Japanese nearly 10,000 men. However, step by step, the Japanese advanced and the world followed with admiration mixed with horror the stages of a struggle in which the heights of heroism were reached.

Days and weeks passed and the main position had not yet been conquered. Often the Russian cruisers and destroyers came out and fired their long-range guns at the Japanese regiments. If things continued in this way, Nogi's army risked annihilation before the end of the year. Meanwhile the Baltic fleet was steaming at top speed for Formosa.

Aged fifty-six, in the full dress-uniform of an admiral, the colossus, Rodjesvensky, was a dazzling sight. Gilt epaulettes decorated with monograms and black eagles shone on his massive shoulders. Rows of medals covered his large chest. Above this bedizened body rose a severe face framed by a short pepper-and-salt beard. Black eyes expressed untameable willpower. Admiral Count Rodjesvensky had never commanded a fleet in battle. This was not his fault, but that of history. It was, doubtless, as a result of this injustice that this high-ranking officer was so quick to anger and terrorised his staff.

On 14 August 1904, at Kronstadt, he hoisted his flag on the battleship *Souvarov*. The second Pacific fleet was going to begin training. At Port Arthur the first fleet had practically ceased to exist four days previously.

The Japanese bombardment of the roadstead by indirect fire became so continuous and so telling that Admiral Whitheft had decided to wager everything on running Togo's blockade to try to get back to Vladivostok.

Whitheft had the reputation of being a scholar, a hard worker and, above all, a scrupulously honest man. But he was no sailor and certainly not a fighting admiral. His nomination to this position had terrified him.

'I'm no commanding officer for a fleet,' he said to himself as he took over his duties.

Several times the squadron had manoeuvred as if to make a sortie, but on each occasion its commander's indecisiveness had led to no more than a half-turn.

Togo was waiting. 'They have refitted,' he said. 'We will watch.'

On 10 August before dawn, the black steel colossi left the inner basin of Port Arthur and slipped slowly out to sea.

The bay was bathed by uncaring Nature in splendour. The green waves rippled gently, the seagulls played around the masts uttering their cries, the golden clouds of morning were disappearing behind the hills where the first barrages of gunfire were beginning to reverberate. But already the radio waves were filling the air with the news from the Japanese ships on guard. Togo took stock.

'Minesweepers protected by two gunboats, two divisions of destroyers, the battle-cruiser *Novik*, the fastest of them all; the *Cesarevitch*: the flagship; six battleships, three large cruisers... They are coming out.'

Grey-green like the waves, beneath their thin trails of smoke, Togo's battleships began to move at seventeen knots towards the extreme tip of the Shan-tung peninsula, as if to cut across the path of the Russian squadron. Then, suddenly, Togo ordered them to steam south on a course more or less parallel with the Russian ships. Togo feared lest if he engaged in a conventional stern chase a moment might come when one or two of his leading ships would be exposed to the combined fire of all the Russian battleships, while the rest of his ships, inevitably strung out in a chase, were not yet within range.

Ship for ship, most of the Japanese vessels proved better than the Russian ships. They were better maintained, partly because of the difficulties of getting repairs done at Port Arthur.

'This time, I've bet £500,' confided the Englishman to sub-lieutenant Yoshihita. He lit his pipe with sensual pleasure.

In the first stage of action, the Russian gunnery was better aimed and the Japanese line of battle began to suffer. Through accidents and direct hits five out of the sixteen twelve-inch guns were out of action by the end of the engagement; several guns on the flagship, the *Mikasa*, had been silenced. Togo rose above this setback.

'Excellent,' he admitted, with very British sang-froid.

In the chase, Togo was gaining on the enemy, but not on the setting sun. Darkness might mean the escape of the enemy. At 5.45 pm Togo decided it was now or never and turned in to open fire.

'Rapid fire!'

It was the first time that the Russian fleet had experienced the rate of Japanese firing. Makaroff had trained his crews to fire accurately, but they were not prepared for the effect of the shells which burst in a shower of incandescent fragments, starting fires everywhere. Soon, the *Sebastopol*, the *Peverest*, the *Retvisan* and the *Cesarevitch* were riddled with huge holes, and fires, fanned by the wind, blackened them with smoke. Their riddled funnels trebled their consumption of coal.

After they had been hit, the big battleships were shipping water through the holes which had been opened in their sides. They slowed down, but Togo's situation remained critical. He had guns which were unusable and, worst of all – this was the disadvantage of rapid firing – there was practically no ammunition left for the big guns.

'Did Nogi lose his two sons for nothing?' he wondered.

It was six-thirty that evening that the *kami* heard them. A 305 projectile, one of the last, hit the *Cesarevitch* between the lower and the upper bridge, killing the admiral and the majority of the staff officers. The next shell burst in the conning-tower, killing all the men who were in it and causing great damage to the steering mechanism.

Then the battleship, no longer in control of her steering, and with a twelve degree list, turned in a complete circle and bore down upon the *Peverest*.

The greatest confusion reigned at this moment among the ships of the Russian fleet. The new commander, Admiral Prince Oukhtomsky, could not rally his ships and withdrew, with the *Peverest*, the *Pobieda* and the *Retvisan* to Port Arthur, where he remained. The other ships, pursued all night by a swarm of Japanese destroyers, escaped. The *Cesarevitch* ran aground in the Bay of Chiao-Chou where the Germans disarmed her: of Admiral Whitheft only one leg was found.

Togo saluted his memory in the wardroom by emphasising the excellence of his last manoeuvre.

From Saigon, where the French allowed the Russians only twelve hours to refuel, to the Kuril Islands, where the fine cruiser, *Askold*, was destroyed, the wrecks of the Russian fleet stood out as landmarks in the seas of Asia.

On 14 October 1904, flags were flying from all the windows in the Baltic port of Libau. Women fainted as the Cossacks galloped past, and gun salutes shook the port. An enormous crowd overflowing on the rooftops contemplated the grandiose spectacle of the roadstead where the black colossi were riding at anchor, their flags fluttering in the wind, heavy clouds of black smoke trailing behind them.

Martial music rang metallically through the cold, grey air. On the bridge of the *Souvarov*, the sovereign and the lay representative of the Holy Synod were preparing to give their blessing. Around the ship, relatives of the sailors were crowding in bobbing craft, their faces lifted towards the high steel armour-plating.

The long-awaited hour was approaching. The priest raised his long, thin arms to the skies. Nearby, Nicholas II, pale and handsome as a wax statue, murmured a few inaudible words.

A final salvo thundered out, the anchor chains grated, and the propellers turned in the oily water: slowly, the vessels made for the open sea. On the bridge stood the officers gazing towards the land, the swarming crowd, and the Tsar's pale face.

Between 14 and 22 September Nogi overran the High Mountain and begun to fire on part of the port. The fortress was about to fall: the water was polluted and the only meat available was horse-flesh. Between the end of July and the end of September, 20,000 of its defenders had been put out of action.

A new phase of the siege began with the arrival of the 280 mm howitzers which Nogi had been awaiting. The first projectile, loaded with ten kilogrammes of powder, destroyed the concrete arch of a casemate as if it had been made of straw.

On 27 November the Japanese began to attack, determined

to make an end of the siege. There were terrible scenes of carnage: column after column of little men in dark blue uniforms with white gaiters fell and were so swiftly replaced that the Russians, in rags, began to think that dead men were rising again. The distance between the adversaries was not more than fifteen paces. They wielded bayonets and grenades in savage hand-to-hand fighting, and when finally they were empty-handed they ended up biting or strangling each other.

On 6 December the Japanese took the High Mountain by force of arms. Nogi had lost 11,000 men to conquer this position, but from there he could pulverise the Russian fleet, cowering at his feet.

The great howitzers were lifted into position and the massacre began: the *Poltava*, the *Retvisan*, the *Peverest*, the *Pallada*, the *Pobieda*, the *Bayan* ...

'The fleet at Port Arthur no longer exists,' Nogi cabled to Togo.

'Rodjesvensky has reached Madagascar,' interrupted Togo when this message was read to him. 'His German coal-ships are late.'

Day after day, the Japanese admiral followed the progress of his new enemy. He had already noted on the chart where he would appear and a cross marked the place where he would end up in the middle of the Straits of Tsushima. Togo had two months to complete the overhaul of his ships, to get new engines and to replace the stocks of his guns.

The war was going to continue at sea, though on the land it was coming to an end.

'Great sovereign, we did all that was humanly possible. Pass judgment on us, but be merciful.' It was by this telegram to the Tsar that General Stoessel announced that he was going to capitulate. During the night of 2 January 1905 two of the four last Russian destroyers had succeeded in running the blockade, carrying off the army's most precious treasure: the flags of Port Arthur.

The Japanese laid down their conditions: the officers could keep their weapons, but not their horses.

Nogi and Stoessel met in the little village of Suchan to sign the surrender. The conquered general expressed his sympathy to his conqueror for the loss of his two sons who had fallen at the foot of the High Mountain, but the Japanese showed no regret.

'I am happy that my sons were able to give their lives for their country,' he said simply.

'Shall we ever be your equals?' murmured the general.

Thirty-four thousand Russians and fifty-eight thousand Japanese had fallen there.

A poem was written which had a great success in Tokyo:

> We fought while we lived,
> We fought when we were dead,
> For our spirits accompanied our comrades.
> Now the flag of the Rising Sun flies over Port Arthur,
> Our task is completed, we have rejoined our ancestors
>   and taken our place among our blessed heroes.

In the Nossi-be roadstead, Rodjesvensky was quelling a mutiny on board the *Malaya*: his sailors had learned of the shootings at the Summer Palace in St Petersburg and of the rebellions among the Black Sea fleet. The admiral, thinner and dragging one leg, was recovering from illness.

The maritime exploit of his enormous fleet's long voyage was acclaimed by the whole of the European Press. Togo could even read in his favourite English newspaper, the *St James Gazette*: 'We underestimated Rodjesvensky and we now salute him with all the respect due to bravery and energy: never has such a large number of steamships been taken so far from their bases.'

Togo knew the multifarious difficulties that the Russian admiral had encountered during this voyage. Japanese informers had been following the fleet through binoculars for him until the day when...

'They have disappeared, Your Excellency.'

Togo forgot to take off his pince-nez in the presence of his general staff.

'He can't pass through the Straits of Malacca: it's like a funnel. I shall wait for him here in the Sunda Straits.'

He waited for three weeks. One evening, very annoyed, Togo called in one of the English engineers, a technical adviser, for a cup of tea.

'What do you wish to know, Admiral?' the man finally asked, filling his pipe and thus shocking Togo.

'You, a Westerner, which way would you go, coming from here?'

'By way of Malacca, Your Excellency. I've bet £100 on it. But you are suspecting a trick where there is none...'

'I see that you know the Japanese.'

'Excuse me... I'm learning to know them, through Japanese girls!'

Togo condescended to smile.

At this moment a cable arrived. 'The second Russian Pacific fleet has just sailed past Singapore in battle order. The third left Djibouti on 7 April.'

This third fleet under Admiral Nebogatoff consisted of reinforcements – old ships which were being sent by way of Suez to swell the numbers of the second fleet. It was composed, in fact, of all the motley collection of old and obsolete ships which were still afloat in the Baltic: a millstone round Rodjesvensky's neck.

'Old tubs! Floating coffins!' he cursed.

On 12 April the anniversary of Makaroff's death, Togo had located his third white admiral.

'This is the night of destiny,' he said to his wardroom.

The battle plan which the samurai of the sea had devised was ready.

'I am awaiting a fleet of fifty ships in the Straits of Tsushima. Rodjesvensky has eight battleships, I have four, but his are old-fashioned in design, and I have at my disposal eight very powerful armoured cruisers, whereas he has only three. As far as cruisers and destroyers are concerned, we are about equal....'

The largest part of the Japanese fleet was moored at Masampo on the Korean coast of the Straits of Tsushima on 26 May. At 4.45 a cruiser sent out this radio message: 'Enemy squadron square 203.'

'At last!' roared Togo. 'Get under way instantly!'

'203!' shouted a sub-lieutenant joyfully. 'That's the coast of the High Mountain at Port Arthur! A good omen!'

Twenty-thousand miles from his departure port, Rodjesvensky was advancing into the Sea of Japan with a sort of tragic solemnity. His ships were pitching violently in rough seas, but the weather remained fine and bright.

'There's a lot of radio activity, Admiral!'

'We have been sighted.'

In the distance, indeed, the attentive escort of Japanese cruisers appeared, their transmitters crackling.

At 13.39 hrs Togo saw at last with his own eyes the sight which he had so often imagined during the past months: in the middle of the stretch of greenish water, amid the foaming crests of the waves, the slow dark hulls of the Russian fleet were moving beneath thick columns of black smoke.

'You will aim for their yellow funnels.'

Leading the Japanese line of battle, the flagship *Mikasa* ploughed strongly through the waves. Foam spread over her forecastle. Togo's glance fell affectionately for a moment on the young gunner who was adjusting the chin-strap of his cap. The Admiral slipped a message to his chief of general staff and a signal was hoisted from the *Mikasa*'s yardarm.

'The fate of the nation rests on the outcome of this single battle! Our country expects every man will do his duty.'

Lieutenant Yoshihita smiled, thinking of his English friend. 'Togo has a Nelson touch': this was so true that he had repeated word for word Nelson's famous signal at Trafalgar.

The Englishman was no longer on board, but this time he bet £1000.

Togo added to his Nelson signal:
'Banzai!'

The two fleets headed towards each other swiftly, on opposing and parallel routes. Togo did not want his adversary to escape: he barred his way.

'Turn to alter course in succession!'

This was the time for the most delicate manoeuvre: while it was being executed the Imperial fleet was nothing but a target offered to the Russian gunners. It was 1408 hrs. Rodjesvensky gave the order that he had been waiting to give for a whole year, indeed for his whole life. Trembling with excitement, he yelled:

'Fire at will!'

The sea was boiling around the *Mikasa*. Spray splashed the flagship and the air was filled with a rumbling thunder.

The Japanese line continued to perform its evolution impeccably without firing a single cannon. For three minutes...

One: Togo wiped his pince-nez with a large white handkerchief, hopping about from one foot to the other as a result of the staggering blows of collisions with the battleship. Showers of splinters struck the conning-tower like hail.

The young gunner, hit in the middle of his forehead, sank gently down at his post, leaving a trail of bright red blood on the bulwark: Togo's eyes were dimmed with tears.

'It's the smoke,' he said.

Two: Captain Ayatsushino, captain of the cruiser *Asama*, had got a bamboo flute out of his dolman. To pass the terrible time of waiting he began to play a very gentle air, of the sort one improvises in springtime under the cherry-trees. A terrific explosion which destroyed the superstructure made him play a wrong note. Embarrassed, he smiled, and began again.

Three: Lieutenant Yoshihita realised that he was holding something hard in his pocket: it was the Englishman's pipe: a present. He sniffed at it for some time: what was English tobacco like? he wondered. He crouched down, leaning towards a sailor who was smoking, and took a puff at his pipe.

'Have you started to smoke?' asked his captain.

'Only recently,' said the young man, very embarrassed.

'Fire!'

With rage, with fury, but also with a precision beyond the Russians' capacity, and with extraordinary speed, the Japanese guns replied all together. A final Russian 305 shell managed to hit the *Mikasa*'s bridge: fifteen officers fell wounded beside Togo. The admiral's compass was smashed before his eyes. He did not frown, and a melancholy smile still played on his lips.

It was the turn of his guns now. They were aiming at the *Souvarov* and the *Osalbia*. The Japanese missiles were loaded for the first time with 'Shimosa' powder, mixed with an explosive as yet unknown to the Russians. These shells tore through armour-plating as if it were paper. They exploded at the slightest contact when they touched a shroud, a funnel or even the surface of the sea. They lit sheaves of flames and spread a poison gas which suffocated the men.

The Japanese gunnery officers were sighting accurately at a rapidly decreasing range. They had opened fire at 6700 metres; now the lines had drawn closer and the distance was no more than 4500. The situation in the leading Russian ships was becoming chaotic. From his bridge, Togo was obviously not able to know the destructive effect of his shells on the enemy, but after half an hour he noticed that the return fire was scattered and ineffective.

On board the *Souvarov* two gunnery officers had been hit in the conning-tower which had been all but destroyed. One of them was killed as he was making for the last usable rangefinder. The admiral was hit by shrapnel. The mainmast, which had been shot off, fell into the water.

In the *Osalbia*'s sickbay the ship's doctor and his assistant were operating without chloroform. Amputated limbs were lying on the floor. Soon the ship took on a list and the wounded started to shout, jostling each other as they made for the escape hatches.

The Japanese fleet kept its line in perfect formation while

the Russian fleet was going to pieces. Togo edged round and began a merciless movement to surround the leaders of the enemy line.

At 1510 hrs the *Osalbia* capsized and sank. White-uniformed Russian sailors could be seen clustered like strange-looking swarms of bees against the ship's listing bridge. Then they slid into the sea. The Japanese sailors watched closely this sight, which they had never seen before: a great battleship sinking as the result of their gunfire.

After this the Russian formation began to break up more rapidly and its shells never really hit their targets again. Battleships and cruisers moved about in disorder inside a small area around which the Japanese were circling. The *Souvarov* had been exposed to bombardment for five hours. She had repelled two destroyer attacks and only one of her '75' guns was still firing, but she was still afloat.

'Bring up Captain Fujimoto's destroyer flotilla!' ordered Togo.

It was a death sentence.

The flagship sank majestically. At the same moment an explosion shook the *Borodino*, which sank within minutes. The *Alexander III* had preceded her, without a single survivor. Lines of troopships were sunk by gunfire like so many shooting targets. The two hospital ships were captured.

Night fell.

'Cease fire!' ordered Togo.

The action was broken off and a rendezvous was ordered for the next day in the Bay of Matsushima. The night was spent in clearing the decks and in counting the casualties: 100 dead and 530 wounded.

'That's very few,' said the admiral simply. 'We have sunk three of the four battleships of the *Souvarov* class: in St Petersburg they are considered to be invincible.'

The Russians were throwing their dead into the sea, caulking enormous holes in their ships' sides, and still hoping, dazed by battle. Their respite lasted only an hour, for suddenly a sound of engines rose in the darkness: the sound of propellers emerging from the swell. They were coming back! The Russians were overwhelmed by despair: it was the destroyers.

The little black monsters pursued their already wounded prey relentlessly. They launched their torpedoes and returned several times to the attack by the light of searchlights. The battleship *Navarin*, hit twice, sank with nearly all her crew. The battleship *Sissoiveliki* and the cruiser *Admiral Nakhinov* crept painfully towards the shores of the islands of Tsushima, where they were scuttled.

Day was breaking. Some Russian ships were still returning fire. The gunners, their foreheads bandaged and their hands burned, had been working all through the night: they had sunk two Japanese destroyers and damaged four. These survivors were still trying to make for Vladivostok, but, once again, Togo blocked their way.

Soon, what remained of the Russian battle corps was tightly hemmed in before the Japanese admiral. Firing resumed on a devastating scale. It had lasted for nine minutes when one of the officers in the admiral's entourage whispered to him something about the *Nicholas I*.

Something was happening on board this ship: the battle flag was jerking at the top of the mainmast as if it was about to be struck. Moreover, a signal was raised on the yardarm: XGH. 'We wish to negotiate,' the signal officer translated. Togo did not move: he seemed turned to stone. The pounding continued mercilessly. The officers surrounding Togo looked at him, and he, staring vacantly, watched the enemy ships being hit. The Russian ships struck their national flag. Another flag was hoisted on some of them: the Rising Sun, the emblem of Japan.

It was a heart-rending sight. These men wanted it understood that they were surrendering, and yet the hellish firing continued. The Japanese officers' throats were constricted, their hearts were beating fast and their hands were moist. Some of them felt their eyes smarting. Slowly, the yellow admiral turned his head towards them for a moment, and then turned back to watch the Russians again, and their agony. He seemed to be wallowing in it. His lips moved, and he muttered something: 'Kagoshima.'

His chief of general staff could bear it no longer. He took up his stand firmly, his eyes speaking volumes. 'Admiral, they are surrendering. What you are doing is contrary to the spirit of *Bushido*.'

The expression in Togo's dark eyes became gentle and amused, as if he was suddenly waking up. He looked at the signal from the *Nicholas I*. 'Cease fire!' he whispered.

Then Togo ordered all his ships to form a circle round the enemy. The time was 1045 hrs on 28 May 1905. He sent the destroyer *Kishi*, with one of his officers, Captain Akiyama, accompanied by Lieutenant Yamamoto, a French-speaking interpreter.

'Bring the Russian admiral back to me,' he said to the young man.

But when they boarded the *Nicholas I* it was Nebogatoff, the rear-admiral of the 'floating coffins', who came forward. It was he who had taken the responsibility for surrendering – to the fury, moreover, of most of the Russian officers.

Togo received him politely and drank a glass of champagne with him to celebrate the end of the war.

'My officers did not wish to surrender. Will they be freed?'

Togo agreed.

'May the crews keep their weapons in captivity?'

Togo shook his head.

'Will they be well treated?'

'We are not barbarians.'

Rodjesvensky was lying in the destroyer *Biedovy*, inert and only half-conscious. He had been carried, badly wounded, from the *Souvarov*, which had already half-capsized, and taken on board the destroyer *Buiny* at the height of the battle: but this latter vessel had been damaged in its turn.

Suddenly the Russian admiral opened his eyes: there was no more firing: the *Biedovy* had been taken in tow by a

Japanese destroyer which was making for Sasebo. Rodjesvensky would regain consciousness in Japan, heavily bandaged.

He was lying exhausted and half-asleep when a Japanese officer came into his bedroom:

'Admiral Togo asks you to do him the honour of receiving him.'

'His wishes are my commands.'

The samurai of the sea came close to him and stared intently and silently at the feverishly bright eyes of his wounded adversary. They gazed at each other for a long time. At last Togo took the emaciated hand of the vanquished admiral. He spoke very gently, like a doctor.

'Defeat can be the fate of any one of us. What counts is to have done one's duty. You have done yours. May I express my high regard for you? I hope that you will recover quickly.'

'Thank you,' answered the white admiral. 'I am no longer ashamed to have been defeated by you.'

Briskly, the yellow admiral left the hospital and went back to the quays where an enormous crowd drew aside to let him pass through. Wearing his sword rather higher than the regulations laid down with a Western uniform, he walked so fast that the officers who followed him were soon out of breath.

Fanatics, drunk with victory and *sake*, threw cherry-tree branches beneath Togo's barouche. Lost in the crowd, alone and unknown, a man in the prime of life, dressed in a simple kimono, watched this triumph. Toyama Mitsuru was the only man to know that the admiral was a son of the Black Dragon.

The conqueror of Tsushima made for the Russian cruiser *Orel*, which was lying at her moorings after being badly battered in the battle. A young lieutenant-commander was in command of this prize. Out at sea, on the way back, he had given full military honours to Captain Yug, who had died of his wounds. He had been buried at sea wrapped in the flag of St Andrew.

The young Japanese officer appeared on the gangway, dressed in white, and introduced himself in the regulation manner: 'Captain Togo. At your service, Admiral Togo.'

For the first time since the beginning of the war, father and son talked and walked together.

'They knew how to die, but they didn't know how to fight. Our troops have been victorious at Mukden, too, but we are going to lose the peace after winning the war, for the country has lost five hundred thousand of its sons. But that doesn't matter. The Land of the Rising Sun will be glorified for ever, and the white man will not reign again in Asia.'

Amaterasu, the Sun Goddess, brought a brilliantly fine day up out of the sea.

The years which followed were glorious ones for Japan. As the result of her energy and her sacrifices she had shown herself to be the equal of the great nations. The Emperor Mutsuhito, who had been the principal author of this rediscovered greatness was to die in 1912. The Meiji era ended with his death and the Taisho era began with his son, Yoshihito.

At the moment when the first gun-salute resounded, announcing that the Emperor's funeral *cortège* was setting out, his most faithful servant, General Nogi, dressed in a white kimono, committed *seppuku* with a short sword. His wife plunged a knife into her breast. Beside their bodies a poem was found:

> Abandoning a fleeting life,
> My sovereign has risen to be among the gods
> I follow him, my heart full of gratitude.

The Heroes with the Bamboo Poles

ON THE other side of the Amur river – the 'Black Dragon' of the Japanese secret societies – stretches Siberia. Boundless areas of steppe swept by winds where, from time immemorial, bands of riders appearing out of the sunshine or from the ice have been swallowed up.

Siberia is still Asia, but it is already Europe. The great river formed a frontier between Japanese Manchuria and Russian Siberia. But from 1917 there were no more Russians. There were only Reds and Whites.

As in a vast cauldron, armies, which were still only bands of soldiers, were swirled around in the sandy wind. Guerrillas, deserters, pillagers . . . The Bolsheviks stepped up the numbers of their terrorist attacks and the Tsarists set up a government in Omsk; German and Austrian prisoners sought freedom or adventure, while the fifty thousand Czechs formed a veritable army fighting now against the Reds, now against the Whites, to reach Vladivostok and the open sea.

The French, English and American contingents, who were supposed to keep order, were soon outflanked. Then they called on their Japanese allies. They asked for eight thousand men. Ten times that number were disembarked, plunged into the continent, and pushed on as far as Lake Baikal, thus making Toyama Mitsuru's old dream come true.

The Japanese leaders had found an excuse: 'We are supporting the white generals, Semenov and Kalminov.' They also supported Admiral Koltchak and the adventurer Ungern, the old Baltic soldier who took himself for Genghis Khan.

The whole adventure was to end in a blood-bath. The Reds advanced towards the East. Bands of Siberian soldiers massacred, raped and pillaged. On 14 March 1920 there was the carnage of Nicolaevsk, where the Japanese garrison was annihilated after the murder of the consul and the suicide of his wife and daughter. After a final battle, General Dietrichs, the last white leader, beat a retreat with his Japanese protectors.

In this way the Empire of the Rising Sun's participation in the First World War ended. It was a bitter victory....

In all the garrisons the officers gave vent to their anger: 'We have been fighting for nearly thirty years and have had nothing but success. And now we have nothing as a result, or so little....'

The situation bore out what they alleged: after her victory against China in 1895 Japan kept only Formosa and the Pescadores. Ten years later her unbelievable triumph over the Russians brought her only a few concessions in Manchuria. And now the Imperial Army was not to keep even the fortified town of Ching-tao, won from the Germans in 1915!

The officers had no difficulty in deciding who was to blame.

'We used to be a land of samurai, and now we have become a nation of politicians.'

Ministers, financiers and profiteers were all lampooned. A booklet with the evocative title *Nihon-kaizo-hoan-taiko*, or 'An Outline Plan for the Reorganisation of Japan', was in great demand. Its author, Kita Ikki, became the inspiration of all the young activist generation. Not only did he belong to the secret society of the Black Dragon, but he remained one of Toyama Mitsuru's favourite disciples. He had assimilated perfectly the society's spirit with its inextricable blend of thought and action.

Kita, who had begun his career as a spy on behalf of the Imperial Army's intelligence services, had 'worked' for a long time in China to the satisfaction of his chiefs. Faithful to his master, Toyama, he dreamed of bringing about a *rapprochement* between the Chinese Nationalists and the Japanese Imperialists. A secret agent, but of the intellectual type, he had read a great deal, even Karl Marx, whom he revived to make of him one of the prophets of Japanese National-Communism. *Das Kapital* plus *Bushido* . . . The mixture was explosive.

At the time of the publication of his manifesto, Kita Ikki founded a secret society which he called Yuzonsha, 'The Association for Permanence'. He took as his chief lieutenant a man named Okawa, an almost professional conspirator, who kept telling him: 'Theory is useful, but only direct action matters.' Okawa ended up, a few years later, by leaving Kita to found a purely activist group, which rejoiced in a very poetic name: 'Society for the Way of Heaven and Earth.'

Toyama Mitsuru, who now wore a bushy white beard, remained in the background of all the small activist groups. With his Black Dragon, he was still the guarantor of the old Japan of the samurai. However, the young terrorists met in an atmosphere of modernism. They dreamed not of yesterday's Empire but of tomorrow's. What they asked from the *ronin* of heroic legend was an everlasting example and a practical illustration of *Bushido*. Faced with a moral code of this sort, notions of right and left, which were beginning to become accepted in Japan with the coming of parliamentary government, did not in fact mean very much.

The Japanese activists of the twenties would never be able to distinguish very clearly between left and right. This scarcely mattered, however. As in the time of the samurai, both the right and left hands held a weapon. They would be the 'two swords' of the twentieth century. Now they were crying out for blood. On 28 September 1921 Yasuda Zenjiro, who was known as the richest man in Japan, was assassinated by a young fanatic. The murderer had only one explanation for his action. He gave it as a funeral oration for his victim: 'He was a capitalist.'

But who was the modern *ronin*? A member of the Yuzonsha, the nationalist 'Association for Permanence', or of the Gyomin Kyosanto, the 'Communist Party of the Dawn'? No one will ever know to which secret society Nakaoka Ryoichi, a railwayman and a professional terrorist, belonged. On 4 November in the middle of Tokyo station this fanatic stabbed to death with a dagger Hara Kei, the Prime Minister. He, too, had only one explanation for his action: 'He was a scheming politician.'

Nature, too, was to participate in this period of violence and death. On 1 September 1923 a catastrophic event took place, making a gigantic backcloth to the time of the assassins. A massive earthquake ravaged Tokyo and Yokohama. Whole buildings were engulfed in smoking fissures. Fire broke out and flames followed the earth tremors. Thirty thousand people were burned alive on one stretch of waste land where they had hoped to find refuge. It was impossible to estimate the numbers of victims who were crushed, burned, drowned or suffocated. There were hundreds of thousands of dead.

And three years later, at the end of 1926, there was another death. Not of a man, but of a god: the Emperor Yoshihito.

The Taisho era had ended. The Showa era followed with Hirohito, a young sovereign of slight build, whose drooping moustache and owl-eyed expression behind large spectacles in fine frames was henceforward to incarnate the divine power. The God Emperor was only twenty-five years old.

The following year his Prime Minister, General Tanaka Giichi, the new president of the conservative party, Seiyukai, presented him with an explosive report – the Tanaka Memorial.

Over sixty years of age, Tanaka seemed to have made himself the leader of all the malcontents. He was taken for a moderate, but he proved to be a reactionary. His plan was a simple one: to ensure control of Manchuria and Mongolia; then to launch an attack on China, as the first stage of a whole series of conquests: India, the South Seas, Asia Minor, Europe. He intended to rule the whole world, after eliminating the USSR and the USA.

In the background there was the Japanese drama: there were eighty million people in a tiny, barren archipelago. To find land overseas, the peasants of the archipelago would have to become soldiers.

The powder kegs were in place in the very heart of Manchuria. Only a spark was needed. It was to be struck at the end of a long, dusty summer's day on 4 June 1928.

A train was whistling through the Manchurian countryside. The iron dragon was carrying, amid clouds of steam and the din of pistons, one of the last warlords of eternal China, to the Manchurian capital, Mukden, Chang Tso-lin, the marshal-dictator, was lounging on the cushions in his saloon-coach. He seemed to be dozing, his eyelids heavy with opium. From time to time he glanced dully at the plain which stretched interminably on either side of the convoy. There was a great feeling of insecurity, and body-guards, armed to the teeth, were on watch on the footboards of the special train. The marshal was a protégé of the Japanese and an enemy of the Chinese Kuomintang, but in Asia things are never so simple. . . .

They had already reached the outskirts of Mukden. Felt tents had given way to brick houses. A few factory chimneys rose behind the bamboo hedges. The dictator, his collar unbuttoned, sighed. The journey was ending.

Suddenly there was a lightning flash and a terrible noise. The train seemed to have been picked up by a giant hand which was crushing it before flinging it into the air – in a thousand pieces. The iron dragon had been blown up by a booby trap.

All that remained of the lord of Manchuria was a few scattered, bleeding pieces of flesh, which the surviving general staff officers tried to reassemble, while they muttered abuse about 'the terrorists'.

Manchurian guerrillas? Communist partisans? Brigands emerging from the depths of the steppes and of the ages? Twenty years were to pass before it was known who had organised this outrage.

His name was Komoto and he held the rank of colonel in the Imperial Japanese Army. At that time he was attached to the general staff of the Kuan-tung Army which was occupying the Port Arthur region to supervise the South Manchurian railway. The outrage was merely a provocation. He wanted to create an atmosphere of insecurity. The Japanese army would then have a pretext to set in motion a policing operation and to occupy all Manchuria.

Colonel Komoto succeeded in avoiding capture and maintained silence until the end. It was not even certain if his immediate superiors had known about his plan.

The tidal wave which was about to submerge Japan did not originate with the generals, but with the young officers. None of the conspirators who were going to breathe fresh life into the spirit of the samurai held a rank above that of colonel. They did not belong to the great families but came from the country people. Patriots and mystics, they claimed to be both proletarian and peasants. Without knowing anything about the West and even in reaction against it, they were devising a genuine 'Japanese national-socialism'. These modern *ronin* had absolutely no need of a leader or of a party. The Japanese State was to be conquered by a spirit and a system. Power would be gained in a strange way, in successive waves. When the whole country had been submerged by a sea of militarism there would be war.

The officers disbanded by the reactionary government of 1924 had almost all asked to become teachers. There were eighteen hundred of them. What interested them was neither the money, nor the job, nor the holidays, but the power freely to indoctrinate young people at the State's expense. By means of these men and of their comrades who were serving officers, the many secret societies were to weave the threads of incessant conspiracies.

Excitement was growing in the barracks. Conversation among the officers became animated: 'Down with political parties!' The young activist captains now treated the conservative Seiyukai and the liberal Minseito with the same contempt. After sneering at politicians they went on to denounce the profiteers: 'Down with the *nouveaux riches*!'

Soon all the capitalists were being destined for hanging. 'Down with the multi-national trusts!'

Rice-alcohol inflamed them. They dreamed of a nation of peasant-soldiers capable of cultivating their own land and of conquering that of others. But there was still an obstacle: power had passed into the hands of civilians, who did not all understand these dreams and who wanted to turn Japan into a land of tradesmen.

One man incarnated this idea of 'civilian power': the Prime Minister, Hamaguchi, whose left-wing government had just succeeded the right-wing government of General Tanaka. The son of a humble State-employed forester, and leader of the progressive Minseito movement, Hamaguchi Osachi was no better and no worse than anyone else. But he became a symbol.

On 14 November 1930 the Prime Minister was at Tokyo railway station. A twenty-year-old student, Sagoya, fell upon and mortally wounded him. The assassin was a member of the 'Society for Love of our Country' (Aikokusha). His action followed in the tradition of political murder and the assassination occurred in the very place where, nine years previously, the Prime Minister, Hara Kei, had been killed.

Now the violence had to be organised.

Some twenty young officers met in secret. They formed the 'brains trust' of activism. All were inspired by the samurai spirit. The youngest were captains and the oldest colonels. They easily recruited some of their friends. Soon they would number a hundred. Their spirits rose to wild excitement.

'We are going to attack the Diet with ten thousand men!'

'We shall explode our bombs in every district of Tokyo!'

They had begun by finding a name for their group: the Sakurakai or 'Society of the Cherry-Tree'. The oldest had already fought with the Kinkikai or 'Society of the Imperial Flag'. Quite naturally the conspirators had chosen as their emblem the cherry flower 'Because it dies in full bloom, like the young samurai who dies for his Emperor'.

The conspiracy took shape. The *coup d'état* was decided upon. But a general must be found to whom power might be entrusted. One of the conspirators mentioned a name: 'General Ugaki.'

'But he's a moderate!'

'Exactly, we don't have to worry about him.'

All of them agreed on the name of the future dictator. All that was needed was to obtain his assent and to ask him to direct the operation, planned for the first day of spring 1931. However, not only did Ugaki refuse to sponsor the enterprise, but further he threatened those who had come to see him. 'Stop this plotting or I'll have you all arrested. For my part, I am leaving the Ministry of War for the government of Korea.'

The cherry-blossom was cut down even before its flowering.

But time was on the side of the new revolutionary generation. Henceforward, the heart of the conspiracy was not in the metropolis but in the colony. The explosion was to be in Manchuria and the bomb the Japanese army of occupation. Only the detonator was missing.

They thought they had found a pretext in a martyr. But an obscure captain shot on a distant frontier was not enough to make the people revolt. Only his comrades understood that his death heralded something irrevocable. For by not striking back immediately, the Imperial Army appeared to have lost face. Its revenge would be all the more terrible. All the officers kept saying, as they impatiently clutched the sheaths of their swords, 'We swear to avenge Captain Nakamura Shintaro one day.'

He was an intelligence officer who 'worked' on the frontier between Manchuria and Mongolia. Surprised by a Chinese patrol when wearing civilian clothes and carrying false papers, he was shot in June 1931. The faithful of the 'Society of the Cherry-Tree' made his death their symbol. For the thirty thousand soldiers of the Kuan-tung Army who ensured the safety of the Trans-Manchurian railway, he was one of their own who had just died at the hands of the enemy.

One could describe the men at the heart of the conspiracy as 'the three samurai': Colonels Itagaki Seishiro and Ishihara Kanji and Major Hanaya Tadashi, all serving at the general staff headquarters of Port Arthur. The youngest was not the least determined of the three. After Captain Nakamora's death, he had made a secret journey to Tokyo to meet 'some comrades on the general staff and in the Imperial guard', all members of the 'Society of the Cherry-Tree', naturally.

But their secrets were all known, beginning with the military conspiracies, and the Minister of War could not do otherwise than protect himself vis-à-vis the Government. He wrote a letter to the Commander-in-Chief in Manchuria, asking him not to let himself become involved in any plot and to be wary of his turbulent subordinates. He took a strong line, but employed a curious messenger. General Tatekawa made no secret of his extremist opinions. It was he who had welcomed the activist Major Hanaya during his recent visit to Tokyo and he had encouraged him to act. Tatekawa took his time and reached Mukden during the morning of 18 September. Colonel Itagaki, one of the chiefs of the local conspiracy, was waiting for him at the station.

'You must be very tired after your long journey, General. Come along and have a rest in a geisha house.'

The two officers seemed to prefer love to war. For war was about to break out...

During the evening an explosion shattered the darkness. More sabotage on the railway lines. The damage was so trivial that the train was not even one minute late, but Japanese propaganda immediately transformed the large squib into a deadly bomb. The name of the saboteur was learned only years afterwards: Captain Imada Shintaro, of both the Imperial Army and the 'Society of the Cherry-Tree'.

At last the detonator had been found. Then came the explosion. Before dawn, Japanese troops had occupied the Chinese barracks in Mukden and several other garrisons.

The civilian cabinet in Tokyo tried to control the situation. It recommended an attempt to avoid aggravating the conflict.

To 'prevent the conflict from spreading', the Japanese military decided quite simply to do away with their potential adversary. The Chinese garrisons were attacked one after the other. Soon, the Japanese were masters of the 'three Provinces' which made up Manchuria.

The young officers were wildly excited. They had found the solution to all ills from which their country and their pride had been suffering: 'We shall rip Manchuria from China and offer it to Japan. And if the Emperor doesn't want it, we will make it an independent state: the first samurai colony of Great Asia!'

The escalation had begun. In exactly ten years' time the Japanese would see the beginning of the Second World War.

The booby trap on the railway line, the taking of Mukden and the occupation of the whole of Manchuria had preceded the tragedy. Afterwards the curtain was to rise on the taking over of power in Tokyo. In October 1931 the members of the 'Society of the Cherry-Tree' decided on action. The most curious aspect of this exploit was that the inspiration of the group did not come from the army but from a civilian, employed, it is true, at the general headquarters. Okawa Shumei came from a long line of conspirators and he was constantly establishing new cells. He knew how to insulate the members of his conspiracy and none of the groups appeared to have any link with the others, except, perhaps, the cult of Toyama Mitsuru, his ideology and his wishes, for he was the moral conscience of them all.

The civilian was more excited than the soldiers at the headquarters. He was full of plans, each more audacious and more bloody than the last.

'We must assassinate all the Emperor's councillors.'

'How?' asked the young officers.

'At one stroke. All we need is an aeroplane to attack the hall where the council meets. With a good pilot and a large bomb, not one of them would escape.'

The soldiers did not like the seat of authority to be vacant. After the cabinet had been pulverised they needed to put in power a man of whom they could feel certain. They did not wish to repeat the blunder which had resulted in the fiasco with General Ugaki. Okawa Shumei, who knew everyone at headquarters, was well placed to suggest a name.

'General Araki is your man.'

This choice pleased the officers. Director of the Military School, Araki was a resolute officer and a fanatical patriot. A robust fifty-year-old with a shaven skull and a ragged moustache, Araki Sadao cultivated the manners of an old-style warlord. His skin was stretched so tightly on his face and his cheekbones were so high that he bore an irresistible likeness to some knight of ancient Japan, chiselled by the sun and the snow of all his distant conquests.

The general did not mince his words and his enemies had found a name for him: 'The babbling Fascist'. He took no notice and continued to chew over, between his formidable jaws, trenchant phrases of the style of: 'If it is necessary we will throw everything in the sea, down to the last machine. We will kill everyone down to the last banker. And we will return to the Family Nation of the year 1000!'

He talked endlessly, walking up and down. Standing up he looked unexpectedly smaller than at his work table. At times an attack of sciatica would double him up. But this dry little man had a will of iron and his eyes glowed with a sense of purpose.

Araki Sadao had only one phrase on his lips: 'the samurai spirit'. The ancient samurai spirit. And also the new one, that which might spring from the people. He loved repeating it to all these young officers who listened to him passionately and called him, between themselves, simply: 'Him.'

'My father was a poor school-teacher. My samurai blood came from my mother. But my grandfather held the schoolteacher in such high esteem that he adopted him after giving him his daughter. This did not prevent him from continuing to teach.' What Araki Sadao did not say, but all the world knew was that he had been a poor child, obliged to earn his family's living from the age of twelve by working as a clerk. Everyone knew his military career by heart: he had entered the Military School as a cadet in 1896, fought against the Russians in 1905, and become military attaché in St Petersburg in 1909.

His career as a diplomat had ended with an incident which reveals his whole character. Araki was arrested in the coach of a train on the Trans-Siberian railway because he was making notes and sketches. Taken with all his baggage into a guard room at the side of the railway line, he was ordered to give his name and rank:

'Araki Sadao. I have no rank.'

'No rank? Really?'

'No. Nobody has ever arrested a Japanese officer alive.'

He stood up calmly and drew his sword from its sheath. The Russian interrogator, Colonel Grakov, pulled out his revolver. The Japanese reassured him. 'It isn't to kill you, but to kill myself.'

Faced with the prospect of a diplomatic incident, they released him with apologies.

Araki came back, in 1916, to fight against the Austro-Germans on the side of the Russians. Later an important post awaited him. But he made the point: 'I am the most plebeian graduate of the Military Academy.'

Now one of the principal chiefs of the army, General Araki still retained the habits of a young sub-lieutenant. Every day he practised two of the martial arts of the samurai: fencing and calligraphy. His favourite turn of phrase was simple yet striking: 'There is only one way which will enable the Japanese to overcome their many difficulties, and that is to realise that they are Japanese.'

His political ideas? Fifty per cent anti-capitalist, fifty per cent anti-communist, one hundred per cent National-Socialist, which he translated in Japanese by 'Imperial-Marxist'. He, too, had founded his little group, half-party, half-sect, giving it the name of Kodogikai, or 'Society of the Imperial Way'.

He announced his programme: 'Japan, like all other nations, and perhaps more than they, needs to surmount the world crisis. This can be done only by turning away from both international Bolshevism and parliamentary democracy.'

That was the official statement, which was, all in all, quite moderate. When he was among close friends the general screwed up his penetrating little eyes, smoothed his large black moustache, stroked his sugar-loaf skull, and prophesied: 'Our country has decided to disseminate its national ideal across the seven seas, to propagate it over the five continents, even if we have to use force. We are the descendants of the gods. We must reign over the world.'

One of General Araki's theories was the disastrous union of the extremists of the right and the left. 'The progressive students would be able to achieve everything if they joined with the nationalist officers.'

Wild talk? Not at all. There was a large left-wing party, the Minshuto, which was social-democratic in inspiration. The secretary general, Akamatsu Katsumaro, decided to break with parliamentary democracy. He spread panic in the executive committee and involved half the members in an historic split. They then founded the Japanese Kokka Shakaito or 'Socialist Party of the Nationalist State'.

The old militants were very upset: 'These youngsters don't know what they are doing!'

Akamatsu was slightly over thirty. He was a hefty man with a bull neck above an open-collared blue shirt. He had the style of a fascist leader. His words tied in quite naturally with those of General Araki. 'It is the agricultural masses whom we must save from poverty. For these six million families there is only one hope: a greater Japan. I have complete confidence in the anti-capitalist movement of the young army. We shall found the only movement of peasants and soldiers and it will create the socialist and Imperial State.'

Pamphlets were circulated in the Japan of the thirties. They all said the same thing: 'Peasants, workers, soldiers! Return to the protection of the *Tenno* and build a new Japan!'

The security services were on the alert. 'Five hundred conspiracies are thwarted each year. If we weren't the best police in the world we should have a hundred political assassinations each month.' But the conspirators, over-confident of success, boasted in every barracks and in all the villages. Even the most serious of the conspiracies, that of Araki, had become an open secret.

The government decided to defend itself and had three colonels arrested. The civilians and the moderates finally crossed swords with the military and the extremists. If they wanted to check the nationalist revolution they had to strike quickly and hard. They chose the exactly opposite method. The only punishment meted out was to transfer those most deeply implicated to provincial garrisons. Among the conspirators there was only one cry: 'We will carry on!'

The war, started by a provocation, was to be resumed because of a further provocation.

At the end of January 1932 Chinese demonstrators attacked Japanese pilgrims in Shanghai. From insults they moved quickly on to blows. The first wounded were still lying in their blood when marines of the Japanese Navy landed and intervened. However, they were immediately surrounded by Chinese infantrymen.

To free them, the Imperial general staff ordered the artillery and the air force to intervene. Shells and bombs fell on the overcrowded districts, burning houses and killing civilians. Refugees tried to reach the International Concessions. Within minutes there was appalling panic, which turned into suppressed terror.

Before withdrawing under pressure from the Great Powers, the Japanese decided to achieve some military successes so the fort of Wong-Song was taken. All that could be seen of Shanghai was blackish clouds of smoke, sometimes reaching towards the grey sky, while loud explosions were heard.

It was not quite war, but neither was it peace.

The Chinese were solidly entrenched. From the Japanese positions little could be seen: rolls of barbed wire, fixed to stakes and tangled like the hair of a drowned woman. Beyond, a deep ditch, then the trenches, protected by sand-bags, the outlines of which could scarcely be seen in the morning mist.

Every time a Japanese soldier showed himself, long bursts of machine-gun fire broke the silence. The Chinese proved to be not only good diggers, but also good shots.

On 20 February 1932 the headquarters of the Kurume division decided to switch to the attack and to capture the enemy's position. An order was sent to the front lines, naming the objective and the time of zero hour.

Captain Matsushita Tamaki, who was in command of the assault unit, assembled his NCOs. They joined their chief in a shelter close to the front lines. All of them guessed the reason for their being called together.

The captain said only: 'It's for tomorrow morning. At five-thirty.'

They knew the disposition of the enemy's troops and they knew also that the Chinese machine-guns were sweeping all the network of barbed-wire entanglements. If the Japanese assault troops did not get across quickly, complete failure was certain.

'Shall we be using grenades?' suggested a young soldier.

'They are not enough to make a breach,' answered the captain drily. 'No, I think I have a better idea. Come and see!'

Matsushita Tamaki had ordered twelve-foot-long bamboo tubes to be prepared. He felt the weight of one carefully. 'Look! It is stuffed with explosive right through!' A smile contorted his face: 'Tomorrow, when the assault troops go in to the attack, the way will be open.'

They still had to put these unusual weapons in place. Volunteers came forward to run through the enemy fire and slip the explosives over the barrier of barbed-wire entanglements. In small groups, at intervals, they rushed forward. But flares were lighting up the front as if it were broad daylight, and the Chinese machine-guns brought them down as they jumped out of their trenches with their enormous bamboo poles, which made them look like samurai armed with spears.

As the day dawned, Captain Matsushita Tamaki realised that his plan was going wrong. Dozens of bodies had already fallen in front of his trench. And these soldiers had covered only a few years before collapsing, faces to the ground, hands clenched on their bamboo bombs.

The officer repeated in a low voice: 'We have to succeed. . . . An order is an order.' Then he shouted once more: 'I am asking for three volunteers.'

He did not even see the faces of these men to whom their comrades were passing more explosives. He saw them jump, cat-like, out of the trench, seemingly unencumbered by their diabolical poles. The captain threw himself at a loophole, pushed his helmet back, wiped his field-glasses and followed through them the progress of the volunteers. They seemed like old soldiers who knew how to fight. They leaped forward, as during their training, jumping across shell-holes, then running between each pause, their bodies doubled up.

The Japanese machine-guns started to fire in their turn, to cover them as best they could. Then came the mortars whose shells fell on the Chinese positions, glowing and rumbling heavily.

Were his men going to get through? Captain Matsushita Tamaki lost sight of them sometimes in this night which the dawn seemed unwilling to end.

Suddenly, he started up joyfully: he had just seen, far off in no-man's-land, a tiny reddish glow: one of the soldiers, who had reached the objective, was lighting the fuse of his bomb.

Matsushita Tamaki could not resist shouting the old victory cry of the Japanese: 'Banzai!'

But it suddenly seemed to him that the old shout had given a signal to the enemy artillery. A dozen guns sounded from behind the Chinese trench. These artillerymen had found their targets and everything fell apart: wires and men, barbed wire and attackers.

A volunteer was flung into the air, another was cut in two and the third disappeared.

Failure – once again!

Captain Matsushita showed neither surprise nor anger. In the glow of the explosions, the soldiers of his comany saw that his face was still impassive, constricted by the chin-strap of his helmet. He snapped his fingers in an impatient gesture, and repeated, once again: 'Volunteers!'

Three men stepped forward immediately, pushing even comrades aside to get to the officer. Their names were to become veritable symbols of courage for all the youth of Japan: Eshita Takeji, Kitagawa Yosaburo and Sakue Inosuke. But they did not yet know what Captain Matsushita Tamaki was going to ask of them – something which no other officer had yet asked of his men.

'Your comrades have been killed before they had time to light the fuses. Therefore there is only one solution: to do it before you make your final dash.'

The dangerous mission had become a desperate mission. The volunteers were to be blown up at the same time as the bamboos filled with explosive.

Not one of the three soldiers protested. They stood to attention and exchanged their rifles for the bamboo poles.

Matsushita said simply: 'In the name of the Emperor, carry out your orders!'

It was still dark when they went over the top of the Japanese trenches and crept towards the enemy. Suddenly all hell was let loose: they had been discovered. They ducked into a shell-hole.

Bursts of machine-gun fire continued. The hits made the earth fly everywhere. But the Chinese were not the only ones to fire and the Japanese replied. Bullets crossed each other above the shell-hole where Takeji, Yosaburo and Inosuke were crouching.

There remained only ten minutes until zero hour. Would

they be able to go on and destroy the barbed-wire entanglement?

Captain Matsushita Tamaki looked at his watch with wild impatience. Suddenly he could not repress his delight: 'They're off again!'

This time they lit the fuses and the small flames could be seen in the greyness of the dawn.

But the Chinese machine-gunners had also located the three men. One of them fell, but his comrades went on, carrying the long bamboo poles.

They reached the barbed wire. They pushed their bombs under the wire and these exploded almost immediately.

This time everyone could shout: 'Banzai!'

The breach had been made. Just in time for the attack. A bugle sounded the charge. The infantrymen swarmed from the trench and rushed on the enemy, through the gap which had been made by the three volunteers for death. The Japanese losses were fearful. But it seemed that the attack could not be stopped. It became as irresistible as a tidal wave and the Chinese position collapsed like a sandcastle when the tide comes in.

The heroes with the bamboo poles had triumphed by their sacrifice. But almost nothing of these men survived. Their explosive had blown them to smithereens. Their comrades collected a few pieces of human remains and put them in small scarlet wooden boxes. The next day the entire Kurume division would march past these relics.

A marching song, a film and a play were to make widely known, in even the smallest villages of the Empire, the action of the 'three bamboo bombers' whose bronze statues were erected in Tokyo. The spiritual chief of the army, General Araki Sadao, delivered the finest of funeral orations for them.

'They fell according to the spirit of *Bushido*.'

Three simple soldiers of peasant stock had been admitted, after their deaths, to the caste of the samurai.

The Mikado's Falcons

GROUP OF schoolboys in severe dark-blue uniforms with gold buttons were being herded by their masters across Tokyo. Each child held in one hand a small white flag with a red sun on it. As they came to the end of their 'walk', all bowed before the bronze monument which commemorated the sacrifice of the three 'heroes of Shanghai'.

'They were the purest incarnation of the Yamato-damashii (the Japanese spirit),' said the teachers. 'You must be worthy of these soldiers, you who will be soldiers yourselves one day.'

Popular imagery aroused a great burst of fanaticism throughout Japan.

In the minds of the leaders of the secret societies, political assassination must now precede the inevitable military *coup d'état*. The two first victims of the wave of terrorism were not men of the left, but, on the contrary, men of the right. In the spring of 1932, within one month, both the financier Inoue and Baron Dan were to be assassinated by young peasants.

These victims seemed well chosen. The first had been Minister of Finance and was capitalism incarnate. The second controlled the Mitsui Trust and appeared as the symbol of monopoly control. But Inoue had formerly been a supporter of reductions in military credits and Baron Dan had been president of a group of business men opposed to the expeditions to Manchuria and Shanghai.

Three other assassination attempts failed narrowly. One on the former Prime Minister, Wakatsuki, the others against Prince Saionji and Baron Shideara.

It was necessary to strike again, and to strike harder and higher. One name was on all lips: that of the Prime Minister,

Inukai Tsuyoshi. He had held his post since December 1931, and symbolised all that the young army detested. This old man thought he could redeem his youth as a militant progressive by flirting with conservative military men of the type of Tanaka. So far as the moderates were concerned, he was a liberal. For the extremists of both the right and the left, he was a traitor.

The young officers were not entirely wrong to pass such a severe judgment. Inukai seemed to have decided to stop the conflict between China and Japan at all cost. His country found itself arraigned before the League of Nations and for him there remained only one solution: negotiation with the enemy.

In deep secrecy, Inukai entered into relations with Chiang Kai-shek. His proposal was simple: 'We will evacuate Manchuria.' 'We' meant both the Japanese and the Chinese.

This was to sign his death warrant, but who would dare to do the deed?

The Japanese Army thought of itself as the élite of the nation and the Fleet Air Arm considered itself the élite of the Army. This corps, which was in the process of formation, needed traditions, and found them quite naturally in the most glorious past of Japan. In a dozen years it was to give birth to the *kamikaze*. At this time it dreamed only of regenerating the *ronin*.

The cadets of the Fleet Air Arm thought of themselves as young samurai. They lived outside Tokyo in curious surroundings: only the throbbing of aeroplane propellers broke the silence of the countryside. In this rural area, where traditions had remained more alive than elsewhere, pilots and peasants got on well together. They met together frequently, to talk politics and dream of a greater Japan. Students and officers sometimes joined them.

Any society produces a leader. The one who was to appear was not a warrior, but a priest of the Nichiren sect. A strange priest, moreover, who had started his career as a spy in China. Inoue Nissho had moved directly from the life of a spy to that of a Buddhist monk, but he repudiated nothing of his past. In his temple he had opened a school for terrorists to which all the extremists of the province gravitated.

A group was formed. They had only to find a name for it. The monk-spy suggested Ketsumeidan. The name expressed aptly what he wished to say: 'The Blood Brotherhood'.

The faithful became initiates. Inoue Nissho made them take an oath: 'You will write the text with a brush dipped in your own blood.' The red lettering on the white parchment looked like Japanese flags in shreds after battle. Inoue Nissho also wanted to avenge his brother, a well-known pilot, who had just fallen in combat over Shanghai.

Behind its romantic façade the Ketsumeidan was soon seen as a very highly organised society. The eternal conspirator, Okawa Shumei, who wanted to take his revenge for the abortive conspiracy of the autumn of 1931, had given it the funds it needed. He watched the progress of the 'Brotherhood' with the avid expression which he assumed as soon as he heard talk of a conspiracy. This one also enjoyed the moral support of old Toyama Mitsuru, who ensured liaison between the old members of the Black Dragon and the young of all the secret societies.

The monk-spy Inoue Nissho was not a man to be content with prayers. What he wanted was action, and for him action meant killing. He chose the best of his followers.

'Thirteen Brothers of the Blood will assemble on Friday, 13 May, close to the Fleet Air Arm base.'

The chief gave his orders after choosing these symbolical numbers.

'The action will take place the day after tomorrow.'

15 May 1932 was a Sunday. It was very fine and most of the town-dwellers had made tracks for the country. Tokyo seemed to be empty....

The thirteen were now only nine. But they were still as fanatical, still as determined. The eldest of them was twenty-seven years old, the youngest twenty-three. All were cadets in the army or navy. Their leader's name was Koga: he was the only lieutenant in the group.

They were to meet at the Yasukini shrine in Tokyo. There, in that high place of heroic Japan, the souls of heroes killed in battle lived on. Slowly, as tradition demanded, the cadets bowed in the direction of the sacred mirror.

Dawn broke. For them it was the day of sacrifice and death.

The modern *ronin* had come in taxis and these vehicles were waiting for them, engines running, to take them to their destiny. Their leader ordered: 'To Sanno!'

On this hill stood the residence of the Prime Minister, a modest building in red brick which was made attractive by splendid flowers. As it was Sunday, most of the guards were off duty. Furthermore, no one seriously feared an attack on Inukai: this old socialist was thought to be in the hands of the generals, but for the junior officers he was just a scheming politician. His death was to act as the detonator of a national explosion.

The nine cadets leapt out of their taxis, knocking over the guards and breaking down the doors. Now they were running through the Prime Minister's house, revolvers in their hands.

Empty rooms, closed doors . . . Their steps echoed in the corridors and they jostled each other to be the first to reach their goal.

Finally, the last room of all! Premier Inukai saw them come in. He was a small, bearded man, thin and grey. He bore his seventy-five years lightly and drew himself up proudly. He also knew how to die like a samurai.

He lifted his eyes from his papers and stared with a strange intensity at those who had come to kill him. After a long silence he spoke: 'Take off your shoes! You are walking on my matting.'

The conspirators had been in too much of a hurry to bother about the usual niceties. They hesitated, and were probably going to obey the old man, when a second group, led by Lieutenant Yamagishi, irrupted into the room. Inukai stared steadily at his assailants. Now he lit his pipe with a hand which did not tremble. The smoke narrowed his eyes still further as he looked at them with an expression as calm as a mountain lake.

Finally, he decided to come to the root of the matter. He did so with infinite politeness, as if it was not a question of his life – and his death.

'Allow me to speak to you.'

The cadets hesitated.

'I am sure you will understand me . . .'

But they had to silence him at all costs. The time was not for words, but for action. And first of all the simplest action.

'Fire!' Lieutenant Yamagishi yelled, and fired immediately.

His comrades followed suit. The room was filled with acrid smoke. Inukai collapsed slowly, watching his assassins. He had taken the opportunity to knock out his pipe before the first shot.

His daughter-in-law, who stood motionless holding her baby in her arms, had been present all the time without uttering a cry.

Now, on the mats of the Sanno palace, blood gradually covered the mud left by the assassins' shoes.

While the pistols crackled, bombs exploded. Inukai's murderers were not the only ones to act on this Sunday, 15 May 1932.

This time it was not cadets, but students and peasants, who formed commandos and attacked public buildings. There was an explosion at the conservative party's headquarters, an explosion at the home of Count Makino, keeper of the privy seal, an explosion in the home of Admiral Suzuki, Grand Chamberlain of the Court, an explosion at the central police station. Symbolic explosions which demonstrated the will of the conspirators to put an end to all authority. For them, there must be no other power than their own in Japan.

But the *coup d'état* took a strange turn.

The conspirators, after throwing their bombs, went to . . . the military police. 'We have come to give ourselves up.'

That same evening another group went to the military headquarters. Young officers, members of the 'Society of the Cherry-Tree', asked to speak to the military leaders. All the military leaders momentarily stopped discussing the assassination of the Prime Minister by the cadets to hear what their comrades were asking. But they were not asking, they were demanding.

'We wish the army to rise up and take power.'

'Have you a leader?'

A third name followed that of the timorous General Ugaki and that of the imprudent General Araki: 'General Mazaki.'

But the latter felt that the conspiracy had come into the open too soon and that the assassins were only precursors. He guessed that it would be necessary to wait and he declined the young officers' offer.

'I have to refuse . . . but you have my sympathy.'

The *coup d'état* had failed, but the conquest of power was beginning.

In refusing to follow the extremists, the army was able to act as an arbitrator. In every barracks the manifesto of the conspirators was passing from hand to hand:

Appeal to Our Compatriots

> Friends and fellow-countrymen! Look at the present state of our well-beloved country! In political spheres, in the diplomatic service, in the national economy, in education, in thought, in the Army, and in the Navy, where shall we rediscover the real face of our sacred Empire of the Rising Sun? All that we see is political parties who are concerned only with wrangling over power; the capitalists are associating themselves with the parliamentary representatives to exploit the blood and the sweat of the masses. That is not all. There is, besides, the authority which protects this exploitation and which is demanding more and more of the people. There is an outrageously self-indulgent diplomatic service, demoralising education, a corrupt Army and

Navy, garbled ideas, the intolerable suffering of the peasant and working classes, and on top of all this there are increasing numbers of demagogues.

Japan is on the point of falling into an abyss.

This is the moment to cure these ills! If you do not rise up now, all that will remain for our country will be a road leading to ruin. Friends and fellow-countrymen, to arms! For the salvation of the land of our birth, direct action is the only remedy which is left to us.

Friends and fellow-countrymen, destroy, to defend the Emperor, the dishonest courtiers who surround him! Annihilate the enemies of the nation, political parties and financiers! Castigate these corrupt practices!

Defend Japan, the patrimony of our ancestors! And, under the aegis of the Imperial Intelligence, return to the spirit of the founder of our country. Re-establish Japan, refreshed and joyful under a regime of autonomous communities! Japanese masses, in order to build anew, we must first destroy. Let us utterly destroy ugly and evil things! Total destruction is necessary and inevitable before we can build a magnificent new Japan!

Those of us who deplore the present state of our beloved country can light the flame of the Showa restoration by sacrificing ourselves and in the expectation of your co-operation.

The fate of our beloved Japan will not depend on the success or on the failure of our advance guard endeavours; it will depend on you and your decision, on you who will carry on our work in the same spirit and in the same direction.

Rise up! Rise up! And build the true Japan!

A group of young Army and naval officers; a group of peasant volunteers.

In sealing this manifesto with their own deaths, the new *ronin* did not doubt for a single moment the value of their example.

The action of a naval officer the following year had a similar significance. The Japanese government had just refused to allow in the 1933 budget for the construction of two battle-cruisers. In a sleeping car on the night train from Tokyo to Shimonoseki a passenger felt warm, sticky drops falling on his face in the middle of the night. He switched on the light. The man in the upper couchette had just committed ritual *seppuku* and was threatening with his sword those who were trying to come to his assistance. Lieutenant-Commander Kusuhara was denouncing his Minister's attitude by committing suicide in this way.

A week later the Minister headed the officer's funeral procession and then went to bow before the Imperial tombs. And the two cruisers were allowed for in the Navy's budget.

The Japanese armies were making progress in Manchuria where propaganda followed the artillery. The Japanese military had an idea which was to be used frequently in the future: they created a puppet state: Manchukuo. Better still, they gave it a sovereign.

One of Toyama Mitsuru's disciples Tanza Komei who had spent ten years in China as 'honourable correspondent' of the Black Dragon, landed at Dairen (Ta-lien). As if by chance a week later in the town of T'ien-chin, Captain Doihara, a member of the 'Society of the Cherry-Tree', romantically abducted a retiring young man, Henry Pu Yi. He had been known formerly as His Majesty Hsuan-t'ung, and he was the last Emperor of China. ...

On 1 March 1932 he agreed to become head of the republican government of Manchukuo under the supervision of the Japanese. Two years later his 'protectors' were to appoint him Emperor, with the name of K'ang-te – that is, 'Tranquillity and Virtue'. But the real master of Manchuria was an 'attaché at the Imperial Palace', Yoshioka Yasunori, a loyal member of the Black Dragon, as was proper.

Order prevailed in Mukden, as it would soon in Tokyo also.

General Araki, in whom the young officers had reposed all their trust and all their hopes, became Minister of War in the new Cabinet. He took as his right hand General Mazaki, who had assured the conspirators of 15 May 1932 of his entire sympathy. From now on Mazaki possessed a redoubtable weapon: the promotion list, of which he had become the master, and which allowed him to promote the extremists in the military hierarchy.

The *putsch* had succeeded from the inside. However, a crisis was developing among the conquerors. From now on, two groups were manoeuvring for power: first, the young officers, the 'National-Socialists', who had risked everything for the revolution and were determined to carry it through to a successful conclusion. They formed what they called the Kodoha, or 'Group of the Imperial Way'. More and more their enemies became the conservatives, without whom they would not have reached the corridors of power.

The latter had chosen for their organisation a symptomatic name: Toseiha or 'Control Group'. They were the oldest of the officers, who shared the nationalist sympathies of their juniors but had difficulty in accepting their revolutionary and anti-capitalist ideas. In their view these young men were going to spoil everything by their impatience and their desire to 'serve the people'.

A struggle became inevitable, more especially because conservatives and revolutionaries were opposed to each other in the field of foreign policy. In the first place, the former were anti-Chinese and the latter anti-Russian. These groups were watching each other and polishing their weapons when, at the beginning of 1934, General Araki fell ill. His replacement gave the old guard the opportunity to regain control of the army. General Nagata, who succeeded him, was to act as a brake: the promotion list was now working against the 'young Turks'.

The most excitable were transferred. The rest had to content themselves with marking time, waiting for promotions which would never come.

Aizawa Saburo was just an officer like all the others. Lieutenant-colonel in the garrison at Fukuyama, he belonged, with many of his comrades in the regiment, to the 'permanent conspiracy' of the Japanese officers. He resented as a defeat the departure of General Araki and as an affront the promotion of General Nagata. For him, the only valid candidate was General Mazaki, the one who had not concealed his sympathy with the conspirators of 15 May.

Inspector-General of Education for the Army, Mazaki the revolutionary had a great moral influence on the young officers and NCOs, and especially on the cadets. Moreover, Nagata the conservative was trying to eliminate him. This was like taking a match to a powder magazine.

On 11 August 1935 Lieutenant-Colonel Aizawa left his garrison. He took the train and went first to the shrine of Ise. He wanted to collect his thoughts before the Imperial mausoleum which dated from the sixth century and was still the most sacred place in Japan. Before making the irreparable gesture, he wanted to meditate at length: 'I am nothing, the Emperor and the Empire are everything. What I do, I do for them. Help me, I beg you. Give me strength in this hour of my most desperate need!'

Having arrived in a temper, he went away calm and collected. He even stopped for a moment in front of the shops grouped together near the temple. He bought lucky charms for his four children. Then Lieutenant-Colonel Aizawa took the train again. The train for Tokyo.

He had still one more evening. He met some army friends and they went to dine in a tea-house on the bank of the Sumida river. From the windows, lights on the other bank could be seen and the sound of oars could be heard. Boats were floating on the quiet water and passing beneath the wooden bridges. Nothing seemed to have changed in this scene since the time of the samurai....

There were five officers listening to the geishas' songs. When the young women had left them, they sipped rice-alcohol and talked politics: that is, they talked conspiracy.

'The Emperor is deceived by his councillors. And the worst of them all is General Nagata.'

Before separating, the officers evoked again the memory of the *ronin*. They had to do something which would be worthy of their warrior ancestors.

Aizawa decided to make this gesture and asked his companions to rely on him. The next day, at dawn, the lieutenant-colonel went to the shrine of Meiji; then he took the road to the office of military affairs.

General headquarters offered no comfort. Rickety staircases, unpainted walls and broken panes. Everything which was not directly useful to the war effort was regarded here as a useless luxury. Aizawa crossed through the barrage of secretaries with haughty self-assurance and, without knocking, went into General Nagata's office.

He was not unknown to the head of the Army Department.

'You here again! You know that I have transferred you to Formosa and that I shall not go back on my decision.'

Aizawa seemed very worked up. 'It isn't a question of myself, but of General Mazaki and of all our friends. You are betraying the army! You are betraying the nation! You are betraying the Emperor!'

He unsheathed his samurai's sword and threw himself at his chief.

General Nagata did not manage to rise from his armchair and the blade struck him across the neck. Blood gushed out, soaking the papers on the desk which the wounded man knocked over with a violent kick.

A colonel of the military police was in the room and tried to intervene. Aizawa prevented him from moving by slashing at one of his arms and his face. Then he returned to his victim. Nagata seemed to be gravely wounded and scarcely breathing. The assassin jumped in and finished him off with a terrible slash from his bloody weapon. Then he calmly wiped the blade on his victim's clothes, as is recommended by tradition, replaced his sword in its sheath, and left the room. Nor did a single one of the headquarters' secretaries dare to block his way this time, either.

Lieutenant-Colonel Aizawa was glad to have killed an enemy of the Empire, but he never forgave himself for having had to make two attempts. One thought obsessed him! 'For a former fencing instructor, this was shameful.'

Arrested by the police on the day of the murder, Lieutenant-Colonel Aizawa had decided to turn his trial into a veritable 'booby trap' for the conservatives. From being the accused, he became the public prosecutor. He claimed to speak for all the young army. But he denied that there had been any conspiracy and claimed to have acted alone! 'In the name of all my comrades. But without accomplices.'

Both the prosecution and the defence avoided investigating the meetings which Aizawa might have had before his action. There was no question of suggesting a probable interview with General Mazaki, who would thus have been thought to have engineered by remote control his enemy's execution.

The court martial seemed to have decided to list the accused's explanations and to give them all the necessary publicity. The whole court-room appeared to favour the assassin who was setting himself up as a judge, denouncing inefficient politicians and corrupt civil servants.

Aizawa quickly became popular. Thousands of encouraging letters reached the court-room and his lawyer brandished them like trophies. The defence would be simple: 'I admit the gravity of Colonel Aizawa's offence. But I ask the court to take into consideration the absolute sincerity of this great patriot. Never for a single moment did Colonel Aizawa think of himself. He thought only of the supreme good of the Empire.'

The lieutenant-colonel went further than his lawyer: 'His Majesty the Emperor is the living God who reigns over the universe. The aim of existence is to grow up in accordance with the wishes of the God-Emperor. The world today is being destroyed by opposing forces: capitalism, communism, atheism and anarchy!'

The accused benefited not only from the support of the army, but from that of the people. The humble country people loved this sort of talk which reminded them of olden times and heralded new times for them, times of victory. For the Japanese were suffocating in their islands, and needed a continent on which they could escape from poverty and hunger.

For one audience after another, Aizawa painted a terrible picture of the situation and evoked an Empire fallen into the hands of corrupt men, in the first rank of whom he placed military men like Nagata, whose promotion was a symbol of decadence. The colonel spoke with gloomy and poetic exaltation: 'The teaching which I received in youth, which exhorted every man to sacrifice his life for the Emperor, blossomed strongly in me. The shadows vanished from my mind, as when the sun dispels darkness.'

The trial, which had begun in December 1935, was still not finished at the end of February 1936. A principal witness was then called before the court: General Mazaki.

But he immediately adopted a haughty attitude: 'I refuse to answer any questions, no matter what they may be.'

This refusal gave the court the pretext – not unexpected – of adjourning.

Aizawa's trial was not taking place only on the floor of the court. It was reverberating through the barracks and the streets. The 'public prosecutor's' lawyer had warned the judges, and through the military magistrates, the whole country: 'If the court cannot understand Aizawa's thinking there will be a second and a third Aizawa....'

The government had thought to calm the agitation by deciding to transfer the Tokyo division – the most restive and the most politically minded in the army – to Manchuria. Their departure had been set for the beginning of March. But before then there was the 'second Aizawa'. He was Captain Nonaka Shiro.

At four o'clock in the early morning of 26 February 1936, the soldiers of the first division assembled on the barrack square. They were in field-service uniform with knapsacks, canvas tents, and three cartridge pouches. The men in the infantry sections already had fixed bayonets. At their head were only lieutenants and captains.

A colonel rushed on to the scene and spoke to the revolutionaries. Their leader, Captain Nonaka Shiro, greeted him coldly: 'You would render a greater service to the Empire by going home quietly instead of opposing a sacred mission.'

The colonel tried to make himself heard, but the captain did not even listen. Then the senior officer made to strike him: he raised his fist. The captain took a step backwards and drew his regulation Nambu 88 mm revolver:

'I have told you to go home.'

The colonel made a last attempt to resist. He yelled to the soldiers: 'Arrest your captain! He is a mutineer.'

Standing to attention, the soldiers did not move.

The colonel had lost the contest. He had also lost face. He knew the consequences: he went home and committed suicide.

Snow was falling in Tokyo.

Captain Nonaka seemed to be master of the situation. He had under his command 1500 men, that is, a tenth of the Tokyo garrison. Some of them even belonged to the Imperial guard.

The leader of the conspiracy set up his HQ at the Sanno palace. And he sent his companies out all over the capital.

Most of the official buildings were occupied without difficulty: the police headquarters, Parliament and the Ministry of War. But the most important task was to render harmless the adversaries of the young officers' political views. Squads of soldiers climbed into military lorries: each of their officers had been given a precise address: that of a man to kill.

The financier Takahashi was killed by swords and General Watanabe – Mazaki's successor – by revolver shots. Admiral

Saito, Imperial councillor, had just come home from a reception given by the US ambassador when the assassins burst into his flat. His wife tried to block the barrel of one of the submachine-guns with her hand. She was wounded and her husband was killed.

Admiral Suzuki, the Grand Chamberlain, tried to argue with a captain who was in command of a group of assassins. It was a waste of breath. And so the admiral did not insist. 'You have nothing more to say to me? Well then, you have only to use your weapons...'

The officer fired. The admiral, hit by three bullets, collapsed. But by a miracle he survived and was even to become Prime Minister in 1945 at the time of the capitulation of his country.

Prince Saionji, personal councillor to the Emperor, was also on the black list, despite his eighty years. However, forewarned in time, he succeeded in escaping from his country home in Okitsu.

His colleague, Count Makino, Minister of the Imperial Household, and a former negotiator of the Treaty of Versailles, had also been warned. But he was old and could walk only with difficulty. Leaning on his grand-daughter, and escorted by a nurse, he tried, nevertheless, to escape. The road he took ran along a cliff and he stumbled at every step. Suddenly he heard the sound of voices and the clatter of weapons. His assassins were there. He tried to hide, but his pursuers had set fire to his house and the flames lit up the night. He had only the choice between his enemies and the precipice. His granddaughter stood in front of him and spread out her arms to protect him with the rampart of her body. Moved by such heroism in a child, the conspirators withdrew without using their weapons.

The last group of assassins arrived before dawn at the house of the Prime Minister, Okada Keisuke. But the guard greeted them with gunfire. They had foreseen this reaction. Their leader ordered: 'Put the machine-gun into action!'

The automatic weapon riposted swiftly. A hail of bullets shattered the front gate.

'Forward!'

There were only four policemen to protect the Prime Minister. Two were killed at the gate, two others while trying to take refuge in the house.

The Prime Minister had to be found. The conspirators were smashing down the panels in the Western-style door when a man ran out of the apartments, a gun in his hand. The leader of the conspirators shot him down.

The killers bent over the body: they shone electric torches on it.

'It's him! It's the Prime Minister. It's the traitor, Okada Keisuke!'

It was, however, only his brother-in-law, Colonel Matsuo, who looked uncannily like him, and who had voluntarily flung himself at the assassins in order to save his relative. The Prime Minister, Okada, was hiding in a cupboard. Before this night of blood had ended he was already thinking of vengeance.

At dawn, snow was still falling on Tokyo, exactly as it had done during the affair of the forty-seven *ronin*. Large white flakes began to cover the machine-guns, and those manning them, the collars of their greatcoats turned up, their faces drawn by fatigue and sleepiness, brushed the flakes away with the backs of their hands.

The revolutionaries had built barricades and crowds wandered round the soldiers who stood motionless in the snow.

The division of the Imperial guard appeared to be on the whole loyal to the government and had encircled the mutineers without firing a shot. Both sides watched each other.

Captain Nonaka Shiro had just issued a manifesto to explain the insurgents' action. His friend, Captain Ando, had helped him to draw up this text, which began by extolling the Emperor and the divine mission of the Japanese nation. All the 'enemies of the people' were then denounced: the parliamentarians, the capitalists and the bureaucrats. It was they who were distorting the Emperor's intentions and weaving a veil of lies between him and his subjects.

The young captains did not hide their intentions:

'The Imperial duty will not be fulfilled if we do not take proper measures to safeguard our country. We can do so only by killing those who are responsible for the *Showa* Restoration ... Under these conditions, we consider it our duty to eliminate the pernicious influence which surrounds the throne, and to destroy the group of statesmen who hold the Emperor under their influence. It is our sacred duty as subjects of the Emperor.'

The end of the manifesto was an appeal to the tutelary divinities of the Shinto religion.

'May the gods bless us and aid us in our task of saving our glorious country from the disaster which lies in wait.'

The snow continued to fall. Barbed wire had been stretched across the roads. By whom? By loyalists or revolutionaries? The Emperor seemed as walled up in his silence as he was in his palace. From time to time military lorries bristling with armed soldiers passed quickly through the deserted streets. Had the killers finished their work?

The Prime Minister, whom everyone thought to be dead, was beginning to get the situation in hand again.

His house was occupied by the conspirators: they thought that the body over which they were going to keep vigil was definitely that of their worst enemy. Okada gave the order to his servants to have 'his' body laid in state, and to clothe it with the kimono used for funeral rites. Then, with the permission of the guards, he sent invitations to his friends to ask them to come to the funeral. He would profit from the confusion to escape in disguise among the weeping *cortège* which was fol-following 'his' funeral.

Okada soon renewed contact with his friends and the news seemed to him to be fairly reassuring:

'The navy has remained loyal. The first fleet is being concentrated in the Bay of Tokyo.'

'And the army?'

'Only the first division has revolted. The Imperial guard is holding out and troop reinforcements should arrive from the provinces.'

For four long days the troops were to watch each other without firing a shot.

But the government was regaining control. Goto Fumio, Minister of the Interior, took over the functions of Prime Minister, and established himself in the Imperial palace, defended by the guards.

A dialogue began across the barricades.

'In the name of the Emperor, disperse!' said Goto Fumio.

'We alone speak in the name of the Emperor,' replied Captain Nonaka.

Meanwhile, the funeral of the Prime Minister was taking place. Among those who followed the *cortège* was a man in a morning coat and top hat, his face covered by the muslin mask worn by the Japanese to protect themselves during epidemics. This man, who looked like a Japanese version of 'the invisible man', was none other than the Prime Minister himself, Okada Keisuke. He approached 'his' corpse and bowed low before the mortal remains of the brother-in-law whose sacrifice had saved his life.

In the streets the situation was becoming tense, but the storm did not break. The military chiefs refused to order the loyal troops to crush the rebel units. General Kashii, military governor of Tokyo was categorical: 'Soldiers never fire on other soldiers whose only crime is love of the Emperor and the country.'

However, the *Tenno* did not approve of this mutiny which tended to force his hand. He calculated the number of men loyal to him. The navy did not move and even declared itself ready to march against the army. It was a good opportunity for them to settle the quarrel between the two great forces which had smouldered since the beginning of the Meiji revolution.

The army officers were more cautious. Some military leaders met the young rebels. Talks began during the morning of 29 February.

The High Command was afraid of being superseded. It did not give the order to attack the barricades, but began a psychological offensive. By means of leaflets and loud-speakers, General Kashii addressed the mutineers: 'It is not too late to return to your posts. Those who continue to resist will be shot as rebels. Your families will weep because you wish to become traitors.' Entire groups of soldiers began to leave the Sanno hill to give themselves up. Captain Nonaka accepted the consequences of these desertions: he committed suicide. From then on it was a rout. The loyal troops captured the barricades and arrested all those who showed any signs of resistance.

Seventeen officers were shot after a summary trial. Colonel Aizawa was taken before another court. His trial, swiftly and secretly held, ended in a sentence of death, immediately carried out. Sixty-five other conspirators were imprisoned.

General Mazaki himself was arrested. He was to spend eighteen months in a cell, and was then set free without having been tried. For the new Prime Minister, Hirota Koki, shared all the conspirators' ideas. A member of the Kokuikai, the 'Society for the Defence of National Prestige', he had just created another ultra-imperialist association, Dai Kyokai, the 'Society of Great Asia'. And then another general's star began to rise. His ideas did not differ radically from those of the mutineers. But he had been prudent. His name was Tojo Hideki . . . He also wanted to revive the time of the samurai.

The officers – sons, in the main, of poor peasants – were to constitute a new nobility. The army to which they belonged had its roots in the past, but also professed to be the most modern of its time.

And the officers knew that a regiment exists only by virtue of courage, discipline and endurance. They knew also that if their leaders were not the very best, the men would no longer follow them. And so the training of cadets was to be ruthless. Young fanatics would spend ten years to win the honour of becoming officers – the samurai of the twentieth century.

The ordeals undergone at the cadet schools were terrible. At Tsuchiura, the Fleet Air Arm cadets turned themselves into acrobats. They had to be able to stand on their heads for ten minutes, to remain underwater for a hundred seconds, to catch flies in flight, and jump from a car speeding at a hundred kilometres an hour. They had also to be able to locate all the stars in broad daylight.

And then, one morning, with the badge of a second lieutenant fastened to the tightly buttoned collar of their green pea-jackets, they joined their units. Their service began immediately. In winter they were up at 5 a.m., in the darkness of night. In summer, at 4 a.m., before the sun had risen. The day did not end for them before 10 p.m.

During exercises they had to be living examples. Tightly buttoned up in their uniforms, wearing their boots and chin-straps, and with their swords on their belts . . .

Imperturbable, frugal, solitary, they discussed only military matters among themselves. They compared endlessly the precision of their shooting and the speed of their marches. Strange records were set up: 'My company is capable of covering 100 kilometres at an average of eight kilometres an hour.' 'Mine can swim fifty metres in thirty seconds.'

Soldiers and officers shared the same menu: rice and rye mixed together, pickled vegetables, occasionally fish, and meat once a week. They drank tea and despised fat people. They were men of hard muscles, abrupt gestures and few words.

The new samurai wanted to cross deserts and jungles, to lead their men to the ends of the world, but not before bowing, at the head of their units, before the images of the *kami*, protectors of Japanese warriors. Then, after an exhausting march, soldiers and officers, their faces white with dust which made them look like masks in the *kabuki* theatre, would chant the slogan of the Imperial army: 'Duty is heavier than a mountain. Death is lighter than a feather.'

From now on Japan was on the road to war. The only virtues became those taught by the *Bushido*.

The ink with which the diplomats signed, on 25 November 1936, the anti-comintern pact between Imperial Japan and Hitler's Germany took on the colour of blood. Three weeks previously the Rome–Berlin axis had been created.

Then came the time of alliances and betrayals. In China, nationalists and communists united against the Japanese. But already the Japanese were everywhere. An incident was to transform the cold war into hot war. During a night exercise a Japanese company ran into a Chinese unit. It was midnight on the Marco Polo bridge near the village of Lukuchiao. Shots rang out through the darkness. Nobody obeyed the cease fire, not even when dawn broke.

The skirmish developed into an ultimatum. The ultimatum became an invasion. Within forty-eight hours Peking had been taken. Then the Japanese seized Tien-chin and Kalgan, reaching the Great Wall. During the summer of 1937 Shanghai was in the heart of the battle. The Japanese were fighting one against ten, but forced a victory. They even threatened Nanking, whither the Chinese government had fled.

There was someone else, too at the service of those Japanese who were taking up Toyama Mitsuru's old dream of a great Asia. The white-bearded old man who had recently been receiving in Tokyo the leaders of liberation movements – the Chinese, Sun Yat-sen – and the Indian Subash Chandra Bose, inspired all the propaganda which followed the victorious progress of the flag of the Rising Sun.

'We must drive out the Whites!'

Nothing seemed capable of stopping the Japanese now, neither treaties nor guns. On 12 December 1937 their aeroplanes bombed the American gunboat, *Panay*, and the British gunboat *Ladybird*, in the Yangtze. The next day, Nanking fell in its turn. Chiang Kai-shek fled to Han-chou.

The year 1938 was to see the birth of the 'new order' in the Far East. Prince Konoe, the Prime Minister, was at the helm like a real samurai of the sea. He had chosen General Araki as Minister of Education. Two years later he asked General Tojo to become Minister of War...

China had been seized by the throat in the North, in the centre, and in the South. The world put no obstacles in the path of Japan, which decided to create the 'Greater East Asia Co-Prosperity Sphere': China, Manchuria, Mongolia, Indochina, Thailand, Malaysia, Burma, Indonesia, the Philippines, and even India and Australia.

The old 'Tanaka Memorial' was gradually becoming a reality. From the end of 1940 there were no longer any political parties in Japan, but a single movement, the Taiseiyokusan-kai, or 'Association for the Service of the Throne'.

In the autumn of 1941, when their German ally had been attacking Soviet Russia since the first day of summer, General Tojo became President of the Council, Minister of War and Minister of the Interior.

A few weeks later – on 7 December – came the attack on Pearl Harbor.

The overwhelming successes of the Japanese soldiers during the first month of the war could make it seem that the new samurai were invincible. Names such as Bataan, Corregidor, Singapore, Wake Island, Guam, Rangoon, Mandalay, Surabaya, Bandoeng and Guadalcanal rang out like bronze bells exalting the courage and the daring of the Japanese soldiers.

But the Battle of the Coral Sea was indecisive and the Battle of Midway favoured the Americans. For a moment the fate of the war seemed to hesitate. Then there came a turn of the tide. The Japanese were to be even more faithful in defeat to the old spirit of the *Bushido* than they had been in victory.

Soldiers, sailors and pilots went to their deaths singing. They sang of death. Not the death of their enemies, as the French soldiers did. Not even the death of their comrades, as did the German soldiers. No, they sang of their own deaths, their dark eyes riveted on a goal beyond the horizon which had at first seemed awe-inspiring, and had then come to appear ridiculous: the conquest of the world. The words of their death song rang out over all their immense Empire from Korea to Java. The refrain was taken up again ceaselessly, putting rhythm into the fatigues and the battles, from dawn to dusk, from victory to defeat:

> Let my body float on the waters
> Or lie on a hillside.
> I want to die for the Emperor . . .

Volunteers for the Jibaku

THE MIDSUMMER sun of 1944 was shining in the highest part of the sky when some Japanese fighter planes, coming from Yokosuka, landed on the small island of Iwojima in the Marianas archipelago to reinforce the aerial defence there.

The longest day of the year was also, for the Empire of the Rising Sun, one of the hardest: since the previous day, an American Navy squadron had taken the offensive. In an infernal rotation, planes had been taking off from half a dozen aircraft-carriers to hurl themselves on Iwojima. In the torrid heat of June, and under the brutal assault of the United States Air Force, the whole island seemed to be on fire.

Landing in a cloud of red dust, the Japanese fighter planes immediately joined their comrades among the bomber pilots and the torpedo men, who had been under great pressure for several days. The newcomers numbered only about thirty: nevertheless, they were welcomed as saviours.

'On each mission we lose more and more men and planes. Everyone is absolutely at their last gasp.'

From now on the American attacks followed each other without any let-up, pinning the Japanese planes to the earth Before they had even been able to take-off.

After a few days, only eight 'Jill' (Nakajima B 6 N, Tenzan) bombers and nine 'Zero' (Mitsubishi A 6 M 2) fighters were left at Iwojima. In any case, they were nearly all damaged. Anguish followed fatigue.

Commander Nakajima, of the general staff, called together the last pilots and did not hide from them the gravity of the situation. But his ambition was as great as his despair: he wanted to destroy the American fleet, which was cruising more than 800 kilometres south of Iwojima!

'All available planes must take part!' That meant only

seventeen. The odds seemed so great that there could be no hope of return for anyone. Therefore it would be necessary to inflict the greatest possible damage on the enemy before being overpowered.

Commander Nakajima did not hide what was in store for the pilots. 'I have no illusions about what we are asking of you, so it is useless to pretend. You are going to an almost certain death. But the decision has been made. You will carry out this mission. May good luck go with you!'

After these few words the officer drew a sheet of paper from his pocket and read out slowly the names of the pilots chosen for this real suicide-mission. One by one they stood up and went to their quarters to get ready. Some wrote letters to their families, others listened to music, or put their papers in order. In one corner, four officers were calmly playing cards.

All at once an orderly rushed in: 'All pilots report to the command tent!'

Captain Miura Kanzo, chief of the air force at Iwojima, was waiting for them. He seemed deeply moved, but kept very calm.

Climbing on to a small dais, he spoke slowly to all these pilots who stood around him already wearing their flying-suits and leather helmets. The captain looked at them one by one. He could not hide his infinite sadness. He knew that almost all of them must die.

One of the few to survive, Sakai Saburo, would never be able to forget the words of Captain Miura Kanzo:

'You are going to return the enemy's blows. From now on the period of defensive fighting is ended for us. You are the elect of the pilots of the Yokosuka squadron, the most famous in all Japan. I am counting on your conduct today being worthy of the glorious tradition of your unit . . .'

The captain paused for a moment. The pilots watched him with unusual intensity. His words were addressed not only to them but to all Japan at this tragic juncture of the war.

'In order to defend our honour, you must accept the task that your officers have prepared for you. You cannot hope to survive. All your thoughts must be directed towards one single aim: to attack!'

The officer went on, looking at each of the young men, one after the other: 'There are only seventeen of you and today you will face a naval force defended by hundreds, possibly, of American fighter planes. You must therefore eschew individual battles. You must not strike as if you were alone. On the contrary, it is most important that you should remain in close formation, that you manage to get through the enemy fighters, and then . . . all together, you will dive on to the American aircraft-carriers! You will dive with your torpedoes, with your bodies, and with your souls.'

Captain Miura paused for a few moments. Then he explained the new tactics:

'A normal attack would not be any use. Even if you managed to evade the barrage of enemy fighters you would be brought down on your way back and your deaths would have served no purpose. It would have been a wasted sacrifice. We cannot allow it. Before reaching your objectives, no fighter pilot will do battle with the enemy planes. No bomber pilot will release his torpedo in flight. Whatever happens, you will stay together! Wing to wing! No obstacle must deflect you from the accomplishment of your mission. Your nose-dives will be made as a group in order to ensure their effectiveness. I know that what I ask of you is difficult and that it may even seem impossible. But I am certain that you will be able to do it, that you will do it, that each of you will dive directly on to an aircraft-carrier and sink it.'

For the first time, a Japanese officer was sending his men on a suicide attack. A heavy silence hung over the air force headquarters at Iwojima. The air which was circulated by a huge fan seemed leaden. Captain Miura Kanzo ended his short speech with a brief phrase: 'Those are your orders!'

No 'Banzai' was shouted, as was usual, to salute his peroration.

The silence became unbearable. With a gesture of his head the officer indicated that the meeting was ended.

The pilots chosen for the suicide mission walked slowly back to their quarters. Those of their comrades who were to remain grounded joined them and offered them small gifts. Already the seventeen pilots were no longer part of this world and were honoured as heroes.

They took off from Iwojima punctually and their departure caused general emotion. Many officers stood at the edge of the runway to salute those who were going to their deaths.

The formation took the southern route and soon met clouds and sudden showers. Shaken by violent turbulence, the pilots continued their flight towards death, teeth clenched and hands tensely gripping the controls.

More than 100 kilometres from their objective, they were attacked by a host of American fighters. With unbelievable numerical superiority, the 'Hellcats' attacked the 'Zeros' and the 'Jills'.

Single combats took place and many Japanese planes were shot down into the sea : a column of white foam swallowed the plumes of black smoke. The waves closed over the engulfed fuselages. The surviving planes took refuge in a huge cloud. The storm was now very violent. Thunder and lightning followed the attack and the enemy fire.

The ruse succeeded and those who had escaped death found themselves suddenly in a serene sky. But they were only five out of seventeen and they had missed their objective. Rather than fall into the sea for lack of fuel, they decided to return to their base at Iwojima.

The next day their planes were destroyed on the ground by another American bombing raid. The first attempt at a suicide flight had finished in failure. But the Japanese pilots quickly found other means of fighting according to the ancient motto of their ancestors : 'A samurai lives in such a way that he is always ready to die.'

In the heat of a burning summer, the Americans attacked the Mariana Islands. The Japanese fell back.

Vice-Admiral Kakuda died leading his men. He was in command of the first naval air squadron, the spearhead of the Japanese fleet.

Admiral Teraoka succeeded him. A goatee beard below a rather plump face, a physiognomy which would have looked flabby, had it not been for his animated expression.

The new chief set up his HQ at Davao, on Mindanao, the southernmost island of the Philippines. He landed on 12 August and the first conference of the general staff revealed to him the extent of the disaster.

'How many aircraft do we have?'

'Barely three hundred.'

Not only were most of the Japanese planes badly damaged, but they were almost all outclassed by the Americans. Admiral Teraoka knew very well that for nearly a year the famous 'Zero' fighter plane had not been able to match the Brunman F 6 F.

Every day brought new difficulties. 'Admiral, we've no spare parts . . . Admiral, our ammunition stocks are very low.' Worse still, the air fleet was in danger of running out of fuel though it had already been reduced by half as a result of the systematic bombardment of all its bases. Soon Teraoka would have only 100 aircraft, at a time when the American attack on the Philippines seemed imminent.

If these last Japanese planes were not able to put the enemy ships out of action, the 'bolt' of the archipelago would give way. Losing the Philippines would not be just losing a battle, it would be losing the war. All the pilots knew this. For them it was no longer a question of risking their lives, but of giving them. The only problem was how to die a useful death.

In Japan the living are not decorated, but the dead are automatically promoted to a superior rank. Lieutenant-Commander Kanno Naoshi wrote on a wooden box containing his personal effects: 'Property of the late Commander Kanno.' He was thus giving himself the rank which could be his only after his death.

Kanno, like all his comrades, was looking for the most

spectacular exit. One summer's day he attacked alone with his fighter plane an enormous American bomber. Kanno quickly realised that he could not shoot it down, either with his machine-guns or his cannon. So he decided to bring it down . . . by colliding with it. Coolly he gained height on the enemy and then dived in the direction of the tail-unit. Twice he missed his target. At the third attempt he struck the American plane, tore off its rudder, and succeeded in making it drop like a stone. But he had torn a wing off his own plane and went into a spinning dive. He succeeded in righting the plane as he approached the ground and even in landing successfully. Death had not yet called the 'late' Commander Kanno, who was to be killed in aerial combat only two months before the end of the war.

On 15 October 1944 the Americans appeared to the east of the island of Luzon.

With great difficulty the chief of the Japanese Fleet Air Arm had succeeded in camouflaging a few planes and in keeping them in reserve for the day of sacrifice.

The order was a simple one. All the pilots had been waiting for it for weeks:

'Scramble!'

But what a pitiful force to face the American armada: thirteen bombers and sixteen escorting planes, inadequately supported by seventy fighters.

One of the Japanese squadrons, the twenty-sixth, was under the command of Rear-Admiral Arima Masabumi. He was still a young man, slim and upright, with a short moustache and a broad forehead. He was known to be fired by fierce patriotism and pure mysticism. He re-read endlessly the same book dating from the time of the samurai: *'The Seven Stages along the Path of the Warrior'*, and explained to his aides-de-camp: 'This book, of which the cover and the first pages are missing, was my grandfather's course in tactics.'

For several days, Admiral Arima had seemed to pray to an

idée fixe. He had left his home in Manila where he had his official residence in order to share completely in the frugal life of his crews. He was only one pilot among the rest. He did not even wear badges of his rank and had scratched out with a penknife the word 'Admiral' on his binoculars. He slept on a simple mat and ate cold food. But he wore a strange expression of burning intensity. He knew that there was now only one way of stopping the American advance. He announced to his officers: 'It is not enough to perfect new methods, like this system of ricochet bombing. We now have to go farther.'

'How can we go farther, Admiral? If not by placing bombs by hand?'

Arima Masabumi did not answer. But he himself took over the controls of the first of his 'Suisei' (Yokosuka D 4 Y) medium bombers which took off to intercept the enemy.

The enemy was nearly four hundred kilometres from Manila. The American aircraft-carriers were protected by innumerable fighter planes, whose wings seemed like a steel rampart. And the guns of the anti-aircraft defences formed a curtain of flames. But Admiral Arima had decided to cross all these barrages. His bomber defied the bullets and the shells. He forced his way through the double defence and flew on towards the American ships.

The eyes of all the Japanese pilots were riveted on the admiral's plane which nothing seemed to stop. But what was it doing? It was diving on an aircraft-carrier without firing its torpedo. Now it was too late. Amid the roar of his engines, Arima Masabumi threw himself on the enemy ship. He crashed on the bridge in an immense cone of flames. His torpedo exploded on the great ship. The American aircraft-carrier *Franklin* was mortally wounded. It was 15.30 hrs on 16 October 1944.

The survivors of the suicide attack were to tell their fellow-pilots about the incident for a long time afterwards: 'Then the admiral threw himself right on to the aircfaft-carrier. He dropped like a stone. Or, rather, like a torpedo. He wasn't a man, he was a bomb.' Rear-Admiral Arima Masabumi had accomplished the ancient *seppuku* in its most modern form: the *jibaku* by diving on the enemy.

The death of this authentic samurai was doubly significant. It initiated a method of attack which was formidably effective. It also proved that now the Japanese had a secret weapon to set against the enemy's material superiority. This weapon consisted not only of steel and gunpowder, but also of flesh and blood. The secret weapon was the pilot himself.

Vice Admiral Onishi Takijiro was not noticeable for a particularly martial bearing. With a round, somewhat fleshy, face, he occupied a position which did not demand extraordinarily warlike qualities. In the autumn of 1944, while the war was raging in the Philippines, he was directing the manufacture of aeronautical equipment for the Ministry of Industrial Production. He had only one obsession: to build more and more planes. Aviation was his whole life.

When one knew him better, one saw the leader in him: even harder on himself than on others, his courage bordered on foolhardiness. His friends knew that he was the first Japanese military man to become a skilled parachutist. They remembered, too, his role in the attack on Pearl Harbor under the orders of Admiral Yamamoto.

More than anyone else, he knew that American superiority in that auumn of 1944 was irreversible. Never would he be able to produce enough planes to keep them out of the skies. But Admiral Onishi was not the sort of man to despair. 'Since ordinary means will not allow us to conquer, we must employ special means.'

Eventually he grasped quickly that only one counter-stroke was possible: that suggested by Captain Jo Eiichiro.

This officer had written to his superiors at supreme headquarters after the heavy fighting of summer 1944:

'There is now no hope of destroying the enemy aircraft-carriers which are too superior in numbers. I ask you, therefore, to form immediately a special air corps whose pilots will hurl themselves directly on to the enemy ships, and to place me in command.'

Before his request was granted, he was to be killed on the bridge of the aircraft-carrier *Chiyoda,* sunk on 25 October. His report had not, however, been lost and Admiral Onishi had re-read it so often that he knew it by heart. But what could he do in an office in Tokyo?

Fate, however, was awaiting such a man because on 9 October 1944, he learned that he had been appointed Commander-in-Chief of the South-West Fleet. He it was who was to face the attack on the Philippines. It took him a week to reach Manila: the skies became more American every day. The Japanese planes based on Formosa were henceforward outclassed.

Admiral Teraoka, from whom he was to take over, said in greeting him at the aerodrome: 'You are as welcome as rain in the desert.'

The interview between the two men took place in an atmosphere of politeness deriving from the warrior tradition of earlier times. 'I beg your forgiveness for leaving you so few planes fit to fly.'

'Thank you for all the trouble you have taken in such difficult circumstances.'

A silence which seemed endless: then Admiral Onishi blurted out: 'I intend to carry on as you have done: to do my best.'

Later, in the office of the naval commander in Manila, the two admirals could not hold back their tears. The scene unfolded without witnesses and their emotion was intense. The two men clasped each other's hands for a long time.

Left alone, Onishi decided to put his plan into action immediately: he was going to create a special flight of volunteers who would fight and die as Captain Jo had envisaged and as Admiral Arima had done a few days previously in throwing himself on the enemy in that death leap which is called *jibaku.*

The American ships, countless as the stars, were sailing

towards the Philippines. All the Japanese reconnaissance planes were sending alarmist messages.

'They're coming!'

It was the invasion. The island of Suluan had been taken. Now Leyte was being threatened.

On 19 October Admiral Onishi Takijiro, accompanied by one aide-de-camp, went to the air force camp at Malabacat, some hundred kilometres from Manila. The day was well advanced and no message had announced this official visit. The setting sun was lighting up the airstrip with its last rays.

The Admiral said to the duty officers who rushed to meet him: 'I want to go to the headquarters of 201 squadron.'

This HQ consisted of a tattered tent where Commander Tamai Asaichi, second-in-command, was preparing operations for the following day. But he had only about thirty planes left.

Without a word the admiral sat down, and waited in silence. Then he let it be understood that he had come about a 'very special' matter. He proposed, in an unusual tone of voice: 'Might we go to the unit's quarters, I want to talk with the officers and ask their opinion.'

The meeting was to take place on the first floor of one of the green-shuttered houses in the town of Malabacat which had been requisitioned by the air force. The admiral sat down at a simple wooden table. The folding beds which the crews used had been stacked against a wall. Night was falling and it was growing cooler, but the mosquitoes and other insects were unrelenting. The air was still humid and even linen clothes clung to the skin.

Half a dozen officers surrounded the new chief of the air fleet in the Philippines: Captain Tamai Asaichi, temporary commander of 201 squadron, Lieutenant-Commanders Yokoyama and Ibusuki, flight leaders, and two or three general staff officers, among whom was Inoguchi Rikihei.

The announcement which Admiral Onishi wanted to make was quite short. He reminded the officers of the manoeuvre of the great Japanese naval squadron, 'You all know that if the *Shô-gô* plan fails the military situation could become very serious. It is essential that all the forces of the first air fleet should ensure the success of Admiral Kurita's manoeuvre by protecting him during his advance.'

Certainly the mission seemed cut and dried. But how were they to make it succeed? The admiral knew better than anyone.

'Unfortunately, we are outclassed in aerial warfare. However, there is still a last possibility: we could prevent the American planes from taking off from their aircraft-carriers even if it were only for a week.'

He waited for this idea to be accepted. Clearly he would have preferred the proposal which he was about to put to them to have come from the pilots themselves. Finally, Admiral Onishi announced, letting his words sink in, with all their mad grandeur:

'I am convinced that the only way we can do this is to load 250-kilo bombs on to our fighter planes, which will then crash deliberately on the targets. What is your opinion?'

His audience seemed petrified by his words. They felt at one and the same time both an uneasy joy and a dull fear. The first to break the silence was the young second-in-command of 201 squadron, Tamai Asaichi: 'What can a fighter plane do, even if it is carrying a bomb, if it crashes on an aircraft-carrier?'

It was a general staff officer named Yoshioki who answered him: 'It would certainly not sink it, but it could put it out of action for several days, perhaps even for several weeks.'

Tamai bowed. Then he made an odd request. 'I am only Captain Nakajima Tadashi's substitute and before I give you an answer I should like to talk alone with my subordinates.'

'As you wish,' sighed Admiral Onishi. 'We will wait for you.'

The officers of 201 squadron left the room for a few moments to go to Tamai's quarters. No one made any comment on their departure: they could not order men to commit suicide. Whatever their answer might be, no one would hold it against them.

Finally, the officers of 201 squadron came back to the conference room. Captain Tamai Asaichi bowed slowly before his chiefs and then, standing to attention, he announced in a jerky voice, sometimes husky with emotion:

'My officers and I have decided to accept the admiral's plan. Moreover, we ask you to entrust to 201 squadron the honour of organising this special assault unit.'

Admiral Onishi looked as if he were waking from a dream. He uttered only one word: 'Right.'

Witnesses of the strange scene have never forgotten the expression on his face: they detected in it as much satisfaction as there was sadness.

This incredible decision had still to be announced to the men of the squadron. Tamai decided first to choose those whom he thought the best. These were the men of the ninth term, whom he himself had trained. He decided to call them together in the middle of the night.

They were summoned by an orderly to the villa in Malabacat where the conference had been held. There were twenty-three of them, all very young, and all good pilots, all good patriots, tempered like sword-blades. For three days they had been talking among themselves of nothing but the action of Rear-Admiral Arima. A legend was being born and they felt that henceforward nothing in the Japanese Fleet Air Arm would be exactly the same as before.

Captain Tamai glanced at them to assure himself that all of them were there, and then he repeated to them in a few short sentences the analysis of the situation which Admiral Onishi had just made. Then, very quickly he came to the conclusions.

The idea of the *jibaku,* the death leap, seemed to arouse the young pilots' enthusiasm. Their eyes shone, in the room which was lit only by a naked bulb trembling at the end of a wire. Tamai added: 'Naturally, I asked that the honour of the first mission should fall to our squadron. And I have chosen you to be the first to go.'

There was not a single cry of anger or surprise. All the pilots simply lifted both their arms as a sign of approval.

Immediately after this extraordinary meeting, Captain Tamai Asaichi met the deputy chief of the general staff of the first air fleet, Inoguchi Rikihei.

'Well, I have just told my former pupils. They have all accepted . . . They have dead comrades to avenge.'

He paused for a few moments, and then added very slowly:

'There are twenty-three of them. Each of them was thinking that the time had come to get his own back. They have themselves well under control and the hot and adventurous blood of youth flows in their veins.'

'They are fine young men,' admitted Inoguchi, 'the best of our race. We shall need many like them.'

'We shall find them, thanks to this example. Courage is always infectious.'

Then they went on to practical details.

'Have you a leader to command them?'

'The best person would, I think, be Lieutenant-Commander Seki Yukio, a former bomber captain who has become a fighter pilot.'

'Would he volunteer?'

'He would not think of anything else.'

So the two officers decided to inform, that very night, the man whom they had chosen for this terrible mission.

The young officer was hastily awakened by an orderly and told what was expected of him. Lieutenant-Commander Seki did not reply immediately. His lips tightened and the muscles of his jaws moved. Then he hid his head in his hands as if the better to conceal his expression. Time seemed to stand still: seconds became hours.

At last Seki Yukio smoothed back his hair. He looked at the two officers as if he had just woken up. He had only been saying farewell to life. Then he murmured: 'I believe you can entrust this mission to me.'

Outside, in the Philippines sky, the moon came out from behind the clouds and illuminated the town of Malabacat with an unearthly light. The palm-trees trembled in the warm night breeze.

The Kamikaze of the Philippines

AT THE end of the night of 19–20 October 1944, Captain Inoguchi Rikihei was to announce to Admiral Onishi the results of his conversations with the officers of 201 squadron.

Lying on a simple camp bed, the chief of the Philippines Air Force was not asleep. He switched on the light immediately and strode up and down. Then he asked Inoguchi: 'Have you found our pilots?'

'Certainly! I've also found their leader, Lieutenant-Commander Seki, a former pupil of the Naval School. And I have at last found a name for this new formation.'

Inoguchi, after taking a deep breath, said very quickly, in a ringing voice: 'Admiral, may I ask you very respectfully to baptise the special assault formation the *Kamikaze* Corps?'

Onishi Takijiro replied immediately: '*Kamikaze*: the divine wind! One couldn't think of a finer symbol for these young heroes.'

The two officers of the Fleet Air Arm had the same thought: 'In those days...'

History seemed to them a never-ending 'now'. A simple name, and the centuries fell away. Each of the pilots who was going to join this suicide unit revived the legend, which was soon to seem more real than history.

All Kublai's fleet destroyed within sight of the Japanese coasts... Three thousand ships sinking... A typhoon. Certainly! But who caused the storms to blow up, who wrecked the hulls, who tore the sails? Who, if not Amaterasu, the protective goddess of the Empire of the Rising Sun? That raging wind, which whipped up the sea as faith moves mountains, and which had saved Japan twice already, in 1274 and 1281, was a Divine Wind. It would always keep its name which rang out like a hope and a challenge: *Kamikaze!* Could history repeat itself? That night in the Philippines everyone believed in the miracle.

Admiral Onishi was not only an admirable leader, he was a great scholar. Since Captain Inoguchi had chosen the name of the suicide squadron, he would choose the names of the four flights which formed the first unit of the 'special assault corps'. He drew his inspiration from an eighteenth-century poem by Motoori Norinaga which he loved to recite in a voice full of conviction:

> *Shikishima no Yamato-gokoro o hito towaba*
> *Asahi ni nioo Yamazakura kana.*

The faithful translation is the following: 'If you are asked what is the spirit of eternal Japan, answer thus: it is pure, clear, and deliciously scented, like the cherry-blossom in the first rays of the morning sun.'

And each of the flights was given a name taken from this poem: *Shikishima, Yamato, Asahi, Yamazakura.*

Admiral Onishi, without even waiting for the dawn, drew up by starlight the order for the establishment of the *kamikaze* corps and laid down its combat mission: 'To destroy or at least damage any enemy ships which show themselves in the Pacific.'

The day after this historic night, Admiral Onishi wanted to pay homage himself to the pilots of 201 squadron who had volunteered for the first official suicide mission. There were barely twenty men and they were barely twenty years of age. And yet on this day, 20 October 1944, it seemed as if all the weight of the Empire of the Rising Sun was resting on their shoulders.

Standing at attention at the foot of a cliff which overlooked the airfield, they watched intently as their commander got out of his car with its yellow flag and walked towards them, one hand on the peak of his cap. He walked slowly past the pilots of the four *kamikaze* flights.

The murmuring of the river Banban which flowed past not far from the airfield could be heard. Ears of corn were trembling on its banks. Then the admiral's words rose above the murmuring of the fresh water over the polished pebbles of the watercourse.

'Japan is in danger! Who can save her? The chief of general staff? the admirals? I, myself? No! You know very well that we can escape from this impasse only by the courage of young men like yourselves, brave and pure as children. That is why I am speaking to you in the name of a hundred million Japanese who are putting their fates in your hands, and asking you to make this sacrifice. I pray for your success.'

Not one of the pilots moved. They were like statues. From time to time a flimsy white silk scarf round one of the volunteers' necks fluttered in the light breeze. Lieutenant-Commander Seki stood on the right of his men.

The Admiral had begun his speech in the tone of a leader. Now he finished it, speaking as a father:

'In the eyes of history you are already gods. And, like them, you have forgotten all our poor human desires. You should have the right to know if your sacrifice will have been useful. Alas! My voice will not be able to reach you in your eternal sleep, but I swear to you that we shall do everything to make your actions worth while.'

Admiral Onishi, near to tears, announced with an especially solemn air: 'The Emperor will be informed of your exploits!'

Then, without trying to restrain his emotion, he ended: 'I ask you to do your best.'

The autumn sunshine struck golden reflections on the leather helmets of the young heroes who were going to their deaths. Yes, they were more like gods than men.

Captain Nakajima Tadashi, injured the previous day during an emergency landing, had insisted on taking his place again at the head of 201 squadron. He had completely approved of the decision which had been taken by his second-in-command,

Captain Tamai Asaichi, and had simply said to him, when he returned to Malabacat: 'I would have done the same myself.' Now he was the chief again and gave his orders at the end of the ceremony: 'The *kamikaze* squadron *Yamato* will be based on the island of Cebu.'

Yamato consisted of four suicide-attack aeroplanes and four escort planes, all of the 'Zero' type. Captain Nakajima said specifically: 'I myself will take command of the escort.'

The eight planes took off immediately, to land on Cebu an hour later.

Everyone at the base was talking about the American landing at Leyte. The Battle of the Philippines was beginning. Nakajima Tadashi assembled all the personnel together and told them the broad outlines of the *Shô* plan.

'The Imperial fleet will attack and repulse the enemy. The only danger for our battleships is aeroplanes. Our duty is simple: we have to destroy the American aircraft-carriers.'

The moment had come to announce the great news which nobody, except the four pilots who were going to their deaths, yet knew.

'Admiral Onishi decided this evening on the creation of a special *kamikaze* assault corps...'

In a few simple phrases 201 squadron's commanding officer explained the fatal tactics of the *jibaku*. Everyone had already thought about this and nobody among the men lined up on the Cebu airfield seemed surprised.

The officer continued: 'We shall need new pilots very soon after the death of your four comrades of the *Yamato* flight. So I am going to have forms distributed. Petty officers who wish to volunteer will be able to fill in their names and ranks. The senior petty officer will hand them in to me tonight.'

The captain concluded: 'The *kamikaze* attacks will begin tomorrow.'

And then there was silence in the twilight.

Nobody said a word as Commander Nakajima Tadashi

returned to the operations room where he had set up his camp bed. He had barely sat down at the large table covered with maps when there was a knock at the door. It was one of his best officers, Sub-Lieutenant Kuno. He saluted, clicking his heels, then bowed, remaining silent.

'What do you want, Kuno?'

'You can guess, sir. I'd like to join the *kamikaze* corps.'

'The "Zero" which I was flying is intended for you. The bomb-rack is already installed.'

A smile spread across the young samurai's face. He saluted his chief and went out without a word. Then Sub-Lieutenant Kuno went to the hall on the ground floor, sat down at an old piano, and played for a great part of the night.

Captain Nakajima was to have other visits. Sub-Lieutenant Kunihara Hisato came in, his face contorted with rage.

'Why did you ask only the petty officers if they would volunteer? What about us, the officers?'

'You don't want to volunteer for the *kamikaze* corps?'

'Yes, we all want to, without exception.'

The commanding officer managed to make a joke of it, despite his emotion. 'I knew it. So there was no need for me to ask you.'

And Sub-Lieutenant Kunihara smiled exactly as his comrade Kuno had done.

A senior petty officer of the Fleet Air Arm came in afterwards, bringing the commanding officer a packet of envelopes: the replies from the petty officers. There were only two blank forms out of twenty. The only men who were not volunteering to die were confined to bed and forbidden to fly . . .

It only remained now to find targets worthy of these volunteers.

The following day in the early afternoon the first target seemed to have been sighted. Reconnaissance planes had just sent a message: 'Six American aircraft-carriers and their convoy. Sixty miles east of Suluan.'

Captain Nakajima gave the order so long awaited: 'To the planes!'

The pilots were resting under the mango-trees at the edge of the tarmac. They were astonishingly calm. Most of them were dozing, despite the songs which were coming from an old wind-up gramophone. They all sprang to their feet.

The mechanics installed the bombs and filled the tanks with petrol while the pilots assembled in the map room. But already American aeroplanes were to be seen above Cebu. For an hour they machine-gunned and bombed. When they left there remained only smoking fuselages: three assault 'Zeros' and two escort planes had been destroyed before the first *kamikaze* mission was airborne.

Captain Nakajima merely ordered. 'Get the reserve planes ready.'

There were only three left. The pilots climbed in amid explosions and clouds of smoke. They wanted their revenge as quickly as possible.

Sub-Lieutenant Kuno was in command. Before setting off at the head of the tiny formation he said to his chief: 'If I don't find the aircraft-carriers, I shall go to Leyte. There's no lack of targets. In any case, I shall not come back. I have offered my life to His Majesty the Emperor.' He waved his hand one last time.

The three aeroplanes disappeared. A storm was raging and no one could see his target. However, faithful to his promise, Sub-Lieutenant Kuno never returned to his base on Cebu.

The first suicide attack of the *Yamato kamikaze* flight had ended in failure.

Bad weather followed bad luck. The tornadoes seemed endless, a thick fog rose from the earth and from the sea, black clouds hung over the mountains of the Philippines. The American aircraft-carriers profited from an extraordinary natural camouflage. The wind and the rain were siding against the Japanese.

However, it was absolutely essential to help the fleet: the *Shô* plan seemed to everyone to be the last chance for the Empire of the Rising Sun. The volunteers could not face the idea of not having the chance to die.

At last, on the evening of 24 October, after five days spent waiting, a message reached Malabacat where the *Shikishima kamikaze* flight was based. American ships had been sighted.

Trainee pilot Uemura Masahisa, after making representations for three days and nights, had been allowed to become a volunteer. He leapt towards his 'Zero', but his chief stopped him:

'Sorry! You aren't a good enough pilot for a night mission.'

'Oh, well – it can't be helped, I suppose. But please keep my turn for me.'

Trainee pilot Shiyoda Hiroshi took his place. Captain Inoguchi, who was present at the time, remarked that his eyes were shining 'like those of a kite which has just spotted its prey'.

However, the fighters returned again with an empty bag.

They had to wait until the next day. A final night in the volunteers' camp of simple huts at the foot of the cliff, away from the others, far from those who were going to live. . . .

On 25 October, shortly after 7 a.m., the *Shikishima kamikaze* flight took off. At its head was Lieutenant-Commander Seki Yukio, commander of the first special assault corps.

Before their departure the pilots who were about to die had sung once again the Naval School song:

> If I go to sea,
> My body will float, tossed on the waves.
> If duty calls me to the mountains,
> My shroud will be made of moss.
> Thus, I shall die for the Emperor,
> Far from the peace of my home!

Some of them, as they climbed into their planes, took with them their samurai swords. All of them wrapped the Imperial flag, with its sun as red as fresh blood, round their foreheads.

Lieutenant-Commander Seki Yukio adjusted his leather helmet and lowered his goggles over his eyes. Then suddenly he seemed to change his mind. He made a gesture to his friend, Captain Tamai, who had gone with him to his plane. The din of the propellers drowned their voices. Seki handed his comrade a small packet and succeeded in shouting above the sound of the planes, which were shuddering before take-off, 'For my wife...'

The *Shikishima* flight took off.

There were ten planes flying towards the enemy: five suicide-planes and five escorts.

They were flying due south, lit up by the first rays of the sun which made the metal of the fuselages and the glass of the cockpits sparkle.

A red sun glowed on their flanks.

At 10.40 hrs, ninety miles from Tacloban, they spotted the enemy fleet. This was to be the first of the *kamikaze* battles.

Seki announced: 'Four aircraft-carriers and six cruisers. We are attacking!'

They nose-dived. From an altitude of 1500 metres the target looked minute. Lieutenant-Commander Seki knew that he must set an example. He settled himself comfortably in his seat and looked intently through his sighting instrument at a specific point on one of the aircraft-carriers. He nose-dived with all the strength of his engines and of his own will. He did not want to think about anything except this enemy ship which was growing larger every second and which he must not miss – not for anything in the world.

He was the leader and must set the example. He felt against his thigh the hilt of his samurai sword. Seconds seemed like centuries. He nose-dived. At that moment he himself was the whole of Japan. He had become both a torpedo and a nation.

The wind distorted his face and his skin suddenly looked as smooth as a theatre mask, his cheekbones stood out, he peered through thin, precise slits – like lines drawn by a paintbrush.

The target was growing larger. Now Seki could distinguish enemy sailors running on the bridge. He wanted to shriek like one sometimes did in a fencing bout, when one wanted to terrorise an adversary even before the clash of steel blades.

Shells and bullets outlined his plane like rays of sunlight.

For a fraction of a second, the *kamikaze* was able to see the whites of the eyes of the commanding officer of the aircraft-carrier. He felt as if he were fighting an ancient heroic duel with him : he was going to kill a man and hundreds of others with him.

The 'Zero', piloted according to instructions, crashed at the precise spot chosen by Lieutenant-Commander Seki Yukio, first leader of the *kamikaze*.

It was a terrible collision. Fire spread to the aircraft hangars and the torpedo bay. The aircraft-carrier shuddered and then exploded. It was doomed. Everything was on fire. On the blazing bridge it was impossible to distinguish between the debris of the Japanese 'Zero' and the fuselages of the American planes. Less than an hour after the *jibaku*, the aircraft-carrier *Saint-Lo* sank in Pacific waters.

The four other pilots had imitated their leader's action. One of them followed him and crashed on the same ship. A third sank a cruiser and a fourth set fire to an aircraft-carrier. The fifth pilot of the *Shikishima* flight was shot down before reaching his target. Two of the escort planes were also reported missing.

Wounded, covered with blood and drunk with victory, chief Petty Officer Nishizawa Hiroyoshi led the two survivors back to the base on Cebu. As soon as his aeroplane had touched down, the petty officer rushed to headquarters and reported the battle. All the pilots surrounded him.

Captain Nakajima summed up the brief account : 'Lieutenant-Commander Seki and his comrades died as heroes.' Then, immediately he sent to general headquarters in Manila the first *communiqué* reporting the victory of a *kamikaze* flight.

At the Malabacat airport Captain Tamai found in the

pocket of his pea-jacket the small white packet which his friend had given him. Shortly afterwards he would send it to Seki Yukio's wife. It contained just a lock of the dead man's hair. He felt it, light and fragile in his hand, like a final presence and a last good-bye.

'They have succeeded!'

The first of the *kamikaze* successes provoked a veritable explosion of joy. Suddenly it seemed that Japan's tragic destiny could still be averted. For several hours of the night following this exploit, the pilots of the *Yamato* flight, based on Cebu, studied maps. Now the enemy fleet had been spotted and damaged. Laughing, they thought to themselves that they would be able to finish it off.

Dawn found them tired, but impatient. They had to wait until the end of the morning before they could take off, armed with fresh information. The first group consisted of two attacking planes and one single escort plane. The second, which left shortly after midday, comprised two escort planes and three *kamikaze*.

Uemura Masahisa, the man whom his chief had judged to be too poor a pilot to fly on a night mission, had at last been allowed to participate in a suicide attack. He taxied out along the tarmac, and very swiftly the island of Cebu vanished beneath his wings.

At last he had been considered worthy to die. He was the least skilful member of the flight. He was to prove the most courageous. This former captain of the football team at the University of St Paul in Tokyo saw his comrades again in his mind's eye. But already they were vanishing into the past. The last picture he saw thus of civilian life and of peace-time was not even of his parents or his wife; it was of his daughter.

Motoko was four months old and he hardly knew her. He had written her a letter which she would read frequently later on:

'When you are grown up, you will ask Mummy and your

aunties to tell you about me. It was I who chose your name, so that you should be a nice, good little girl. When you want to see your daddy, you will have to come to the temple of Kudan. Then you will see me at the bottom of your heart. You will be the apple of your grandparents' eye and I am sure you will not suffer because of my absence. I have kept with me in the plane the doll I bought for you when you were born. So you will be with me until the end.'

Uemura looked at this little doll which was trembling with the vibration of the plane. How far removed it seemed from this war and from the tragedy towards which he was rushing! In less than three-quarters of an hour he would have found his target. He remembered the telephone call he had made just before he took off. He had succeeded in getting through to his mother and his wife. He had wanted to hear his daughter . . . But Motoko had refused to cry or to shout. So his wife gave the baby her breast, and then withdrew it from her suddenly. The child began to cry immediately and, very moved, her father murmured: 'Is that Motoko? Be good, don't cry . . .'

Nobody was to cry today. Death must be approached dry-eyed. He must watch the sixty American fighter planes which were protecting the fleet.

Uemura succeeded in crossing the barrage and he crashed on an aircraft-carrier. His plane exploded in a sheaf of flames. Nobody saw Motoko's little doll amid the molten sheet metal.

The five *kamikaze* of the *Yamato* flight were dead, but two of them had succeeded in the *jibaku* and each of them had put one aircraft-carrier out of action.

In his office in Manila, Admiral Onishi re-read the reports of the operation. The tactics which he had advocated were monstrous, but this was the only way of ensuring the success of the *Shô* plan and of reversing the situation. He knew that he would bear a terrible burden of guilt in history and he wondered how he should interpret the Emperor's own words. The chief of general staff had insisted on telling him, in a telegram sent from the Imperial palace at the time of the first expedition, of the sovereign's reaction.

'His Majesty has asked if we really need to do this. He says that, in any case, these young men are heroes.'

Had they really needed to do this? Admiral Onishi was convinced that it had been necessary, even though he was more grieved than anyone else to see the best pilots of the Fleet Air Arm going to their deaths. But what the volunteers of 201 squadron had accomplished had been the only possible counter-attack. Admiral Onishi was so convinced of this that he tried to win over to his point of view Admiral Fukudome, who had just arrived in the Philippines with the second naval air fleet and its 350 aeroplanes.

'The first fleet has only fifty aircraft now. There is no way of continuing the struggle except by special attacks.'

'I do not share your opinion. Conventional attacks in close formation can succeed.'

But Fukudome was to lose his planes and his pilots while achieving only paltry results. The father of the *kamikaze* would not have much trouble in persuading him. 'Your pilots are dead just the same, and have died for nothing.'

At two in the morning, Admiral Fukudome yielded to Admiral Onishi's arguments. He asked 701 squadron under the command of Kisa Tatsuhiro to supply four *kamikaze* flights. 'We will call them *Junchu, Seichu, Chuyu* and *Giretsu*.'

The Inspector-General of the Imperial Air Forces wrote an order of the day for all the *kamikaze*. It was a text the like of which no previous commander had ever written. The young candidates for voluntary death learned every sentence of it by heart, like recruits in all the armies of the world learn the Army regulations concerning their everyday life:

'The Empire is at a cross-roads between victory and defeat. The first suicide unit, resolved to win victory by its spiritual power, will sweep along by its example all the units following it. There is absolutely no question of your coming back alive. Your mission is certain death. You will die physically, but your spirits will live on. The death of one of you will mean the birth of a million others. Do not allow any carelessness to affect your training or your health. You must not leave behind you any cause for regret which would follow you into eternity. One more word : do not be over-hasty in your desire to die. If you do not find the proper target, turn back : the next time you will have better luck. Choose a death which will bring the best results !'

The newcomers seemed determined to show themselves worthy of their predecessors. They immediately imitated their behaviour, that strange mixture of courage and imperturbability.

Lieutenant-Commander Fukabori Naoji had been appointed to lead the *Junchu* flight. He set out the same day on his suicide mission to attack the American aircraft-carriers in the waters off Leyte. But instead of diving on the enemy, he turned back and landed on the airstrip on Cebu. Was he to be the first coward?

As he got out of his plane he said simply : 'I should like to see the commanding officer.'

Captain Nakajima received him immediately and the young officer said : 'The fuse of my bomb has stuck. My sacrifice would not have done any good. I request permission to do repairs on your airstrip.'

A few moments later he took off again.

There was the sound of an engine, an aeroplane which was circling over the Cebu runway, and the approach lights were lit on the airstrip. Lieutenant-Commander Fukabori had come back.

'Well ?' asked Captain Nakajima.

'It was too dark, Captain.'

He spoke calmly. But the officer thought : 'He has come from the cemetery to return there again tomorrow.'

The new arrival asked : 'Will you allow me to spend the night here ? I'll set off again at dawn.'

'Would you not prefer to go back to your base tomorrow and wait for another mission ?'

'You may be right, Captain. But my comrades attacked today. They are dead. My place is with them.'

The next morning the *kamikaze* set out alone for his destiny. He left a letter addressed to his superior officers. After making various technical points he ended: 'Please tell my comrades not to be in too much of a hurry, and to reflect calmly in order to crash in the right place. One usually tends to get impatient and so to risk missing the target.'

His report ended with a postscript paying homage to the comrades who had died before him: 'The pilots, despite their youth, behaved admirably, and the memory of their conduct is engraved on my memory. You have no need at all to worry about the recruitment of *kamikaze* pilots. Farewell, good health and good luck!'

No one ever heard anything more of Lieutenant-Commander Fukabori.

Less than a week after the *kamikaze* corps was established, Captain Inoguchi Rikihei was appointed director of training of the special corps. In an atmosphere of enthusiasm and sacrifice, he found himself at the very heart of what he called 'the Garden of War'.

Every time he met a young volunteer he could not help thinking of the words of an old Japanese poet: 'Sooner or later you will be carried away by the terrible gusts of the storm which is sweeping Japan.'

Often he met young lieutenants who had been his pupils at the Naval Academy. One of them was his own nephew who substituted simply 'Uncle' for the traditional 'Captain'. The boy asked him immediately after reporting at the Manila headquarters: 'Have you any news of my father?'

'I believe he died at his post on the battleship *Musashi*.'

In the Japanese navy it was even rarer than in any other for a captain to survive his ship.

'How strange! Today I flew over the place where he died.'

The young officer said nothing more and withdrew. The

next day a dozen Japanese aeroplanes were about to take off. Lieutenant Inoguchi was sitting beside his uncle in the airport headquarters. Suddenly he leapt up and ran outside. A few moments later a petty officer pilot reported: 'The lieutenant ordered me to give up my place to him and he has just taken off.'

Only one aeroplane returned from this mission and it was not that of young Inoguchi. He died in battle in the same place where his father had died a week earlier. For a long time the captain kept in his desk the helmet, the tunic and the samurai sword which his nephew had left behind when he took off.

But the passing days grew harder and harder for Japan. From this time onwards, the *Shô* plan was to fail. The *kamikaze* force which had been established to gain a difficult victory was to become the very symbol of inescapable defeat. The more desperate the battle seemed to be, the more impatient the young *kamikaze* were to participate in it. Captain Inoguchi was obliged to calm this ardour.

'Whether you fight a little earlier or a little later it is still for your country! The special attacks will continue until the world is at peace and you are only the advance guard of an advance guard.' He added: 'Do not complain if you have to spend a few days here after your comrades have died.'

At that one of the young volunteers exclaimed approvingly: 'You are right, Captain. It doesn't matter. There is no precedence of rank or of order of arrival at the shrine of Yasukuni Jinja, where the souls of soldiers are reunited.'

He spoke of this as of something completely natural. The first pilots to join the *kamikaze* corps were heroes, that went without saying. They were also cheerful. And this good humour, in which politeness and courage were mingled, did not fail to strike all those who came into contact with them, the officers who sent them on their missions as well as the mechanics who maintained their aeroplanes. However, they no longer belonged to this world. They were accommodated separately and they had their own rites and their own songs.

They loved especially this patriotic song which henceforward they alone had the right to sing:

> On our badges the cherry-blossom is embossed.
> We, the trainee pilots, will fly today on the storm-clouds
> Towards the clear cloud of hope
> Which is rising in the sky.

Their song resounded at the edge of the runway where they waited for hours for the order which would send them on a mission from which none of them would return. 'Have you noticed,' asked one of them, 'that our song is one of the few which does not mention death?' And yet death was there, always present, in the Philippines sky.

'Who are you?' a comrade asked Uebara Ryoki, who was to die at Okinawa on 11 May 1945, at the age of twenty-two.

'I am only a fragment of iron drawn by the magnet which is the American aircraft-carrier.'

But already their conversations were ending. Orderlies were arriving, out of breath and nervous: 'All pilots to assemble in the map-room. Captain Inoguchi wants to speak to you.'

The young *kamikaze* hastened to the room and sat down quietly in a half-circle round a blackboard. Imperturbable, their hands lying flat on their knees, attentive, they learned how they were to die.

Captain Inoguchi Rikihei pointed out with a long bamboo stick the enemy ships' weak spots. What he was showing them was the exact place where they should crash, their flesh would be consumed in the explosion of their whole being.

The officer wore spectacles with delicate tortoise-shell frames and his bald head shone in a ray of sunshine which was playing on the palm-trees near the men's quarters. He spoke slowly, as if he were not discussing their own deaths with these boys who were listening with an attention which they gave him more out of politeness than as a matter of discipline.

'The best point of impact on an aircraft-carrier is the cage of the central lift... Exactly here.'

But the instructor knew very well that it is not always easy to hit an enemy ship right in the middle. So he indicated other possibilities. 'Always try to hit the lifts. Either fore or aft.' He paused for a moment and sighed: 'Obviously, the ideal would be to attack each aircraft-carrier with four planes: two to hit the central lift and one for each of the others. But it is too late now. There are not enough of us. . . .'

Captain Inoguchi's voice suddenly became low, almost broken. 'We haven't enough planes now and we haven't enough pilots either. So here is the new formula for the *kamikaze* attacks: "one plane for one vessel".'

And the instructor added, as if he could already see the cone of fire, the thick, black smoke and the aircraft-carrier rearing up, then heeling over, before being swallowed by the waves: 'One of ours to kill a thousand of the enemy. One single second to give ten thousand years of life to the Empire.'

The magic words 'ten thousand years' rang out in the pilots' room like a cry of vengeance in place of the victory cry 'Banzai! Banzai!'

Now the rituals were well established. Each pilot wore the badges of the *kamikaze* on his flying-suit: a red sun on a white armband on each sleeve and patriotic and religious exhortations painted on bright material stuck on the dark-blue harness of his parachute. Short boots and a leather helmet, lined with sheepskin, were part of their equipment, which would not have been complete without the samurai sword from which some of them would never be separated and which would accompany them to their deaths.

Five hundred *kamikaze* had already perished when the traditional ceremony of 31 December took place at the end of 1944. All the pilots bowed deeply towards the east in homage to the Emperor and the Nation of the Rising Sun. But with the new year the American offensive had hardened still further. The threat to Luzon became more explicit.

There were only forty aeroplanes left now. They were thrown into a final attack by Captain Nakajima Tadashi, who for several weeks had been begging to be allowed to take off at the head of his men. Every time he had written his name at the top of the flight plans, but every time his superiors had ordered him to remain grounded to direct the training programme. On 5 January he thought he might be allowed to die. It was finished.

'There are no more Japanese aeroplanes in the Philippines,' a general staff officer announced to Admiral Onishi.

'In that case, the pilots must turn into soldiers and make for the mountains, ready to throw themselves, armed with explosives, on the first American tanks.'

But the mechanics accomplished a last miracle. On the morning of 6 January five 'Zeros' had been made airworthy.

Thirty pilots immediately presented themselves. Captain Nakajima Tadashi assembled them in three rows and announced that this would be the last *kamikaze* raid in the Philippines. All of them wanted to go on it, so it was necessary to choose five men from the thirty volunteers.

One name commanded immediate attention: that of Sub-Lieutenant Nakano Yuzo. He had just come out of hospital still suffering from tuberculosis and he had only one fear: that he would have a relapse before he could offer his life for the Emperor. Captain Nakajima said simply: 'You have asked to go despite your illness. Well, the enemy is now so close that this short sortie will not tax you too much.' It was not worth while dwelling on the fact that there would be no return.

Right up to the time of his take-off the young sub-lieutenant kept repeating: 'Thank you, Captain! Thank you very much!' The plane took off immediately.

But the other pilots did not wish to go without thanking Captain Nakajima in their turn. They throttled down their engines, leaned out of their cockpits, and all four of them shouted: 'Thank you! Thank you, Captain, for choosing us.'

The sun was setting. The commanding officer of 201 squadron, who had created the first *kamikaze* corps, watched the disappearing planes for a long time. Then he turned to those who remained and said: 'They are carrying away part of our souls.'

The Divine Thunder Dies at Okinawa

IN THE first days of 1945 Admiral Onishi, who had received a last-minute order to leave besieged Manila, formed with the 'Zero' fighter planes and the 'Suisei' medium bombers, the first unit of the Taiwan (Formosa) *kamikaze*.

The volunteers were assembled at the Takao aerodrome and their commanding officer said to them: 'Remember always what your comrades have just accomplished in the Philippines. The *kamikaze* spirit assures us of eternal life for Japan.'

The first Formosa special assault corps was comprised of very young pilots who were obsessed by the exploits of their elders. They themselves chose the name of their flight: *Niitaka*. It was also the name of the highest mountain in the island. They would be thinking of this peak at the moment when they dived to their deaths on the enemy ships.

The baptism of the new unit ended with a short meal, which was fairly unusual during these times of rationing. Beef, tinned cuttlefish and a few raw vegetables. It would be one of their last banquets. Admiral Onishi, wearing a uniform of fawn linen, his sword at his side, went from one group to another and insisted on all the young volunteers being introduced to him. At the end of the day there seemed to be neither superiors nor subordinates, but only warriors, all equal and all pledged to death.

The admiral insisted on serving them himself and poured out the ritual small glass of *sake* for each of the pilots. With a smile or a word he eased the tension. No one was to let his feelings show.

The evening of the ceremony was one like any other, marked by a lesson on the theory of the procedures of this special assault.

Once again, they learned how to break through the barrage of guns and fighter planes to reach their targets.

The instruction of the trainee pilots on the island of Formosa had to take only a week. Two days to study take-offs, two days to practise formation flying, and three days to study methods of approaching and attacking enemy ships. Landing had no importance. All that was needed was to avoid the young pilots doing too much damage to the planes during their training. But for their single combat mission, it was not necessary to be able to land skilfully.

Amid the throbbing of the engines, the *kamikaze* learned to take off with a 225-kilo bomb, which threw their planes off balance. The instructors repeated constantly: 'Take off gently – above all, don't zoom, and wait till you have a height of at least fifty metres before retracting your undercarriage.'

Those who were now arriving in Formosa made up the second wave of *kamikaze*. Many were students who had left university benches for the seats of suicide planes. They were full of goodwill and touching in their clumsiness. They had only one fear: that they would not know how to die like their elders from the best classes of the Fleet Air Arm. Sometimes a deep melancholy seized them and sitting alone on their camp beds they wrote long letters to their relatives and poems for their friends.

The trainee-pilot Ichima Yasuo was spending his last night in this world. And he knew it. He noted every moment:

'As I went to bathe, I walked slowly through the countryside. Tomorrow, it is possible that I may receive the orders to set off on the attack. Twenty-three years of life move to their end. I do not feel that I am going to die tomorrow. I am here, in this southern country, but I cannot believe that it is to attack the enemy fleet by throwing myself against their guns and planes.

'Strolling along the edges of the fields, I listened to the song of the cicada and the croaking of the frogs. I remembered my childhood. How beautiful the lotus flowers were under the light of the moon. The countryside was like that of Kawasaki in summer. I remembered the land of my birth and the many walks our family all took together.

'I went back into my room, but there was no electricity. Oil was burning in an old tin and the flame threw flickering shadows of us all on the wall. It was quiet this evening. I went to sleep looking at a little doll.

'I went to gather lotus flowers, but I had no one to give them to.'

The great period of waiting had begun. It was not to last for long. On 21 January 1945 an American squadron was reported.

Admiral Onishi hesitated. The Niitaka flight had been formed so recently. But he decided quickly, because the danger was increasing with every hour.

'I am sending out three assault flights.'

The pilots rushed to their planes, which were rarer now than men. Only seventeen aircraft took off and left Formosa in search of fighters. Four *kamikaze* would succeed in their *jibaku* and crash on their targets. But heroism was no longer enough to save Japan.

Already the American Flying Fortresses were over the archipelago and even the capital. Everything must be done to stop them. Everything.

Lieutenant-Commander Sakamoto Mikihiko had understood this very well and his action had set all the young fighter pilots dreaming. On 21 November 1944 this pilot had taken off to try to intercept a formation of B 29s from China which was preparing to bombard the port of Sasebo. The fighter pilot quickly realised that his opponents outclassed him, and that he could achieve nothing with his machine-guns. But he had thought of different tactics: he hurled his plane against an enemy aircraft. The impact was terrific and the two planes exploded. All that fell down from the sky was some debris, steel feathers from the great birds which had been struck down.

Just as the samurai spirit had formerly impregnated the whole corps of officers, the *kamikaze*'s sacrifice served as an example to every soldier.

Just over 20,000 Japanese were cut off on the island of Iwojima. The islet, rather, for it was only eight kilometres long and three wide. Iwojima seemed to be the advance fortress of the Empire of the Rising Sun.

Lieutenant-General Kuribayashi Tadamichi had dotted the islet with small forts and had dug tunnels everywhere in its volcanic soil. He was an officer with a frosty expression and a short moustache, who seemed to live in another world, he was so merciless. For him, duty was simple:

'We are here to defend this island to the limits of our strength. We must devote ourselves completely to this task. Each of our attacks must kill many Americans. We cannot allow the enemy to capture us. If our positions collapse we will get bombs and grenades and we will throw them under the tanks to destroy them. We will infiltrate the enemy's lines to exterminate him. No man must die until he has killed at least ten Americans. We will harry them by guerrilla attacks until the last of us lies dead. Long live the Emperor!'

The *kamikaze* were not only pilots, but also infantrymen. It took twenty-six days and torrents of blood before twenty-four thousand Marines were able to capture an islet scarcely bigger than Sark.

'The fate of Japan will be decided on Okinawa.' At the beginning of 1945 this phrase recurred frequently in all conversations. The generals, like the soldiers, knew that on the fate of the island hung the future of the entire Japanese archipelago.

Airmen, infantry, sailors, all the defenders had to become *kamikaze*. There were a hundred thousand of them. Every means of resistance had been foreseen. No plans for a withdrawal had been considered. Never had the phrase been more precise: to conquer or to die. Or rather, since the sacrifice was part of the plan, what must be said from now on was: to die to conquer.

General Ushijima Mitsuru did not have any illusions. He said to his officers, and he proclaimed to his men: 'You must realise that in the present conflict material superiority takes precedence over moral superiority. So we are not on an equal footing with the enemy.'

Therefore means had to be found to hold on, and to drag the enemy to his death. The basis of the manoeuvre was simple. The army would dig itself in on the island and would hold down the greatest possible number of the enemy. It would be for the air force to strike the final blow. The air force were to find themselves more than ever in the vanguard of the fighting. The hardest thing was not to die, but to find another new name to symbolise this will to die.

Vice-Admiral Ugaki Matome, who was henceforward in command of the Japanese air forces based on the island of Kyushu, the southernmost of the islands of the Japanese archipelago, wanted his own choice of the word which would describe the purest of the new samurai: 'They are Kikusui, floating chrysanthemums. No flower is more immaculate.' Nor any man greater, perhaps, than these heroes who were to die for Okinawa.

Admiral Ugaki kept telling his subordinates that it was not a matter merely of dying, but, above all, of dying a useful death. He even set out, with the exactitude of a former chief of staff of Admiral Yamamoto at the time of Pearl Harbor, the results appropriate to each sacrifice: 'Each suicide plane must destroy a ship. Each human torpedo must sink a ship. Each soldier sacrificed must cripple a tank or kill ten of the enemy.'

At the end of March, everything seemed ready for confronting the American invasion. Volunteers even had to be turned down for these hopeless missions. Admiral Ugaki put his case clearly with implacable logic: 'We cannot allow ourselves to lose our best planes and our best pilots immediately. Any old crate and any young boy are quite good enough to hurl at the enemy.'

The aerodromes on Kyushu soon began to look like veritable cemeteries of almost unusable ancient kites. Incredible planes were to be seen there, even old training bi-planes. There was to be a shortage of everything from now on, and principally of aircraft fuel. So training flights were reduced to the minimum. Some pilots took off for their last mission who would scarcely have been capable of landing. But this eventuality had been excluded from their calculations to such a point that they did not even take enough fuel for the return journey.

Admiral Ugaki knew that from now on their sacrifices would have to be more sophisticated. Courage must be enhanced by technical skill. More than ever courage would be of no value unless it was also useful. What counted now was not the heroic gesture, but the effective gesture. Death could not serve now as either an example or a challenge: it must be an act of war.

Admiral Ugaki found the man he was looking for in the person of Captain Okamura Motoharu, an old fighter pilot, to whom he gave the command of a new special unit called *Jinrai Butai*, or Corps of the Divine Thunder.

His men flew strange planes which they called 'Oka' (cherry-flower) as a sign of purity. These machines were not really aeroplanes, but rather a sort of flying bomb: six metres long, with two very short wings, just allowing them to dive on the enemy and carry 1200 kilos of explosives in the nose. The 'Oka', carried beneath a twin engine 'Mitsubishi' bomber, was released at a height of six to eight thousand metres at about thirty kilometres from its objective. It glided down and then dived. A simple sight in front of the pilot enabled him to dive to his death on the enemy at an angle of fifty degrees, five rockets giving the machine a speed of one thousand kilometres an hour. This terrific thrust lasted only nine seconds. But it was enough to allow the most terrible of the *jibaku* to succeed.

Captain Okamura had trained his men at Konoike. The 'Oka' pilots soon showed themselves to be even more fanatical than those of the 'Zeros'.

It was the first day of spring, 21 March 1945, when the Divine Thunder Corps faced the enemy for the first time.

An American force had been sighted during the morning. Admiral Ugaki's aide-de-camp immediately gave his chief all the details.

'The enemy aircraft-carriers are 320 miles south of Kyushu.'

It was pointless to add what was to obsess all the Japanese military chiefs from now on: the country was no longer safe from air-raids. Henceforward, any hesitation would be criminal. The air force commander made his decision immediately.

'Call Captain Okamura.'

'You intend to use the "Oka", Admiral?'

'It's our last hope.'

The officer wanted to say that the pilots had not yet even finished their training, but he knew the need to improvise all the time and to work miracles.

So he simply pointed out: 'We have only thirty 'Zero' fighters to escort them.'

Admiral Ugaki did not answer this remark and said only: 'Hurry!'

As soon as he was with his chief Captain Okamura said: 'Without enough escort planes, the transport aircraft will not reach their objectives and will not even be able to release the "Oka".'

The admiral's irritated gesture signified: 'I know that perfectly well, but I can't do any better,' and he asked immediately: 'Who is in command of this first operation of the Corps of the Divine Thunder?'

'Lieutenant-Commander Nonaka Goro. He is our best torpedo expert.'

'I should like to see him.'

The officer learned of his mission with the despairing expression of one who is going to die, but who knows that his sacrifice will be useless. He said simply to his chief: 'I will respectfully draw your attention to the fact that we have very little chance of getting through the enemy barrage.'

'You will have to try.'

Captain Okamura interrupted: 'Admiral, let me go with my first flight. I will lead the attack myself.'

Then it was his subordinate who interrupted. Nonaka said simply: 'Commander, do not withhold this honour from me. Fate has made the decision.'

Now the planes were being assembled on the runway. Eighteen 'Mitsubishi' bombers, each with its 'Oka' machine piloted by a *kamikaze*, with thirty 'Zero' fighters to escort them.

The men in their flying-suits walked slowly to their planes. Admiral Ugaki insisted on reviewing them a last time. He told a drummer to play the roll which had in olden times accompanied the samurai as they went to war. Motionless, bundled up in their flying-suits, the sides of their leather helmets flapping like wings in the light wind of this first day of spring, the pilots of the 'Oka' planes had the feeling that the drum-sticks were beating on their temples. Their blood was stirring. This drum roll heralded that of the Divine Thunder which they were carrying in their machines. The honour of engaging in the first battle of flying bombs was theirs.

It was 11.35 when the drum stopped. The last plane had just taken off from the runway of Kanoya. At the head of the flight was Lieutenant-Commander Nonaka.

When the mechanic closed the cockpit of his 'Oka' which was suspended beneath the bomb-bay of the bomber which was carrying it, he smiled for a long time as if he could see wonderful things in another world. And then he said simply. 'We are going to our deaths.' But he surmised that he would not have the luck to kill before dying. . . .

The formation was attacked by a wave of American fighters at 100 kilometres from its objective. The escorting 'Zeros' tried to counter-attack, but the enemy were more than fifty strong and outclassed their opponents.

The battle was very fierce. The bombers were obliged to

release their 'Oka', which were lost in the sea with their *kamikaze* pilots. They in their turn were shot down one after the other. Half the fighter planes also disappeared in the course of this battle. There would be only about fifteen survivors to tell how the first pilots of the Divine Thunder had died.

Never had a sacrifice been so useless. Admiral Ugaki could not hold back his tears when he learned of the total failure of the first attack. Captain Okamura was even sadder. For it was he who had trained the sixteen *kamikaze* who had died.

The syllables of a *haiku* echoed in the head of the commanding officer of the 'Oka' corps like a drum-roll. The *haiku* had been written by Yamaguchi Teruo, who had fallen in battle at the age of twenty-two.

> May we die
> As in Spring-time
> The cherry-tree flowers,
> Pure and lustrous.

The Battle of Okinawa was raging and the *kamikaze* did their best to support their comrades who were defending the island, metre by metre, in hand-to-hand fighting.

A young sub-lieutenant of the *Jinrai* flight was entitled to a short leave before setting out on his last mission. He went to Yashiro where his parents lived. But time pressed and he had soon to leave the house where he had been born. His parents, who wanted to keep him with them as long as possible, decided to go with him by train half the way to his base.

The officer did not dare to tell them that this would be their last meeting and that this leave preceded a *kamikaze* attack. However, he wanted his parents to understand all that he was feeling. He took out a sheet of paper from his tunic, which was decorated with six cherry-blossom buttons, and wrote a short poem:

> Life allows but a single road,
> That of remaining faithful to one's destiny.

His mother looked at him without speaking. Then, in her turn, she wrote some lines:

> You are leaving, we are remaining.
> You are doing what you think best,
> So who can complain?

His father also remained silent. He read what his son and his wife had written on their knees, jolted from side to side by the train as it whistled through the countryside. And he added just two lines:

> You have to die and your soul will be immortal.
> I must congratulate you on your departure.

The pilots who were arriving at the Kyushu aerodromes had never been so young or so fanatical. They knew that from now on they were not going to die to conquer the world, but to defend their country.

On 31 March the first suicide-plane crashed on the bridge of the heavy cruiser *Indianapolis* and put it out of action. The next day the great invasion began.

Admiral Ugaki took a week to launch a colossal suicide-plane attack. He managed to get 355 planes off the ground and among them were eight 'Oka' flying bombs.

Hundreds of men came to watch the departure of their comrades. They bowed slowly in salute to the volunteers who were flying into the sky amid the roar of their engines. The spectators waved streamers and caps. The scarlet suns made patches of blood on the immaculate white of the Japanese flags. Those who were about to die had bound round their foreheads the same emblem, which lit up their faces with its crimson glow.

At the beginning of the afternoon, three *kamikaze* crashed on the bridge of a destroyer and sent it to the bottom of the sea. Three others took care of another destroyer which had come to its assistance. Nothing seemed able to stand up to the

Japanese armada whose wings were darkening the sky. At 14.50 hrs a message announced the attack.

'Target in sight. We are releasing the 'Oka'.

The suicide-planes tried to dive on the enemy, but more than a hundred of them were shot down far from their target. Inexperienced pilots failed in their attempts at the *jibaku* and were swallowed up by the sea. Some of them were injured as a result of their dive and could no longer control their planes. However, several American ships were sunk and others were damaged.

The attack lasted all the afternoon. Night had fallen more than an hour before the first heavy *kamikaze* raid finished amid the smoke of fires and the din of explosions. The sea was covered with debris. The American fleet which had attacked Okinawa had paid a high price, but 250 Japanese planes would never return to their base.

Only a few dozen escort fighters landed that night at the Kyushu aerodromes. However, Admiral Ugaki estimated that the balance was in their favour. He took to thinking aloud: 'Perhaps we shall manage to save Okinawa . . .'

Vice-Admiral Ito Seiichi, in command of the 2nd Fleet on the high seas, did not share the optimism of the chief of the air force. He, too, had just been given a *kamikaze* mission:

'The 2nd Fleet will make for Okinawa. The ships will be beached and will form artillery positions. The sailors, after landing, will take the Americans in the rear. No fuel has been allowed for a return journey.'

'What an incredible mission for the largest and the finest battleship in the world!' murmured the Admiral. And for a long time he gazed at his flag which was flying on the battleship *Yamato*, doomed now to become no more than a hulk. He knew the name of the operation: *Ten-go*. As he spoke this name he could already taste in his mouth the bitterness of defeat.

One of his flotilla chiefs, Rear-Admiral Komura Keizo, had insisted on assembling all his ships' captains on the cruiser *Yanagi* before they set out to die.

'It is a *kamikaze* mission, but unlike those accomplished by the air force we have no chance of destroying an important objective.'

All his officers disapproved of the mission planned for the 2nd Fleet. Admiral Komura went on board the flagship again and when he returned after a second general staff conference he assembled his officers once more and told them almost brutally:

'I have accepted the orders which come into force immediately. For more than an hour I tried to make known your opinion, insisting on the fact that I shared it. But Admiral Kusaka assured me that this sacrifice would not be in vain.'

Nobody seemed very convinced, but one of the naval officers asked to speak: 'Our country is offering us the opportunity to die with honour. A samurai is always ready to give his life.'

The 2nd Fleet got under way the next day, 6 April 1945. Two days later, attacked by nearly four hundred American planes, it was almost completely destroyed. The battleship *Yamato* and the cruiser *Yanagi* sank with most of the escort ships. Only three small destroyers managed to return to the port of Sasebo.

Admiral Ito died in his control room. The Imperial fleet had ceased to exist. Now the war seemed really to have been lost.

However, four days later, Admiral Ugaki launched a fresh suicide-attack with 350 planes. But luck had definitely run out for the Empire of the Rising Sun. A few aircraft-carriers and battleships were certainly badly damaged, but only one destroyer was sunk. Hit amidships by an 'Oka' flying bomb, her back was broken in two.

Out of 350 Japanese planes which took part in this engagement, 330 did not return to their base that evening.

After this, Amiral Ugaki could not launch another mass attack and his *kamikaze* had to employ harrying tactics. The nerves of the American sailors were sorely tried, but they gritted their teeth and kept their eyes steadily fixed on the victory which was soon to be theirs.

The *kamikaze* no longer felt the tranquil enthusiasm or the cold hope of the Battle of the Philippines. Newcomers knew that the present battle was not without honour, but that it was without hope. Before taking off they sometimes wrote letters, certain that these would be their last, and that when the flimsy sheet of paper reached their relatives and their friends they would be no more. So it was a matter of describing things calmly, exactly as they were. Life becomes simple when it is already the same as death.

On 28 April 1945 Otsuka Akio took up his pen for the last time. He was twenty-three and had left the Chuo Faculty of Law in Tokyo to join the *kamikaze* corps. Otsuka was not a volunteer. Not altogether. But he was brave. Totally. This is what he wrote at daybreak on his last day.

'This morning I got up at six o'clock and I breathed in the pure mountain air. It was the last time I shall breathe the morning air. Everything that I do today I shall be doing for the last time.

'The briefing will take place at 1400 hrs. We shall take off at 1500 hrs.

'It's strange. I feel that I want to write many things but when I try I find I have nothing to say. I no longer feel that I am going to die. I am relaxed and light-hearted, as if I were setting out on a journey. I look at myself in the mirror; my face is not that of a man who must soon die. . . .'

The month of May was even more terrible than that of April. The suicide-pilots had decided to do anything to break the vice which was closing on Okinawa. But their sacrifice was to prove vain. The fate of the island was sealed. On 29 May the Marines reached Naha, the capital of Okinawa. During the first days of June the first white flags appeared above the Japanese trenches.

But there was no question of the Emperor's soldiers and

sailors surrendering. They sent officers carrying flags of truce to the enemy. These officers were wearing uniforms in rags and were covered with mud and blood. When they stood before the Americans they bowed low and made this following incredible request:

'We ask you to suspend your firing for a few minutes. Our men wish to commit suicide quietly.'

What happened on the Oroku peninsula was unbelievable. From the cliff-tops the Marines saw Japanese soldiers killing themselves to escape defeat and capture. The officers carried out the traditional actions of the *seppuku* and committed suicide according to the old medieval rite. Their men blew out their brains with pistols or lay down on grenades, pulling the pins out as they did so. To be sure that nothing would remain of their bodies, some of them used a whole crate of explosives on which they sat, smiling.

It was a scene out of hell. A hundred Japanese, members of a crack company, bathed naked in the sea, then put on their uniforms again and gathered round a flag spread out on the rocks. Their commanding officer distributed grenades, whose pins they removed as they would have done during their training, and pressed them to their hearts.

On 22 June the two last surviving generals knelt on a white flag. They plunged daggers in their bellies and then, at the moment when they bent over, contorted with pain, their orderlies cut off their heads with their swords.

They were following the hundred thousand soldiers to death. Cut in two by bursts of machine-gun fire, burned alive by flame-throwers, fragmented by shells, suffocated by smoke in caves, dead from colliding head-on with enemy ships, or having killed themselves when they had no hope left but to die honourably – all the Japanese combatants of Okinawa had wished to die as they had lived, according to the precepts of the *Bushido*. The samurai were no longer only an élite now; they had become an army.

The Twilight of the Samurai

THE LAST great battle of the Pacific ended in a terrible defeat. But in all the Japanese schools the children were reciting a poem by one of the soldiers killed by the enemy:

> Even if I fall at Okinawa
> My soul will live to defend
> Our country.

With Okinawa fallen, the last bolt had been broken. The Flying Fortresses could now attack the aerodromes on the island of Kyushu. The sky of Japan was no longer Japanese.

This was the terrible summer for the Empire of the Rising Sun. On 6 August the first atomic bomb fell on Hiroshima. On 9 August it was the turn of Nagasaki. The official authorities had a final proclamation pasted up on walls:

'We knew that we must expect the worst. Now we have to recognise that the worst has happened. The government will do the impossible to defend national unity and the honour of our country.'

The driving force in the new government formed in April 1945 was Baron Suzuki, an old man of seventy who had escaped by a miracle from the bullets of the nationalists. He had wanted to arrange a peace and he had succeeded in ousting General Tojo Hideki.

But the spirit of the samurai would not resign itself to dying.

The Minister of War, General Anami Korechika, held to a simple position which left no room for capitulation: 'Our only chance is to conduct a holy war to save our national independence, even if we have nothing to eat except grass and refuse, and even if we have nothing to sleep on except earth and mud....'

The old leader continued, exalting the spirit of the samurai and of the *kamikaze*: 'If we continue to fight with the will to win, we shall triumph over all the obstacles and find life again in death!'

The Council of Ministers was to sit for two days. Still the country did not panic. Yet processions were forming. Civilians joined the soldiers. Were they demanding peace? No, they were brandishing placards which threatened – 'Death to the traitors to our country!'

On 14 August members of the Supreme Council were summoned to the Imperial palace. Seated round a long table, the military men faced the politicians. Some of them wanted to arrange a peace, the others to continue the war. The Emperor would have to arbitrate. But he had already made his choice.

'We can see only one possible way which will allow Japan to survive. That is what has led us to endure the unendurable, to tolerate the intolerable. We must accept the Allied Proclamation.'

That evening the 'god incarnate' was to record a statement to his people which would be broadcast by the radio.

At nightfall, some of the young officers called to see General Anami. Once again the army was throwing its weight into the balance.

'General, we have come to offer you the means of continuing the war ... until final victory.'

The general did not dare to sanction their proposal, any more than he could oppose it. He managed to get rid of these conspirators.

It was the last conspiracy of the last night of the war. The moving spirit of the revolt had the modest rank of major. His name was Hatanaka Kenji and he also saw himself as the last samurai. With a dozen of his comrades he hurried to see General Mori Takeshi, who was in command of the division of the Imperial guard. Could he persuade him to concur where General Anami had refused?

'General, we have come to ask you to put yourself at the head of the insurrection.'

'It is not my habit to disobey orders. I refuse.'

The conspirators immediately fired their pistols at the old soldier and took away his seal. They were going to use it to stamp a number of orders and have some of the loyalist leaders arrested.

It was not yet midnight and already a thousand armed rebels were occupying the Imperial palace. Some officers of the guard joined the movement and took their men with them. Everywhere the same countersign could be heard: 'We will never surrender.'

Major Hatanaka seemed to be the most resolute of them. His violent coup had succeeded but he still needed the support of the people. He ignored the message recorded by the Emperor. The proclamation which he had tucked into the pocket of his tunic was the victory *communiqué* of those who refused to admit defeat. It had to be broadcast urgently.

He jumped into a car, accompanied by armed and helmeted soldiers: 'Quickly! To the Japanese Broadcasting Company!'

But the duty staff were obdurate: 'No broadcasts are possible during alerts. What's more, to broadcast anything you need the authorisation of General Tanaka Seiichi, who is in command of the military region.'

Major Hatanaka was reassured. This general was one of those who could not accept the capitulation, and he had remained a friend of Tojo, the dictator who had been removed by the politicians. But it was impossible to reach him on the telephone. The orderlies at headquarters said only that he had just gone out.

Major Hatanaka could not broadcast his *communiqué*. He hesitated for a moment, but the radio technicians sheltered behind 'rules' and would not give in. So he had to return to the Imperial palace.

The dawn of 15 August was rising over Tokyo: a grey and

grubby dawn. Never had the rising sun looked so dreary. Everything seemed unreal and abandoned. No guards on the ramparts nor in the gardens. The conspirators seemed to have vanished in the morning mist.

Major Hatanaka strode quickly to the office of the general staff of the Imperial guard. There he found his fellow-conspirators. They had just killed themselves.

General Tanaka, who had arrived at the palace during the night, had asked them not to disobey the Emperor and to accept the capitulation. Four colonels immediately pulled out their revolvers and each shot himself in the head. This was their only way of reconciling discipline with honour. The others had scattered and vanished in the alleyways at dawn.

Major Hatanaka found himself alone in the Imperial palace. His idea of saving the Empire despite the Emperor could end only in a bloody defeat. So he had to accept the consequences. He wandered through the gardens, looking for the place which would seem the most fitting for his death. He wanted to leave this world beneath a tree or by a lake. The report resounded in the calm air, while throughout the country loudspeakers were being set up to relay the announcement of the capitulation from the lips of the Emperor himself.

Other *seppuku* were to follow: that of General Anami who had refused to help the conspirators and that of General Tanaka who had requested them to accept the capitulation. Also that of the old Marshal Fujiyama, former chief of general staff of the army. For these samurai there was nothing more they could do than to die well, either following the most ancient tradition or in the most modern manner.

At dawn on that 15 August, while Major Hatanaka was wandering in the deserted palace in pursuit of his own death, Admiral Ugaki, chief of the last of the air forces, summoned a commander of the general staff:

'Get the planes ready. We are leaving for Okinawa.'

As soon as he had been infomed, Admiral Ugaki's adjutant

went to see his chief. He found him in a basement room behind a simple screen, in a hovel which served him at the same time as bedroom and office.

Commander Miyazaki asked him, with some astonishment mingled with anxiety: 'The duty officer tells me that you wish to send the bombers out ... why?'

'Because I want to fly with them.'

'You cannot give such an order, Admiral!'

'I have given it, nevertheless. And I ask you to carry it out efficiently.'

Two admirals, friends of Ugaki, persisted in trying to dissuade him, but each drew the same reply: 'It is the best opportunity for me to die like a samurai.'

The order to take off on the last *kamikaze* mission was quickly given: 'Three bombers under the personal command of Admiral Ugaki will attack the enemy on Okinawa.'

At noon, the Emperor's broadcast message told them that all was lost. But Admiral Ugaki did not change his orders. The word 'peace' could mean nothing to him if it was to be preceded by the word 'capitulation' or the word 'Defeat'.

The chief called his officers together. He said simply: 'I had hoped for a better outcome. It now remains for you to do your duty after my death.'

Admiral Ugaki then went to the aerodrome, his sword at his side. Eleven planes were waiting for him with their crews lined up. Never before had anyone seen pilots lined up before taking off.

'I asked for only three planes.'

Lieutenant-Commander Nakazuru replied: 'It would not have been seemly to have so few to follow you.'

The admiral walked towards the crews and asked: 'Do you want to die?'

All the men raised both hands. These last *kamikaze* became volunteers among volunteers. Since noon, they had no longer been fighting for an unlikely victory, they were fighting against certain defeat ...

Their gesture had no value other than a symbolic one. Seven

bombers out of eleven were to reach Okinawa. Late in the afternoon, a radio message relayed to the rear base and from there to the whole Imperial Army, Admiral Ugaki's testament:

'It is entirely my fault if the forces I command have not succeeded in crushing the enemy and protecting our country, despite the heroic battles fought by my air-crews in these last six months ... I am going to dive very shortly on to an enemy ship at Okinawa, where so many of my men fell like cherry-blossom in order to respect the traditions of our ancestors and with an absolute confidence in the immortality of the Empire and in the nobility of the *kamikaze* spirit. I hope that all those I command will understand the motive for my conduct and will surmount their future trials and work with all their hearts for the renascence of our great country. May she live for ever! Banzai!'

At 19.24 hrs exactly another message from Admiral Ugaki preceded those of the six other pilots: 'I am diving.'

So died Ugaki, as had Arima and so many others. Four thousand six hundred and fifteen names of *kamikaze* are written on rolls of rice-paper placed in two statuettes of goddesses in the Kannonji temple in Tokyo.

But there was one man who did not come on 5 May each year to honour their sacrifice. The 'father' of the *kamikaze*, Admiral Onishi, had not wished to survive these hundreds of young heroes.

On 15 August 1945, on the evening of unconditional surrender, Admiral Onishi invited to his home some of his fellow-officers, veterans of the First Fleet. This invitation was not exactly an order. The admiral was no longer of any importance in defeated Japan. No, this invitation was almost an entreaty. Those who arrived that evening numbered all the survivors. Nobody will ever know what happened during this reunion of former *kamikaze* chiefs. It ended at midnight.

Admiral Onishi had a few hours before he died. He did not

want to see the dawn which would herald the first day of his country's defeat. He took off his uniform so that he could put on the traditional clothing of those who choose to commit *seppuku*. He could not end his life as a samurai in any other way. But first he wanted to speak to his *kamikaze*. To all of them. The dead who were so numerous and the few still alive. All were youngsters, and never before, probably, had a leader loved his men so much and yet sent them deliberately to their deaths.

The fine brush moved easily over the smooth paper. The August night, so short and so sad, surrounded the house with invisible presences. The *kami*, those protecting souls of the Empire of the Rising Sun, wandered around Admiral Onishi's deserted residence.

His testament was written straight out and the black ink, in the light of a candle, took on reflections like blood,

'I speak to the élite which the *kamikaze* represent. They have fought heroically. We were strong in our faith in final victory, but, nevertheless, their sacrifice did not make it possible for us to triumph. I offer my death to the souls of my subordinates and their families. I address myself also to all young people. May they learn a lesson from my death! Life must be taken seriously. Let them obey the Emperor! I commend to them self-respect and steadfastness. Even in defeat they should remain proud of being Japanese.'

Then he added a last phrase, precise as a *Bushido* maxim:

'Children are the country's treasure.'

Finally, Admiral Onishi knelt down and opened his kimono.

Very slowly, he drew the sword from its sheath and the blue steel gleamed dully: then he wrapped the blade in a white cloth, leaving five inches of naked steel at the point....

Bibliography

AKAMATSU, PAUL : *Meiji 1868: Revolution and Counter-Revolution*, Allen & Unwin, 1972.

BUSCH, NOEL F. : *A Concise History of Japan*, Cassell, 1973.

CHALLAYE, F. : *The Soul of Japan*, Routledge, 1933.

COOPER, E. M. : *Japan, an historical and cultural introduction*, Pergamon, Australia, 1970.

CRAIG, WILLIAM : *The Fall of Japan*, Weidenfeld, 1968.

DILLEY, ROY : *Japanese Army Uniforms and Equipments, 39–45*, Almark, 1970.

FREDERIC, LOUIS : *Daily Life in Japan at the Time of the Samurai*, Allen & Unwin, 1972.

FREDERIC, LOUIS : *Japan: Art and Civilisation*, Thames & Hudson, 1971.

HALL, CHAMBERLAIN B. : *Things Japanese*, John Murray, 1905.

INOGUCHI, R. AND NAKAJIMA, T., WITH PINEAU, R. : *The Divine Wind: Japan's Kamikaze Force in World War II*, Hutchinson, 1959.

INOUE, MITSUSADA : *Introduction to Japanese Literature*, KBS, Tokyo, 1962.

KEENE, DONALD : *Anthology of Japanese Literature*, Grove Press, New York, 1960.

KENNEDY, MALCOLM D. : *A History of Japan*, Weidenfeld, 1963.

MCCULLOUGH, H. C. : *Yoshitsune*, University of Tokyo Press, 1966.

MARAINI, FOSCO : *Japan: Patterns of Continuity*, Hamish Hamilton, 1972.

MARAINI, FOSCO : *Meeting with Japan*, Hutchinson, 1969.

MILLOT, BERNARD : *Divine Thunder: Life and Death of the Kamikazes*, Macdonald, 1971.

NITOBE, INAZO : *Bushido: The Soul of Japan*, Tuttle, Tokyo, 1970.

REISCHAUER, EDWIN O. : *Japan: The Story of a Nation*, Duckworth, 1970.

SAKAI, SABURO : *Samurai*, New English Library, 1969.

TANAKA, GIICHI : *Japan and the next World War* (Secret Memorial concerning Manchuria, Mongolia, the United States and the World, submitted by General Tanaka to the Japanese Emperor, 1927, China Critic, Shanghai, 1931.

TANAKA, GIICHI : *Japan's Dream of World Empire*. (The Tanaka Memorial outlining the positive policy in Manchuria, 1927), Allen & Unwin, 1943.

SANSOM, G. B. : *Japan, a short cultural History*, Appleton, New York, 1943.

THIESS, FRANK : *The Voyage of Forgotten Men – Tsushima*, Bobbs, Merrill, Indianapolis, 1937.

SUYEMATSU, BARON : *The Risen Sun*, Constable, 1905.

VARLEY, H. PAUL & MORRIS, IVAN : *The Samurai*, Weidenfeld, 1970.

WOODWARD, DAVID : *The Russians at Sea*, Kimber, 1965.

YEFIME : *Japan*, Vista Books, 1962.

YOSHIKAWA, EIJI : *The Heike Story*, Tuttle, Tokyo, 1956.

COLLECTIVE AUTHORSHIP : *A Cultural History of the Meiji Era* (10 vols.), Pan-Pacific Press, Tokyo, 1958.

COLLECTIVE AUTHORSHIP : *Sources of the Japanese Tradition*, Columbia University Press, New York, 1958.

UNESCO : *Japan, its Land, People and Culture*, Ministry of Education and Finance, Tokyo, 1964.

IMPROVE YOUR HOME AND GARDEN WITH THESE HELPFUL GUIDES FROM CHARTER BOOKS

☐ **FAMILY HANDYMAN'S NEW SIMPLIFIED HOME REPAIR GUIDE** 22706-6 $1.50
(Illustrated)   Christopher Gerould
Everything you need to know about the home repairs you can really do yourself.

☐ **DECORATING FOR AND WITH ANTIQUES**
Ethel Hall Bjerkoe   14202-8 $1.95 (Illustrated)
Fine antiques, displayed with taste and knowledge, are beautiful—and a good investment!

☐ **THE DO-IT-YOURSELF GUIDE TO RESTORING ANTIQUES**   15210-4 $1.95   (Illustrated)
Rosemary Ratcliff
Learn how to restore the beauty of almost any kind of antique easily and inexpensively.

☐ **THE COMPLETE FIX-IT-YOURSELF MANUAL FOR HOME AND APARTMENT OWNERS**   By the Editors of <u>Family Handyman Magazine</u>   11626-4 $2.50 (Illustrated)

Available wherever paperbacks are sold or use this coupon.

CHARTER BOOKS, Book Mailing Service
P.O. Box 690, Rockville Centre, N.Y. 11570

Please send me the titles checked above.

I enclose $_____ . Add 50¢ handling fee per book.

Name_____

Address _____

City_____ State _____ Zip_____

Ab

HEALTH AND BEAUTY—ADVICE FROM THE EXPERTS

☐ **IT'S IN TO BE THIN**   37489-1 $1.95
Lose weight eating hundreds of delicious recipes that are amazingly low in calories.   **Lois Lyons Lindauer**

☐ **HONEY FOR HEALTH**   34267-1 $1.50
Not only is honey a delicious energy source, it's a beauty aid and medicine, too.   **Cecil Tonsley**

☐ **HEALTH THE EASY WAY**   31968-8 $1.95
A complete guide to healthful living from one of the world's leading nutritionists.   **Lelord Kordel**

☐ **DR. CARLTON FREDERICKS' LOW CARBOHYDRATE DIET**   49772-1 $1.95
Don't count calories, eat six meals a day, and still lose up to 15 pounds a week!

☐ **VITAMIN C: THE PROTECTIVE VITAMIN**
86539-9 $1.50
Recent findings about the natural, inexpensive vitamin that can prevent and cure disease.   **James Webster**

☐ **THE 14-DAY MIRACLE MAKE-OVER PROGRAM**   24906-X $1.95
A head-to-toe program for women that promises beautiful results in only two weeks.   **Zina Provendie**

Available wherever paperbacks are sold or use this coupon.

CHARTER BOOKS, Book Mailing Service
P.O. Box 690, Rockville Centre, N.Y. 11570

Please send me the titles checked above.

I enclose $_____. Add 50¢ handling fee per book.

Name _____

Address _____

City _____ State _____ Zip _____

Bb

CHARTER BOOKS—The best in mystery and suspense!
JOHN CREASEY

"Consistently the most satisfying of mystery novelists."
—The New York Post

☐ **A SPLINTER OF GLASS**   77800-3 $1.50
A tiny clue was all Superintendent West had to solve a huge gold theft—and a murder.

☐ **THEFT OF MAGNA CARTA**   80554-X $1.50
Scotland Yard searches for international thieves before a priceless treasure vanishes.

CHARTER BOOKS—The best in guides for healthier living!

☐ **INSTANT HEALTH THE NATURE WAY**   37079-9 $1.50
Put natural foods to work to fortify your body against disease.   Carlson Wade

☐ **HERBAL REMEDIES**   32761-3 $1.95
The classic book of herbal medications, with centuries-old, proven remedies you can make.   Simmonite/Culpeper

☐ **INFANT CARE**   37058-6 $1.95
by U.S. Dept. of Health, Education and Welfare.
The most famous book in America on pregnancy and child care, revised and updated.

CHARTER BOOKS, Book Mailing Service
P.O. Box 690, Rockville Centre, N.Y. 11570

Please send me the titles checked above.

I enclose $_____ . Add 50¢ handling fee per book.

Name_____

Address_____

City_____ State _____ Zip_____

Cb